Studies in International, Transnational and Global Communications

Book Series Edited by:
Carola Richter, Berlin, Germany
Michael Brüggemann, Hamburg, Germany
Susanne Fengler, Dortmund, Germany
Sven Engesser, Zurich, Switzerland

In the face of increasing globalization, understanding communication processes and media developments requires a widening of perspective beyond national and cultural boundaries. A multitude of mediated communications is developing beyond or across national borders. At the same time, it is important not to neglect the enduring force of nation-states, and to identify and explain differences and similarities in media developments in various countries and regions using comparative perspectives. Studies on forms of mediated communication in all regions of the world should help to broaden the view on the phenomena of globalization and their impact on media and communication.

The series is open for a variety of topics related to international and transnational communication, such as foreign and war reporting, comparative journalism research and political communications, public diplomacy, media and transformation, media systems research (media policy, media economics), audience research, media and migration. Theoretical and methodological approaches from different social sciences are welcome. The series intends to include current case studies and country-specific studies as well as broader overviews.

Stefanie Walter

EU Citizens in the European Public Sphere

An Analysis of EU News in 27 EU Member States

Stefanie Walter
Hamburg, Germany

Studies in International, Transnational and Global Communications
ISBN 978-3-658-14485-2   ISBN 978-3-658-14486-9 (eBook)
DOI 10.1007/978-3-658-14486-9

Library of Congress Control Number: 2016942529

Springer VS
© Springer Fachmedien Wiesbaden 2017
This work is subject to copyright. All rights are reserved by the Publisher, whether the whole or part of the material is concerned, specifically the rights of translation, reprinting, reuse of illustrations, recitation, broadcasting, reproduction on microfilms or in any other physical way, and transmission or information storage and retrieval, electronic adaptation, computer software, or by similar or dissimilar methodology now known or hereafter developed.
The use of general descriptive names, registered names, trademarks, service marks, etc. in this publication does not imply, even in the absence of a specific statement, that such names are exempt from the relevant protective laws and regulations and therefore free for general use.
The publisher, the authors and the editors are safe to assume that the advice and information in this book are believed to be true and accurate at the date of publication. Neither the publisher nor the authors or the editors give a warranty, express or implied, with respect to the material contained herein or for any errors or omissions that may have been made.

Printed on acid-free paper

This Springer VS imprint is published by Springer Nature
The registered company is Springer Fachmedien Wiesbaden GmbH

Acknowledgement

This book is based on my Ph.D. thesis "EU Citizens in the European Public Sphere: An Analysis of EU News in 27 EU Member States" in political science at the University of Mannheim. I would like to thank a number of people for their support: Rüdiger Schmitt-Beck and Hartmut Wessler, who supervised my thesis, and my colleagues Mona Krewel, Julia Partheymüller, and Anne Schäfer, as well as Sascha Huber, Sebastian Fietkau and Sebastian Schmidt. Special thanks to Yannis Theocharis, Lucy Kinski, and Sebastian Popa for providing me with support and feedback.

Over the course of my thesis, I have greatly benefited from the training, support, and funding provided by the Graduate School of Economic and Social Sciences, the Center for Doctoral Studies in Social and Behavioral Sciences, and the Mannheim Centre for European Social Research. I am grateful to the PIREDEU team at the University of Amsterdam, which was of great help in the initial phase of this project. Patricia Moy and Christopher Wlezien also spent their limited time providing me with feedback on my work and I would like to thank them for that. Furthermore, I wish to thank the editors of the book series "Studies in International, Transnational and Global Communications" for giving me the opportunity to publish this book, and especially to Michael Brüggemann and Sven Engesser for their feedback.

Last but not least, I take this opportunity to express my gratitude to my parents, family, and friends for their continuous support during my studies. Without their encouragement, this project would not have been possible.

Stefanie Walter
Hamburg, April 2016

Table of Contents

List of Tables 11

List of Figures 13

1. Introduction 15
   1.1. The EU and its Citizens 16
   1.2. EU Citizens and the European Public Sphere 20
   1.3. Aims and Research Questions 23
   1.4. Structure of the Book 25

2. Citizenship, Democracy and the EU 27
   2.1. The Historical Development of the Concept of Citizenship 27
   2.2. Citizenship: The Underlying Concept of This Study 33
   2.3. Citizenship and Political Legitimacy 34
   2.4. Citizenship and the EU 36
   2.5. EU Citizenship: Development of the Concept 40
   2.6. EU Citizenship: The Underlying Concept of This Study 44
   2.7. Conclusion 48

3. The Public Sphere 51
   3.1. An Analytical Definition of the Public Sphere 52
   3.2. Normative Models of the Public Sphere 57
      3.2.1. Elitist Public Sphere 58
      3.2.2. Liberal Public Sphere 61
      3.2.3. Discursive Public Sphere 65
      3.2.4. Participatory Public Sphere 69
   3.3. Conclusion 73

4. The European Public Sphere 77
   4.1. An Analytical Definition of the European Public Sphere 78
   4.2. Extant Research on the European Public Sphere 82
      4.2.1. A Pan-European European Public Sphere 83
      4.2.2. The Europeanisation of National Public Spheres 85
      4.2.3. Empirical Observations: Does a European Public Sphere Exist? 88
   4.3. Extant Research on EU Citizens in the European Public Sphere 95
   4.4. Conclusion 101

5. Research Questions 103

6.	Methodology		109
	6.1.	Data	109
	6.2.	Dependent Variables	112
		6.2.1. Concepts and Measurement	112
		6.2.2. Operationalisations	117
7.	To What Extent are EU Citizens Visible in the European Public Sphere?		123
	7.1.	The Visibility of EU Citizens in EU News	124
	7.2.	The Visibility of EU Citizens Across EU Member States	127
	7.3.	Conclusion	131
8.	EU Citizens in the Light of Normative Public Sphere Theories		133
	8.1.	Aim and Research Questions	134
	8.2.	State of the Art	138
	8.3.	Research Strategy	143
	8.4.	Concepts, Measurement and Operationalisations	146
	8.5.	Results: The Actor Structure in EU News	154
		8.5.1. Horizontal and Vertical Actor Structure	158
		8.5.2. Country Level Differences	162
		8.5.3. Quality of Visibility	173
	8.6.	Conclusion	179
9.	Explaining the Visibility of EU Citizens in the European Public Sphere		183
	9.1.	State of the Art	184
	9.2.	Hypotheses	186
		9.2.1. News Story Related Factors	187
		9.2.2. Media Related Factors	191
		9.2.3. Country Level Factors: Member State's Relation to the EU	196
		9.2.4. Country Level Factors: Independent of EU Governance	206
	9.3.	Methodology	211
		9.3.1. Measures – Dependent Variables	211
		9.3.2. Measures – Independent Variables	212
	9.4.	Results	222
		9.4.1. Bivariate Analysis	222
		9.4.2. Multilevel Analysis	227
	9.5.	Conclusion	234
10.	Excursus: Explaining the Visibility of Fellow EU Citizens		239
	10.1.	Theoretical Background	240
	10.2.	Hypotheses	241
	10.3.	Methodology	246
	10.4.	Results	248
	10.5.	Conclusion	251
11.	Discussion and Conclusion		253
	11.1.	Main Empirical Findings	255
	11.2.	Theoretical Implications	258
	11.3.	Limitations and Suggestions for Future Research	261

Table of Contents

References 265

Appendix I Classification of Media Outlets 283

Appendix II Tables for Results in Chapter 8 287

Appendix III Country Level Scores for Independent Variables Chapter 9 311

Appendix IV Excluded Independent Variables Chapter 9 313

Appendix V Country Level Scores for Independent Variables Chapter 10 321

Appendix VI Correlations of Independent Variables Chapter 10 323

Appendix VII Excluded Independent Variables Chapter 10 325

List of Tables

Table 3.1 Public sphere theories and ideal levels of visibility by actor group 74
Table 7.1 Visibility of EU citizens in EU news 124
Table 7.2 Exclusive and overlapping forms of visibility of EU citizens 126
Table 8.1 Overview of actor coding 153
Table 9.1 Summary of hypotheses 210
Table 9.2 Overview independent variables and operationalisations 220
Table 9.3 Correlation independent variables at news story level 221
Table 9.4 Correlation independent variables at media outlet level 221
Table 9.5 Correlation independent variables at member state level 221
Table 9.6 Bivariate analysis national EU citizens 223
Table 9.7 Bivariate analysis European EU citizens 224
Table 9.8 Explaining the visibility of national EU citizens 230
Table 9.9 Explaining the visibility of European EU citizens 231
Table 10.1 Bivariate regressions 249
Table 10.2 Explaining the visibility of citizens from fellow member states 250

List of Figures

Figure 3.1 The public sphere as a mediating system 55
Figure 4.1 The European public sphere as a mediating system 80
Figure 6.1 Sample selection process 113
Figure 6.2 Overview of dependent variables 120
Figure 7.1 Visibility across EU states 128
Figure 7.2 Visibility of national and European EU citizens across EU states 129
Figure 7.3 Visibility of a country's own and citizens from fellow EU states 130
Figure 8.1 Ideal typical levels of visibility by theory and actor group 145
Figure 8.2 Overall actor structure (news story level) 155
Figure 8.3 Actor structure (actor level) 156
Figure 8.4 Horizontal and vertical actor structure (news story level) 159
Figure 8.5 Horizontal and vertical actor structure (actor level) 161
Figure 8.6 Overall actor structure by EU member state (news story level) 164
Figure 8.7 Overall actor structure by EU member state (actor level) 165
Figure 8.8 Horizontal actor structure by EU member state (news story level) 168
Figure 8.9 Horizontal actor structure by EU member state (actor level) 169
Figure 8.10 Vertical actor structure by EU member state (news story level) 171
Figure 8.11 Vertical actor structure by EU member state (actor level) 172
Figure 8.12 Actor structure based on quotations, absolute (news story level) 174
Figure 8.13 Actor structure based on quotations, absolute (actor level) 175
Figure 8.14 Actor structure based on quotations, relative (news story level) 177
Figure 8.15 Actor structure based on quotations, relative (actor level) 178
Figure 10.1 Reporting about national EU citizens 241

1. Introduction

> The gap between the European Union and its citizens is widely recognised. In Eurobarometer opinion polls carried out in recent years, many of the people interviewed say they know little about the EU and feel they have little say in its decision-making process. Communication is essential to a healthy democracy. It is a two-way street. Democracy can flourish only if citizens know what is going on, and are able to participate fully. (Commission of the European Communities 2006a p.2)

This "two-way street" of communication is considered an essential element of a functioning democracy and refers to the provision of information on European Union (EU) governance to EU citizens, and to the inclusion of the "people's views" (Commission of the European Communities 2006a p.4) in the decision-making process at the EU level. As the Commission itself notes, the latter aspect has received less attention than the former. This study focuses on an issue that is directly linked to the European Commission's concern, the visibility of EU citizens in the European public sphere.

Today, the mass media are seen as the primary forum of the public sphere in societies and modern politics is primarily mediated (Bennett and Entman 2001; Ferree et al. 2002a; Habermas 1974). The argument put forward by this study is that mass media can improve the democratic performance of the EU and function as such a "two-way street" of communication, if the media fulfil two tasks: a) to provide information on EU governance to citizens, and b) to include the views of EU citizens in the news coverage on EU governance so their opinions become visible to policy makers. As such, the mass media constitute a mechanism through which EU citizens' views can be communicated to the decision makers at the EU level (for a similar argument, see Gattermann 2013; Kriesi 2013b). While the provision of information on EU governance to citizens has been at the centre of attention of European political communication research, few studies have analysed the visibility of EU citizens in the European public sphere in a systematic way. Closing this gap in European public sphere research by analysing the visibility of EU citizens in depth is at the heart of this study.

1.1. The EU and its Citizens

When the cornerstone of the EU was set in 1951 with the Paris Treaty establishing the Coal and Steel Community, the primary aim of the European integration was to secure peace and political stability in Europe and to foster an economic upturn and economic cooperation among the European states. The founding fathers of the European project, a small group of politicians and public officials, pushed the European project and "[i]n the politics of the period, still in the shadow of post-war reconstruction, they were able to deliver consent to participate from six countries, and they benefited from the oft-remarked 'permissive consensus' of those countries' populations" (Wallace 2009 p.12). The term *permissive consensus* was first introduced by Lindberg and Scheingold (1970) and is used to describe this phase of the European integration that is retrospectively considered as mainly elite-driven, but that was nevertheless supported by the citizens of the EU member states. At that time, the EU was perceived as legitimate purely on basis of its policy output, especially within the fields of peacekeeping and successful economic policies (Scharpf 1999).

Over time, the range of policy areas located at the EU-level as well as the EU's legislative competences have grown (Pollack and Ruhlman 2009). Today, the EU is even taking decisions in policy fields that have formerly been considered core elements and sovereignty rights of nation states (Jachtenfuchs and Kohler-Koch 2003). A transfer of sovereignty from the national to the supranational policy level took place. As a consequence, European governance is of increased importance for the citizens of the EU member states and decisions made by the EU directly impact their lives (Beetham and Lord 1998). However, "by extending the chains of responsiveness and accountability to additional layers of (supranational) government, the inclusiveness, transparency, and ultimately the responsiveness and accountability of the political process is reduced" (Kriesi 2013a p.207).

Some argue that today a "considerable split has arisen between elites and citizens in the process of European integration" (Haller 2008 p.xxi), because support for the European integration has been stronger among the political elites than among the citizens of the EU member states. Since the 1990s, a decline in trust in the EU and support for the European integration has been observed (Armingeon and Ceka 2013; Thomassen and Schmitt 1999). This has largely been perceived as the end of the time period of the permissive consensus.

Against this backdrop, the distinction between input and output legitimacy is crucial. Input legitimacy highlights the idea of "government by the people" and emphasises that citizens should either directly or indirectly participate in governance (Haller 2009; Scharpf 1999). Output legitimacy, on the other hand, is based on the principle of "government for the people" and political decisions are considered legitimate if they contribute to the general welfare of a society (Scharpf 1999). While the EU has in the initial phase of the European integration been considered as legitimate through its policy output, the lack of input legitimacy and the lack of opportunities of EU citizens to participate in EU governance has in the long run contributed to a democratic deficit of the EU (Follesdal and Hix 2006). Some have claimed that the EU has a twofold problem of legitimacy and democracy, as founders of the European integration project as well as their successors believed that they had "the right vision for the future of Europe (...). Believing that they were, so to speak, in advance of their time, they organized the European Community in a rather elitist manner" (Blondel et al. 1998 p.3). In other words, the involvement of citizens in European governance was not of primary importance to policy makers (cf. Dalton and Duval 1986).

Different normative theories of democracy provide diverse standpoints as to what extent ordinary citizens ought to participate in political affairs (Ferree et al. 2002b; Downey et al. 2012). In general, there are several mechanisms (that are ascribed to varying degrees of importance depending on the respective democratic theory) through which citizens can provide their input, the most obvious one being elections. Citizens of the EU member states were already allowed to vote in European elections in 1979, long before the EU citizenship was formally established. During non-election times, political parties ought to articulate and aggregate citizens' interests.[1] However, research has argued that this mechanism might be problematic at the EU level and that European elections are not an appropriate mean to represent citizens' interests at the EU level (Follesdal and Hix 2006). One reason is that European elections are often not about Europe, but it is national affairs that are in the centre of the election campaign. Follesdal and Hix, for example, argue that European Parliament elections cannot be considered "European", because "they are not about the personalities and parties at the European level or the direction of the EU policy agenda" (Follesdal and Hix 2006 p.536). Furthermore, while governments are appointed as an outcome of elections at the national level, this is not the case in the case at the European level (Decker 2002). European elections are therefore considered second-order national elections (Reif and Schmitt 1980) and it is argued that, as a consequence, the preferences of EU citizens have at best an indirect effect on EU governance (Follesdal and Hix 2006 p.536). Furthermore, compared to national elections, turnout at European elections is low and has been declining (European Parliament 2014).

To compensate for these shortcomings, instead of trying to engage with the EU citizens more directly, the EU followed the ideals of the liberal-representative democratic theory, which focuses on political participation by the means of being represented by collective actors. As such, the EU has identified the development of a European civil society as the solution to the democratic deficit (Rumford 2003). Therefore, the "empowerment of civil society" has been a fundamental priority of the European Commission (Bee and Guerrina 2014a) and the EU has predominantly focused on including and consulting civil society actors in the decision-making process (Commission of the European Communities 2006a). However, civil society is not synonymous with the EU

---

[1] The elitist, liberal, discursive, and participatory democratic theories all consider political parties as important for representing citizens' interest (see also Chapter 3.2). Yet, they vary to the degree that they ascribe importance to additional actors in representing citizens, as well as the need for direct representation, or the lack of it.

citizenry (Fisher 2004 p.502; Persson 2009 p.145). Fisher (2004) and Persson (2009) emphasise that the participation of civil society actors in the decision making process at the EU level does not necessarily improve its democratic functioning, nor can it be considered a cure to the democratic deficit of the EU as such.

There are several reasons why focussing on the consultation of civil society actors only can be problematic. First, the Treaty of Lisbon, which states that citizens and representative associations should be given the opportunity to express their views (Art. 11.1), does not provide any criteria based on which civil society groups that are invited for consultation are selected, but it is the EU itself deciding whom to listen to (cf. Lord and Pollack 2012). As a result, participation at the EU level is not equally distributed among civil society actors (Persson 2009). Furthermore, as Lord and Pollack (2012) point out, even the large scale interest organisations do not possess a mandate by their national members when negotiating on their behalf at the EU level. This raises the question of how those interest organisations can be held accountable themselves when negotiating with the EU (see also Bagchi 2000; Bee and Guerrina 2014b; Persson 2009). It has even been argued that the involvement of civil society has a negative impact on the EU's accountability, since it diffuses responsibility for policies (Persson 2009).

The point here is not to diminish the importance of civil society actors for the European integration process, but to draw attention to potential problems that can arise from a policy approach that uses the term civil society as synonymous with political representation of ordinary EU citizens. The involvement of civil society actors might not be the only cure for the alleged European democratic deficit, but also involvement of ordinary EU citizens in EU governance is needed. It is the aim of this study to draw attention to the EU citizens themselves.

Direct participation of EU citizens in governance at the EU level, however, is more complicated compared to the national level. For example, organising a protest in Brussels requires resources and organisational skills that are often not available (cf. Ruzza 2004). Therefore, research has often focused on electoral participation as the central mechanism of representation at the EU level (e.g., Evans and Ivaldi 2011; Franklin 2001; Mattila 2003). This study makes the claim that there is another, more *indirect* form of representation of ordinary EU citizens that has so far been neglected: The visibility of EU citizens in the European public sphere. This study puts forward the argument that the visibility of EU citizens in the European public sphere constitutes an additional mechanism through which citizens' interests can be communicated to policy makers at the EU level. The main argument is outlined in the following.

1.2. EU Citizens and the European Public Sphere

The European democratic deficit mainly refers to a lack of input legitimacy (Schmidt 2006; Fisher 2004) and is based on the assumption that democratic legitimacy of the EU cannot be derived by its policy output alone. Therefore, making the EU institutions more representative and participatory is often seen as a solution to the European democratic deficit (e.g., Follesdal and Hix 2006). Yet, there is also the possibility that there is a communication deficit between citizens and governmental actors that is located at the bottom-up side of European political communication. For legitimacy of EU governance, policies implemented at the EU level need to be responsive to the will of the European people. Especially given the decline in support for the European integration (e.g., Eichenberg and Dalton 2007; Armingeon and Ceka 2013), it is important that politicians at the EU level take citizens' preferences into account when making decisions. One component of the political system that is not directly a part of the formal arrangement of the EU, but is nevertheless a requirement for democracy at the EU level, is the European public sphere.

The notion of the public sphere has originally been developed in the context of the national state and is considered an essential element of democratic governance (Gerhards and Neidhardt 1991; Habermas 1974; Peters 2007; Wessler et al. 2008). Very broadly, the public sphere can be defined as a communication system that mediates between the citizens at the micro-level and the governmental system at the macro-level (Gerhards and Neidhardt 1991, see also Price and Roberts 1987). The media is seen as the most important forum of the public sphere in modern societies, as they are able to establish a permanent forum for political discussion and are able to reach a vast number of people. Since the European integration has led to a shift in governance from the national state to the EU level, a European public sphere is needed for to ensure accountability and responsiveness and ultimately the legitimacy of EU governance (Koopmans 2007; Meyer 2005; Peters et al. 2005).

As citizens hardly have any direct experience with EU governance, the mass media constitute a relevant mechanism through which EU citizens' views can be communicated to the decision makers at the EU level. The visibility of political actors in the news coverage as such is seen as a precondition for the functioning of representative democracy at the national and European levels (cf. de Vreese, 2003). The media therefore play an important role in political communication by operating as an intermediary between governments and citizens (Habermas 2006).

This study argues that especially in the case of the EU, which a large number of people perceive as a distant and elitist institution (Follesdal and Hix 2006), the visibility of citizens in the news coverage can enhance communication between the institution and its constituents. From a participatory perspective, the visibility of EU citizens in the news coverage about the EU is important, because it makes citizens and their opinions visible to policy makers. Given the decline in support for the European integration (e.g., Eichenberg and Dalton 2007; Armingeon and Ceka 2013), it is important that politicians at the EU level take citizens' preferences into account when making decisions. The visibility of EU citizens in the news coverage can also function as a feedback mechanism for policies implemented at the EU level.

For *national* news, research has focused on and examined different forms of visibility of ordinary citizens in the news coverage. According to this stream of work, citizens can become visible in the news through references to opinion polls and surveys, through inferences journalists make about public opinion – which, however, lack empirical evidence, but also through vox pops, and demonstrations (Brookes et al. 2004). A number of studies have examined the visibility of citizens in the context of news sources (i.e., persons that provide information or accounts of events in news stories) (Dimitrova and Strömbäck 2009; Hopmann and Shehata 2011; Lefevere et al. 2011). If citizens are used as sources, they often provide first-hand information as eye witnesses, or references to citizens are employed to set a human interest frame to a news story, but they are also used to counter statements by official sources (cf. Dimitrova and Strömbäck 2009 p.80). Overall, these studies come to the conclusion that the visibility of citizens is relatively low, though there is some evidence that there is variance across countries and topics (Dimitrova and Strömbäck 2009; van Aelst and de Swert 2009).

Furthermore, the effects that the visibility of ordinary citizens (e.g., interviews with citizens or reporting on polls) in the news can have on public opinion have been analysed (Bosch 2014; de Vreese and Semetko 2002; Daschmann 2000; Lefevere et al. 2011; Moy and Rinke 2012; Ostfeld and Mutz 2014). Here, empirical evidence shows that interviews with ordinary people in the media have "significantly more impact than experts that are being interviewed and, in particular, than politicians that are quoted in the news" (Lefevere et al. 2011 p.115). Against this background, it is surprising that so far, there has generally been relatively little research on the visibility of ordinary citizens in the news media coverage (cf. Hopmann and Shehata 2011). Empirical evidence on the visibility of citizens in the news is also limited as previous research has either been based on single-country studies, or compared only a limited number of countries. More importantly, all of these studies have been carried out with reference to the nation state and none of the studies aimed to find factors that can *explain* variation in the visibility of citizens in the news coverage.

At the European level, citizens have received most attention in the area of attitude research (see, e.g., Boomgaarden et al. 2011; Gabel 1998; Hooghe and Marks 2005). Numerous studies have focussed on the emergence of a European identity among the citizens of the EU member states (Bruter 2004; Risse 2003), and citizens' attitudes in terms of support for the European integration, political participation, and satisfaction with democracy at the EU level have been examined (Sanders et al. 2012). Studies in this area are often based on survey data provided by the Eurobarometer. Contrary to previous research, the present study is not interested in analysing survey data on citizens' opinions on the EU, but it focuses on the visibility of ordinary EU citizens and their opinions in the news coverage on EU governance.

European political communication research has so far mainly neglected the visibility of ordinary citizens. While a number of studies have discussed and theoretically identified EU citizens as relevant actors in the European public sphere (e.g., Meyer 1999; Kleinen-von Königslöw 2010; Gripsrud 2007; Trenz and Eder 2004a; Maier and Rittberger 2008b; Statham 2008), very little is known about their visibility in the news media coverage (for exceptions see Garcia-Blanco and Cushion 2010; Michailidou and Trenz 2013; Wessler 2007). Based on previous research, it can be assume that EU citizens become visible in EU news; however, to what extent, and under which circumstances, has not yet been investigated systematically and in more depth.

1.3. Aims and Research Questions

This study argues that the visibility of ordinary citizens in the EU-related news coverage is important, because the European public sphere fulfils a dual role: It provides citizens with information of EU governance, but it also delivers information on citizens' preferences and public opinion to policy makers. For this purpose, the study focuses on the visibility of ordinary EU citizens in the news coverage on EU governance, which is a necessary, but not sufficient condition for their opinions being reported in the news.

From point of view of participatory public sphere theories, the visibility of EU citizens in the European public sphere is a key requirement for communication flows between the EU and its citizens that contributes to accountability and responsiveness of EU governance. Therefore, it is not only of interest to establish the extent to which EU citizens become visible, but also to understand the factors that hinder or foster their visibility. The aim of this study is to analyse to what extent EU citizens are visible in the European public sphere and to examine which factors foster their visibility. By focusing on this neglected actor group, the primary aim is to this gap in European public sphere literature.

For an analysis of the visibility of EU citizens, a conceptual discussion of the notion of EU citizens in the European public sphere is needed. Hence, the first aim of this study is to provide a theoretical framework for the analysis of the visibility of EU citizens in the European public sphere. The initial research question addresses the extent to which EU citizens become visible and different forms of visibility are discussed. Yet, different democratic theories and corresponding models of the public sphere have diverging expectations as to what extent citizens should be able to participate in the European public sphere. Here, the question is to which normative public sphere theory the empirical levels of visibility of EU citizens correspond best. For this purpose, ideal typical actor structures are derived from the elitist, liberal, discursive, and participatory public sphere theory that are then used for empirical comparisons. Hence, the visibility of EU citizens is analysed from the point of view of different normative public sphere theories as well as in comparison to other actor groups. Beyond discussing to what extent EU citizens become visible in the European public sphere, an important part of this study concerns the question how potential variance in the visibility of EU citizens in different countries and media outlets can be explained and what are the factors that lead to a higher visibility of EU citizens in debates on EU governance.

To analyse the visibility of EU citizens empirically, and to answer the research questions, this study uses a secondary analysis and draws on a large scale content analysis data set of the 2009 European Parliament elections provided by the Providing an Infrastructure for Research on Electoral Democracy in the European Union (PIREDEU) project. The data set includes content analysis data of news reports from 27 EU member states and is therefore ideally suited for the purposes of this study.

1.4. Structure of the Book

The 2nd chapter of this book provides an overview of the development of the concept of citizenship. It then discusses the importance of the notion of citizenship for democratic governance. Although the idea of citizenship has traditionally been associated with the nation state, the European integration led to the creation of a supranational form of citizenship. After a brief summary of the historical development of the EU citizenship, the chapter turns to define the concept of the EU citizenship that is the basis of this study.

Chapter 3 turns to a discussion of the notion of the public sphere and its most important forum in today's society: The mass media. Furthermore, an analytical, structural model of the public sphere is provided and different normative public sphere theories are discussed that have different standpoints as to what extent ordinary citizens should play a role in public discussions. Four normative theories that differ significantly in this regard are the elitist, liberal, discursive, and participatory model of the public sphere. An ideal typical actor structure is derived for each theory that is the basis for further empirical analyses. The 4th chapter then discusses how the concept of the public sphere has been applied to the European level. The chapter starts out by providing an analytical model of the mediated European public sphere that underlies this study. It then discusses how previous research has conceptualised the European public sphere and it provides an overview of empirical findings that help to answer the question of whether such a thing as a European public sphere has emerged.

Chapter 5 outlines the main research questions this study aims to address, before Chapter 6 turns to provide information on the PIREDEU media study that is employed to analyse the visibility of EU citizens in the news coverage on EU governance. Furthermore, the operationalisations of the dependent variables that are the basis of the empirical analyses in the following chapters are discussed. The different forms through which EU citizens can become visible in the EU news coverage are then analysed in Chapter 7. It answers the first research question, namely to what extent EU citizens are visible in the European public sphere.

After establishing the extent to which EU citizens become visible in EU news, in Chapter 8, their visibility is analysed in light of the different normative public sphere theories and in comparison to other actors in the European public sphere. Chapter 9 then turns to the question of how differences in the visibility of EU citizens can be explained and provides a number of hypotheses that identify possible explanatory factors at the news story, the media, as well as the country level. The hypotheses are tested using multilevel logistic regression models and the chapter shows that factors from all three levels are relevant for the visibility of EU citizens in the media coverage on EU governance. The final empirical Chapter 10 moves beyond the general theoretical framework and, in form of an *excursus*, provides a shorter but substantively parallel examination of an additional function that is fulfilled by the European public sphere: The mediation among citizens of the EU member states. The question addressed is what factors foster the visibility of citizens from fellow EU member states in the European public sphere. Following a similar rationale as the previous chapter, several hypotheses are developed and tested in a multilevel framework.

The concluding chapter summarises the main findings of the study and discusses their theoretical implications in the context of the notion of the European public sphere. It goes on to discuss the limitations this study faces and provides at the same time an agenda for further research.

2. Citizenship, Democracy and the EU

The importance of the visibility of EU citizens in the European public sphere s grounded in the role that EU citizens play for legitimacy of EU governance. To better understand the importance of the EU citizenship for democratic governance at the EU level, it is helpful to consider the history of the concept of citizenship in the first place. Furthermore, when interested in analysing the visibility of EU citizens in the European public sphere, a conceptual understanding of the *EU citizenship* and that of an EU citizen is needed. The origins of modern conceptions of citizenship can be traced back to ancient Greece and Rome, but were also influenced by events in the 18th century. To comprehend the importance of the notion of citizenship today, the next section sets out to provide a brief overview of some of the central historical periods and key political thinkers that influenced the modern vision of citizenship in the 21st century. Afterwards, the understanding of the concept of citizenship that underlies the present study is outlined, followed by a definition and discussion of the concept of the EU citizenship.

2.1. The Historical Development of the Concept of Citizenship

Citizenship has been and still is a concept that evolves over time. Historically, the notion of citizenship was associated with the city and not the state (Isin and Turner 2002). It was in the context of the ancient Greek city states (*polis*) that the notion of citizenship emerged (Bellamy 2008; Heater 1999; Magnette 2005). The purpose behind the idea of citizenship was to *"draw the outline of the political community*, by defining who belongs to and who is excluded from the civic body"* (Magnette 2005 p.7, italics in original). Aristotle's writings are a starting point for modern definitions of citizenship. In Aristotle's definition, a citizen is not simply a resident, but a free born man from Athens who possessed property and therefore gained the right to take part in self-government by the people (Aristotle 1995 [350 B.C.]). In this sense, the ancient notion of citizenship was inseparable from participation in governance (Smith 2002). Aristotle derived his definition of a citizen by examining who should be excluded form citizenship: The group of non-citizens consisted of women, foreigners and slaves, but also children and elderly people were excluded from citizenship in ancient Greece (Aristotle 1995 [350 B.C.] 1275a).

Participation in the *polis* had a political and judicial dimension. Citizens were not only responsible for the formation of policies and laws by attending assemblies and holding offices, but also their enforcement by being members of juries in courts that dealt with conflicts related to the city (Heater 2004; Magnette 2005). This form of participation can only be realised in small political communities. Aristotle himself considered the size of the citizenry as important and argued that "in order to decide questions of justice and in order to distribute the offices according to merit it is necessary for the citizens to know each other's personal characters" (Aristotle 1995 [350 B.C.] 1326b) to form a functioning political community. Furthermore, Aristotle argues that there needs to be some kind of bond among the citizens in form of the existence of a common interest citizens agree on (Aristotle 1990 [350 B.C.] p.IX. 6).

Already back then, citizenship and citizenship rights, such as freedom of speech and thought, were closely connected. To participate in the democrat process, citizens had to be able to speak openly in the assemblies when determining policies (Heater 2004 p.25). However, the formal existence of these rights was not sufficient, but citizen's willingness to act upon these rights given to them was also curial.

During the times of the Roman empire, citizenship became a more formal status since citizens were officially registered at birth (Heater 2004). Simultaneously, the notion of citizenship was broadened and was no longer limited to the city state. With the expansion of the Roman empire, citizenship applied no longer exclusively to natives, but was a status also given to conquered people to generate loyalty and foster unification (Heater 2004; Magnette 2005). Yet, citizenship was still not a universal concept, but it was mainly elites that gained the status of a Roman citizen. At that time, a theoretical debate emerged about the possibility of dual citizenship, which was dismissed (Heater 2004). In practice, however, some territories maintained a certain degree of autonomy and their own citizenship practices. According to Magnette (2005 p.21), "the genius of Roman citizenship lay in the unity it produced while letting an important variety of laws and institutions tied with local citizenship remain".

Above all, the Roman citizenship was a legal status and as such, it could relatively easily be extended to conquered territory (Walzer 1989). This is reflected in the definition of a citizen in the Roman empire, who was a person that lived under the guidance of, or was protected by, the Roma law (Heater 2004; Walzer 1989). At the same time, Roman citizens were obliged to fulfil certain duties, including military service and taxation. Citizens benefited from the rights and privileges that came along with their status, such as the right to trade and the respect of their properties. Political participation rights were limited, but included the right to vote for elected assemblies and to take up certain political offices. However, "Roman citizens never experienced the kind of political power wielded by the Athenian citizens in their Assembly in that state's democratic area" (Heater 2004 p.32). Direct political participation was furthermore complicated due to the broad geographic scope of the Roman empire.

In the middle ages, the notion of citizenship was depoliticized in the sense that it no longer referred to political participation and the idea of self-government of the people (Kostakopoulou 2008). Citizens were not seen as a source of authority, but as persons that were protected by the authority (Walzer 1989 p.215). The political order of the feudal system was based on "faith, trust, law-abidingness and allegiance" (Kostakopoulou 2008 p.17). According to the Christian doctrine, the king was seen as chosen by god, exercised authority on his behalf and the people ought to obey. By the end of the 13th century, the term citizenship denoted a privileged status of residents in a city (Heater 2004; Magnette 2005). As in Aristotle's definition, the ownership of property in a city was a precondition for gaining the citizenship status. In addition, guild membership played an important role (Heater 2004; Kostakopoulou 2008). As citizens, people gained, for example, the right to exercise a profession, free movement to trade, and the right to court trials (Kostakopoulou 2008 p.18). In return, citizens were obliged to pay taxes and to participate in the military service.

In the middle ages, approximately half of the population of a city held the citizenship status (Kostakopoulou 2008). In the decentralized feudal system of governance, cities were the most important political communities (Kostakopoulou 2008 p.17) and, by gaining the status of the city, achieved a certain degree of independence with regard to taxation, administration and judiciary (Heater 2004). In this sense, each city defined its own rights and obligations that came along with the citizen status (Magnette 2005).

It was only in the course of the 18th century that the notion of citizenship retrieved its political dimension. It was at that time that the idea of citizenship became linked to the concepts of sovereignty and legitimacy (Kostakopoulou 2008). One of the most influential writers on citizenship at that time was Rousseau. In "The Social Contract", Rousseau argues that people can gain freedoms as citizens by entering into a social contract:

> The public person that is formed in this way by the union of all the others once bore the name *city*, and now bears that of *republic* or *body politic*; its members call it the state when it is passive, *the sovereign* when it is active, and a *power* when comparing it to its like. As regards the associates, they collectively take the name of *people*, and are individually called the *citizens* as being participants in sovereign authority, and *subjects* as being bound by the laws of the state. (Rousseau 1994 [1762] p.56, italics in original)

The government is seen as responsible for guaranteeing these liberties; however, it is only considered legitimate as long as it represents the general will of the people. In this sense, the people are considered as the sovereigns that are nevertheless ought to follow the law in order for society to function. It is the participation in the exertion of sovereignty that defines Rousseau's vision of citizenship (Brubaker 1992 p.42).

It was the French Revolution that gave significant impact to Rousseau's notion of citizenship and some argue that modern (national) citizenship has been an "invention of the French Revolution" (Brubaker 1992 p.35). The French

Revolution brought about the change from a small-scale elitist notion of citizenship based on economic resources towards a more inclusive concept (Kostakopoulou 2008 p.24). It was Robespierre who argued that the citizenship status and rights should not be based on wealth of a person, but citizens should be considered equals (Heater 2004). The French Revolution "institutionalized political rights as citizenship rights, transposing them from the plane of the city-state to that of the nation-state, and transforming them from a privilege to a general right" (Brubaker 1992 p.43). The citizenship status still did not apply to women, Jewish or black people. However, it was during this period of enlightenment that women's entitlement to citizenship rights was raised (Isin and Turner 2007). In the French constitution of 1791, a citizen was defined as a person born in France, but also foreigners could become French citizens after having been a resident in France for at least five years (Heater 2004 p.89). For the first time, a *social* dimension was added to the notion of citizenship and it was suggested that society as a whole should support less privileged citizens, e.g., by offering them work or other forms of support.

The modern notion of citizenship is closely linked to the nation state. The territorial unity and the closure of borders to foreigners to protect citizens from foreign economic competition were important elements of citizenship in the 19th century (Fahrmeier 2007). As modern states advanced, the term citizenship became more inclusive. Former restrictions to the citizenship status based on gender, race, age, property and residence were gradually reduced (Fahrmeier 2007 p.229). "The expansion of citizenship went hand in hand with the expansion of the power of the state. Modern constitutions, courts, police forces, and border controls emerged in the nineteenth century" (Hix and Høyland 2011 p.273). During this time period, citizenship became synonymous with nationality. Sometimes, membership in a nation state is even seen as the defining criterion of citizenship (see, e.g., Janoski and Gran 2002).

One of the most influential scholars that impacted the modern notion of citizenship is Marshall (1964). For Marshall, the central elements of citizenship are citizenship rights and duties. The former is divided into three dimensions, namely civil, political and social citizenship rights. *Civil* rights account for the rights that are needed to guarantee individual freedoms, such as freedom of speech, freedom of assembly, the right to own property and the rule of law. According to Marshall (2009 p.149), civil citizen rights were those citizenship rights that developed first. Next were *political* citizenship rights linked to political participation (Marshall 2009 pp.149–149), but also the guarantee of political protection, e.g., in form of minority rights (Janoski and Gran 2002 p.13). Finally, *social* citizenship rights were established in the context of nation-state building, particularly in European states (Roche 2002, p. 76).[2] Social rights guarantee a certain quality of life and well-being of citizens, for example, by providing access to the system of the welfare state. Depending on the respective political community, the combination and scope of those rights might vary (Isin and Turner 2002). The same applies to citizenship duties, which might, *inter alia*, include military service, jury duty or paying taxes (Isin and Turner 2002 p.3).

For the understanding of citizenship in the context of the nation state, a common language shared by the citizens was usually implied. Mill, for example, wrote: "Free institutions are next to impossible in a country made up of different nationalities. Among a people without fellow-feeling, especially if they read and speak different languages, the united public opinion necessary to the working of representative democracy can not exist" (Mill 1991 [1861] p.310). Nevertheless, nation states are not always homogeneous; some states are multi-lingual and/or possess a federal structure. This characteristic has influenced the modern notion of citizenship in the sense that it is considered as possible that citizens can be members of more than one political community at the same time. To express that citizens are simultaneously members of different political communities, the term "multi-layered citizenship" (Yuval-Davis 1999) is often used. Since citizens participate in the political process at both levels, federalism and layered citizenship ought to strengthen democracy.

---

[2] The order in which citizenship rights developed according to Marshall has been challenged by other scholars. For a criticism of Marshall see, e.g., Turner (1993).

2.2. Citizenship: The Underlying Concept of This Study

Today, there is no single or a standard definition of citizenship. Since the concept of citizenship is evolving, it has been defined in different ways, emphasising different aspects of citizenship considered relevant. Therefore, the following section does not aim to provide a universal definition of citizenship, but outlines how the concept is understood in the present study.

The first defining criterion of the concept citizenship is its legal dimension, namely the official status of *membership in a political community*. Political community in this sense refers to an institutional order based on democratic norms that defines a political system, which is responsible for politics and policy making. In the past, it was the nation state that was seen as the primary political entity citizens belonged to (Déloye 2011; Isin and Turner 2002). Therefore, citizenship has been and still is often associated with nationality and "in most nation-states, this criterion of nationality is still the condition for inclusion in the citizen community" (Déloye 2011 p.238). Secondly, as stressed by Marshall (1964), along with the legal status of citizenship come certain *rights* and duties. Marshall's work has led to a shift in the perception of the notion of citizenship away from a purely legal definition towards an understanding of citizenship that includes a social dimension and stresses the element of political participation.

However, Marshall himself does not distinguish between passive citizenship rights and active participation (Turner 1990). As the previous section has shown, historically, the notion of citizenship has also been closely linked to political participation since the status of a citizen is also an entitlement to take part in collective decision making (Bellamy 2008, p. 3). This is the third criterion upon which citizenship can be defined, namely the active exertion of those rights as well as political *participation* that links the legal status with the importance of citizenship for the democratic process (Dahl 2000; Déloye 2011; Pateman 1970). According to Janoski and Gran (2002 pp.13–14) "[w]ith passive rights alone, a beneficent dictator could rule (…). Active rights bring citizens in a democracy to the foreground in politics". Participation in the political process can take place in various forms, e.g., via voting in elections, running for a political office, but also campaigning or protesting, or by taking part in political discussions.

In sum, the three defining components of citizenship are: membership in a political community, citizenship rights, and participation. Based on these criteria, in this study, a citizen is understood as an *individual who is a member of a democratic political community and is, based on their legal status, entitled to certain rights. An active citizen exercises these rights, and participates in the political community*. What is explicitly left out from this definition of citizenship are identity-related concepts that e.g., require a shared history, culture, religion or language (Cerutti 2003; Etzioni 1995; Walzer 1994). These approaches are usually based on a nation state perspective and citizenship is reduced to nationality (cf. Taylor 1989). However, there is also a constructivist approach to identity that starts out from the assumption that it is politics, not culture, that drives identity-formation (Maier and Rittberger 2008b p.250). As discussed in the previous section, citizenship has existed well before the nation state and these criteria are therefore not necessary preconditions of citizenship, but might rather be a result of the creation of political institutions and living in a shared political community (Habermas 2001; Habermas 2003; see also Kriesi 2013 p.22).

2.3. Citizenship and Political Legitimacy

The concept of citizenship is strongly linked to political legitimacy. The notion of legitimacy concerns primarily the right to govern (Beetham 1991; Coicaud 2004). In this sense, citizenship is the "principle that links the individual to the collective principle of self-governance, or sovereignty" (Bagchi 2000 p.161). In ancient Greece, citizens participated directly in the decision making process and the policy formation. In today's mass democracies, direct participation of citizens is much more complex. Instead, democratic government is essentially based upon the principle of representation. Citizens chose through elections who will govern them and is authorised to use political power on their behalf. "Rep-

2.3. Citizenship and Political Legitimacy

resentative government inevitably establishes distance between the rulers and the ruled, implying the possibility that this distance may attain such proportions that it would be difficult to continue to speak of democracy" (Klingemann 1998 p.2). Therefore, it must be assured that the political process fulfils democratic criteria. *Accountability* and *responsiveness* are two central, and closely related, mechanisms that contribute to democratic legitimacy in representative democracies. Both concern the "idea of a binding relationship between citizens and their representatives" (Persson 2009 p.144), however, their focus is slightly different and explained in the following.

Analytically, democratic legitimacy can be divided further into two dimensions, namely input and output legitimacy (Scharpf 1999). The idea of input legitimacy highlights "governance *by* the people". Here, citizens right to participate in the political process, but also their willingness to act upon these rights are crucial so that the will of the people can be reflected in the decision making process. One central citizenship right to guarantee input legitimacy is the right to vote in elections. If the government is formed and implements policies according to citizens' preferences, the democratic process and governance is considered *responsive* (Markowski 2011; Powell 2004). In this sense, responsiveness functions as a bottom-up mechanism of political representation (Andeweg and Thomassen 2005).

Output legitimacy, on the other hand, concerns "government *for* the people" and is considered legitimate if the political outcome is in line with citizens' preferences. "Since those who exercise power enjoy great status and privilege, they have to be shown to merit it and to use it to serve a more general interest than merely their own advantage" (Beetham 2011). *Accountability* refers to this process that assures that responsibilities can be assigned to political actions and is considered a top-down mechanism of political representation (Andeweg and Thomassen 2005). Accountability goes further than responsiveness in the sense that political decisions not only have to be in accordance with preferences of citizens, but have to be justified and face consequences (Mulgan 2000). Citizens' consent with the government's actions contributes to the legitimacy of the political system. In the event that citizens conclude that their government is not sufficiently accountable, citizens have the option to vote them out of office in the next election. In addition, citizens are, for example, entitled to the right to protest to express their disagreement during non-election times.

What is important is that the concept of legitimacy is not a binary one; political systems are not either legitimate or illegitimate, but the extent of legitimacy of a political system can vary:

> In any society there will be some people who do not accept the norms underpinning the rules of power, and some who refuse to express their consent, or who do so only under manifest duress. What matters is how widespread these deviations are and how substantial in relation to the underlying norms and conventions that determine the legitimacy of power in a given context. Legitimacy may be eroded, contested or incomplete; and judgements about it are usually judgements of degree, rather than all-or nothing. (Beetham 1991 p.20)

In this sense, it is possible that political systems are not illegitimate *per se*, but possess a "legitimacy deficit".

For legitimacy overall, but also accountability and responsiveness of governance, transparency and public communication play a key role and are necessary requirements of representative democracies in two ways: on the one hand, citizens need to be informed about on-going political processes, e.g., to make an informed vote choice. On the other hand, office holders need to be able to perceive citizen's preferences and concerns to act responsively (Gerhards et al. 1998, p. 28). Originally, this communicative process was applied and limited to the nation state. Today, however, the former closely-knit and exclusive tie between citizenship and the nation state is challenged (see, e.g., Kostakopoulou 2008). One prime example is the European integration and the EU citizenship.

2.4. Citizenship and the EU

As mentioned previously, it has primarily been the nation state that was seen as the political community that citizens belong to (Linz 2009; Safran 1997). It is for this reason that there is a close connection between citizenship and nationality. However, as the previous section has shown, the theoretical idea of citizenship is by no means tied to nationality. Nevertheless, research has often identified nationality as the defining criterion for citizenship. In the 20st century, the idea that nationality is the precondition for citizenship and membership in a political community has been challenged (Delanty 2008 p.61). Among the reasons for the transformation of the relationship between the nation state and citizenship are globalisation pressures (Held 1995; 2000). "Globalization challenged the nation-state as the *sole* source of authority of citizenship and democracy" (Isin and Turner 2002 p.4, italics in original). This is what Dahl (1994) calls the "third transformation of democracy":

> The boundaries of a country (...) have become much smaller than the boundaries of the decisions that significantly affect the fundamental interests of its citizens. A country's economic life, physical environment, national security, and survival are highly and probably increasingly dependent on actors and actions that are outside the country's boundaries and not directly subject to its government. Thus the citizens of a country cannot employ their national government, and much less their local governments, to exercise direct control over external actors whose decisions bear critically on their lives (...). (Dahl 1994 p.26)

According to Dahl, this situation results in a democratic dilemma where citizens face a situation where they have to choose between a) their democratic control of the democratic process at the national level, or b) the ability of their government to act effectively at the supranational level.

The European integration bears a resemblance to an advanced form of globalisation (Golub 2000 p.181). One could argue that the dilemma described by Dahl was reflected in the initial phase of the European integration project, where power has been transferred to EU institutions that were not directly accountable to the citizens or their nationally elected representatives (Majone 1999). The involvement of citizens of the EU member states in European governance was not of primary importance to policy makers (cf. Dalton and Duval 1986). Instead, the European integration was for a long time seen as being based on "permissive consensus" (Lindberg and Scheingold 1970 p.38). As mentioned previously, the term permissive consensus is used to describe the initial phase of the European integration that is toady mainly perceived as being elite-driven, but policy outcomes where nevertheless supported by the citizens of the EU member states (output legitimacy). At the time of the initial phase of the European integration, the EU for the most part focused on the introduction of the common market. The EU was perceived as legitimate purely on basis of its policy output, especially within the fields of peacekeeping and successful economic policies (Scharpf 1999). Only when the purely output based legitimacy of EU governance was challenged, a debate on the necessity of an EU citizenship emerged.

Just as at the national level, the notion of democratic legitimacy of EU governance and the EU citizenship are closely related. Today, the EU is taking decisions in policy fields that have formerly been considered core elements and sovereignty rights of nation states (Jachtenfuchs and Kohler-Koch 2003). And in the near future, if not already, the EU will produce more important binding legislation than the national state (Thomassen and Schmitt 1999 p.3). Hence, a transfer of sovereignty from the national to the supranational policy level has taken place. European governance is of increased importance for the citizens of the EU member states and decisions made by the EU have a direct impact on people's life (Beetham and Lord 1998). This makes the case that European governance likewise needs to be accountable to the will of the European[3] people. Otherwise, the transfer of decision making powers to the supranational level will lead to a decrease in democratic control, accountability and ultimately democratic legitimacy of governance. It can even be argued that the EU has to meet the *same* standards of political legitimation that apply to national democratic states (Lord and Beetham 2001).

However, against the backdrop of declining support for the EU, the legitimacy of EU governance has been challenged and a debate emerged about the European democratic deficit. The democratic deficit, *inter alia*, refers to a lack of legitimacy of EU governance, because the EU institutions are not sufficiently accountable and responsive to the EU citizens. The debate about the European democratic deficit has mainly evolved around institutional deficits of the EU.[4]

---

[3] For language sake, Europeans is used as a synonym of the EU citizens and does only refer to the EU member states. Other European countries are not taken into account.

[4] The requirement of a European public sphere is also seen as a part of the European democratic deficit and is discussed in the subsequent chapter.

2.4. Citizenship and the EU

As such, it is argued that the European integration process has led to an increase in power of the executives (Andersen and Burns 1996; Raunio 1999), while policy making at the EU level is beyond the control of national parliaments and the institutional structure of the European Parliament is considered too weak (Follesdal and Hix 2006). The transfer of decision-making powers to the EU level has furthermore made it more difficult for citizens to assess accountability, since it became harder to "identify the *locus* of politics and attribute responsibility" (Lord and Pollack 2012 p.53, italics in original). As a result, research has often emphasised that that there is a "shifting of blame" (Lord and Beetham 2001) taking place, where national governments accuse EU institutions of unpopular decisions.

A second aspect refers to European elections. Here, it is argued that European Parliament elections are not about Europe, since there are no European political parties and European policy issues are often not in the centre of the election campaigns (Follesdal and Hix 2006). Instead, European elections are considered second-order national elections (Reif and Schmitt 1980). As a consequence, Follesdal and Hix (2006 p.536) argue that "the absence of a 'European' element in national and European elections means that EU citizens' preferences on issues on the EU policy agenda at best have only an indirect influence on EU policy outcomes". This has furthermore consequences for the accountability of EU governance, since the lack of EU issues makes it more difficult for citizens to judge whether their representatives acted on their behalf at the EU level (Lord and Pollack 2012 p.55)

If EU citizen's preferences are only insufficiently reflected in EU governance, this has consequences for the responsiveness and accountability of EU governance and impacts the legitimacy of the EU overall. This is where another line of research comes in that additionally sees a democratic deficit at the citizens' level. It is based on lack of support for the European integration and a gap between the EU and its citizens (Kuper 1998). The introduction of the EU citizenship in 1993, after the sharp decline in support for the EU, can be seen as a step that acknowledges that it is the EU citizens that are the ultimate source of legitimacy for governance at the EU level. Since the concept of democracy has been extended to the supranational level, it is only consequential to assume that a concept of citizenship beyond the national borders is needed, as citizens are the source of legitimacy of democratic governance. In other words, supranational governance requires supranational citizenship and EU governance needs EU citizens.

2.5. EU Citizenship: Development of the Concept

One can argue that on critical step towards the EU citizenship was already taken when the Treaty establishing the *European Coal and Steel Community* was signed in Paris in 1951 by France, Germany, Italy, Belgium, the Netherlands, and Luxembourg. The treaty established a common market for coal and steel (Art. 4) and in this context, the right of free movement for coal and steel workers was introduced. The Treaty of Rome from 1957 established the *European Economic Community* and extended right of free movement to *all* workers.[5] It stated that between workers of the member states, any kind of discrimination based upon nationality should be abolished (Treaty of Rome 1957, p. 21). However, as Heater (2004 p.103) correctly notes, none of the founding documents of the EU[6] establish a reference to the EU citizenship. One important difference that distinguishes the right of free movement of workers from the notion of EU citizenship is that it is not universal in the sense that the right did not apply to all individuals living the Community area, but was limited to one specific group, namely one that is defined in economic terms: employees. Everson (1995) uses the metaphor of the "market citizen" to express that the Union citizenship has its roots in economic developments. This initial development reflects that the EU initially started out as a purely *economic* cooperation.

It was in the 1970s that a first shift from an economic integration towards an supplementary *political* integration could be observed (c.f. Wiener 1998, p. 66). The citizenship debate was motivated by "the need to make European inte-

---

[5] With the exception of the public service (see Art. 48.4).
[6] For better readability it is referred to "EU", even though the European Union was officially only established in 1993.

2.5. EU Citizenship: Development of the Concept

gration more relevant to ordinary people" (Anderson et al. 1994 p.106) of the member states. The political origins of the EU citizenship can be traced back to the European Summit in Paris in 1974 (Bellamy et al. 2006), where the need for additional political integration was emphasised. It was decided that a report upon the future developments of the EU should be composed by Leo Tindemans, Prime Minister of Belgium. The Tindemans' report is one of the first documents where the notion of a "European citizenship" appears (Closa 1992 p.1141). The report highlights the gap between public and political support for the European integration and makes the case for more civic involvement (Tindemans 1976). Tindemans argues that the EU must be "experienced" by citizen in their everyday lives and it is proposed that border controls between the member states should be abandoned, the education systems should be harmonized in a sense that diplomas are equivalent, and that there should be mediated exchange of information, so that citizens are able to gain "better knowledge of each other" (Tindemans 1976 p.28). In order to achieve these aims, it is argued that political measures have to be taken. At about the same time, the Commission presented the report "Towards European citizenship", which discussed the notion of European citizenship and argued that each member state should treat citizens that decent from fellow member states as their own citizen (Commission of the European Communities 1975, p. 32).

In the context of the debate of citizenship, the granting of special rights and a passport union were discussed (c.f. Wiener 1998, p. 85). Special rights were defined as political rights and as such the "Act concerning the election of the representatives of the Assembly by direct universal suffrage"[7] was passes in 1976. It paved the way for the first direct elections of the European Parliament, which took place in 1979. Previously, the members of the European Parliament were delegated by the national parliaments. In 1979, citizens of the member states were for the first time given the chance to *directly* participate in the European integration project by casting a vote in the European elections. The passport union, on the other hand, was meant to "enhance the feeling of belonging to

---

[7] The European Parliament only received its official name in 1986, before, it was named European Assembly.

a territory broader than that of a single member state" (Wiener 1998, p. 106). It can furthermore be seen as an attempt to raise consciousness of the European integration among the citizens of the member states (Anderson et al. 1994 p.106). The act was passed in 1981 and established uniform passports.

A more significant step was the *Schengen Agreement* that was signed in 1985 by Belgium, Germany, France, Luxembourg and the Netherlands. It states that national citizens of the member states[8] should be able to cross internal borders to "strengthen the solidarity" between them. It was ten years later, in 1995, that the Schengen Agreement was in fact implemented and the border controls within those states came to an end. By the Schengen Agreement, citizens of the Schengen-area have been able to experience the consequences and benefits of the European integration in their everyday life. Mass argues that the removal of the internal borders is a crucial step for the development of the EU, in the same way had previously played a decisive role for the process of nation state building (Maas 2007a p.233).

All of these steps finally led to the introduction of the European citizenship, which passed in 1992 along with the *Treaty of Maastricht* and entered into force in 1993. The Maastricht Treaty established not only the *European Community*, but also the *Citizenship of the Union*. In the treaty, a Union citizen is defined as person that holds the nationality of one of the member states (Art. 8.1). As a consequence, EU citizens by definition do not share the same nationality (Weiler 1997 p.509). EU citizens are also entitled to certain rights (Art. 8.2): While citizens were previously already allowed to vote and stand as a candidate in European elections, the right was extended to EU citizens who are residents in fellow EU member states. Furthermore, the right to vote and to run as a candidate in municipal elections, in the member state of residence, was added. Additional rights concern free movement and the right to diplomatic protection, the right to apply to the European Parliament and to request the Ombudsman. The duties of citizens, on the other hand, remain undefined. The introduction of the EU citizenship represents a "significant departure from the model of European integration established by the founding Treaty of Rome in

---

[8] As well as goods and services.

that for the first time it defined the EU in terms of a relation to the individual citizens" (Delanty 2008 p.64).

Yet, the legal introduction of the Union citizenship is not the end of its development. In 1997, the Amsterdam Treaty added one more sentence to the definition of Union citizenship, namely that it shall *complement* and not replace national citizenship (Article 2.9). It was amended to reassure fears that the EU would become a sovereign state itself (Maas 2007, p. 242). In 2004, a directive by the European Parliament and the Council further specified the right of residence of EU citizens and their family members within the territory of fellow EU member states (Directive 2004/38/EC). Recently, the EU citizenship has been further strengthened. The Treaty of Lisbon, implemented in 2009, introduced the legal framework for the *European citizen initiative* (Treaty of Lisbon, Art. 8 B.4). The citizens' initiative is a measure of direct democracy meant to increase the democratic functioning of the EU. EU citizens can propose to the EU to take legal actions in a policy area where the EU has decision making competences. The initiative requires one million signatures by EU citizens from at least seven different member states and can be organised on any issue in areas where the European Commission has the right to propose legislation. The Commission itself states that the Treaty of Lisbon has improved citizenship since it "gives EU Citizenship greater prominence by integrating it in the provisions on democratic principles (Article 9 TEU) and creates a stronger link between citizenship and democracy (Articles 10 and 11 TEU)" (Commission of the European Communities 2010 p.2). The articles referred to in this citation highlight that EU is ought to serve the citizen's interest (Article 9 TEU), to value democracy, the rule of law and human rights (Article 10 A TEU). In addition, the common foreign and security policy was established, intended generating "political solidarity" (Article 11.2 TEU) among the member states.

2.6. EU Citizenship: The Underlying Concept of This Study

The previous section has provided a legal definition of the EU citizenship. However, it has also been highlighted that the notion of the EU citizenship as well as European citizenship rights existed well before its legal status. This section aims to provide further discussion on the notion of the EU citizenship and to define the concept from the point of view of democratic theory. In general, the idea that a citizen can be a member of various political communities is not new. Easton (1965) provides an illustrative example for different levels of political community which can be nested within each other: "For a person to say that [s]he is a Parisian, a Frenchman, and a European indicates three different levels of political community to which [s]he simultaneously adheres. Each of these communities stands at a different level, with each lower community nesting within its next higher supra-system" (Easton 1965 p.181). Easton's approach to different levels of political community is well suited to describe the EU citizenship, where citizens simultaneously belong to the national and European level and are citizens of both political communities at the same time. According to Kivisto and Faist (2007 p.124), the idea of nested citizenship is the most compelling approach to account for the interconnectedness of the EU and member state level.

Research has acknowledged that the EU citizenship does not intent to introduce the full range of citizenship rights as defined by Marshall, but complements national citizenship by adding elements that are not usually covered within the scope of national citizenship (Déloye 2000). In this sense, the EU citizenship possesses the characteristic of additionality, meaning that citizenship rights at the national and European level are complementary to each other (Closa 1992). Because citizenship rights are still enacted at the national level, the role of the nation state for citizenship is not becoming obsolete (Isin and Turner 2002). Furthermore, the EU might not impact national citizenship rights directly, but it functions as a mechanism to coordinate and harmonise those rights across the EU member states (Kivisto and Faist 2007 p.124). This is in line with the EU's principle of subsidiarity, which states that the EU is not taking any

2.6. EU Citizenship: The Underlying Concept of This Study

action if the respective issue can be solved more effectively at the national or sub-national level (Article 5, Treaty on European Union) (for a counter argument see Kuper 1998). In this regard, the EU citizenship is comparable (yet not identical) to citizenship in federal states, where citizens are likewise members of both the national and sub-national political communities simultaneously. "In most federal systems, the fundamental laws of both national and sub-national governments define the rights that attach to their own citizenship status" (Schuck 2000 p.216). This might weaken the criticism about the novelty of the European citizenship raised by some scholars, arguing that the Maastricht treaty hardly introduced any *new* citizenship rights (c.f. e.g., Weiler 1997; Kostakopoulou 1998).

Furthermore, the concept of the EU citizenship is innovative since it goes beyond the traditional definitions of citizenship (Déloye 2000; Moro 2012; Preuß 1996). Some argue that the crucial aspect of the EU citizenship is the "conceptual decoupling of nationality from citizenship" (Weiler 1997 p.509), which reflects that the EU as a polity is based on political, rather than on ethnocultural values. Similarly, Preuß argues that:

> [C]lear-cut demarcations in terms of territory and persons do not fit into the conceptual framework of the European Union. Citizenship of the European Union is as novel, unprecedented, imperfect, and evolving as the European Union itself. This is why it can be defined only tentatively and in rather vague and speculative terms. (Preuß 1996 p.549)

The establishment of the EU citizenship has also affected and altered the notion of national citizenship. While it has been argued that "citizens alone enjoy an unconditional right to remain and reside in the territory of a state" and that "the modern state has fundamental interest in territorial closure" (Brubaker 1992 p.24), this holds no longer true for the EU member states, since EU citizens gained the right to move and reside freely within the territory of the member states.

Overall, one can differentiate EU citizenship rights into two dimensions.[9] The first dimension consists of rights obtained by the EU citizenship that apply to the EU level and its institutions directly. I hereafter refer to this dimension as *vertical* EU citizenship. Vertical EU citizenship rights include:

- The right to vote and to stand as candidates in the European Parliament elections
- The right to petition the European Parliament and to complain to the European Ombudsman
- The right to take the initiative of inviting the European to submit any appropriate proposal (Lisbon Art 8B,4)

The second dimension is defined by this study as the *horizontal* EU citizenship. It refers to rights given to the citizens of the EU member states on basis of their status as EU citizens, however, these rights concern the member state and not the EU level directly. Horizontal EU citizenship rights include:

- The right to vote and to stand as candidates in municipal elections in their member state of residence
- The right of protection by the diplomatic and consular authorities of any other EU country

These horizontal citizenship rights are crucial since they reflect the EU's capacity to implement changes at the national level (Delanty 2008 p.65). EU citizens' rights at the horizontal level have furthermore been extended by decisions of the Court of Justice of the EU on the basis of the EU citizenship, mainly in the area of social right and access to the welfare-state (e.g., Case C-85/96 [1998] ECR I-2691 and Case C-184/99 [2001] ECR I-6193). Overall, the court rulings suggest that citizens from fellow EU member states who are residents in other member states are entitled to equal treatment as nationals of that respective state (Bellamy et al. 2006 p.14).

Even though one might argue that this lists of rights obtained by the EU citizenship is rather short, one has to keep in mind that all of these rights are unique and "particularly significant rights since they would never be constitu-

---

[9] The flowing distinction into a vertical and horizontal dimension of the European citizenship has first been introduced by Magnette (2005 p.177). However, what exactly constitutes the two dimensions remains unspecified.

2.6. EU Citizenship: The Underlying Concept of This Study

tive elements of national citizenship" (Moro 2012 p.41). Furthermore, even if the introduction of the EU citizenship and its rights was only a symbolic gesture, past research has highlighted the importance of "symbolic responsiveness" as one form of political representation (Eulau and Karps 1977). In this sense, the legal introduction of the EU citizenship itself expresses an institutional shift of the EU away from an intergovernmental organisation towards a constitutional polity (Delanty 2008 p.64) and an official recognition that democratic governance at the EU level needs to be responsive to the will of the EU citizens. It also postulates a shift from a purely economic to an additional political cooperation at the European level. According to Bellamy et al. (2006 p.10), the "the transformation of the 'European citizenship' concept into something more political" can be seen as a direct result of the Maastricht Treaty and it even initiated a more political orientation of the EU as a whole.

Furthermore, the EU citizenship is not merely symbolic since citizens are, in fact, given rights to actively participate in European governance. The Treaty of Lisbon states: "Every citizen shall have the right to participate in the democratic life of the Union. Decisions shall be taken as openly and as closely as possible to the citizen" (Art. 8A.3). Participation in the political community is the last defining aspect of the traditional notion of citizenship. With regards to political participation in EU governance, one can distinguish between direct and indirect participation. Direct participation refers to the vertical citizenship rights outlined above. Furthermore, according to the EU, it aims to launch policies that explicitly aim to promote an active European citizenry (Council Decision 2004/100/EC). EU citizens also have an indirect impact on EU governance through national parliaments which ought to control their national governments acting at the EU level and by selecting the representatives at the national level that take part in EU governance via the Council of the EU. However, as Fisher (2004 p.502) points out, this form of indirect participation might not contribute to a firm connection between the EU and its citizens.

Based on these considerations, it can be concluded that the three defining criteria of citizenship can be meaningfully related to a concept of EU citizenship. Thus, the three defining components of the EU citizenship are: *member-*

ship in the EU's political community, EU citizenship *rights* and *participation* in EU governance. Accordingly, in this study, an EU citizen is understood as *an individual from the EU member states who is a member of the EU's political community and is, based on their legal status, entitled to certain rights. An active EU citizen exercises these rights and participates in the EU's political community.*

2.7. Conclusion

This chapter set out to present the major developments of the concept of citizenship. While in ancient Greece, citizens took part in direct governance of the city state, over time, as the scale of political communities expanded, citizenship rights became more formalised. With the development of the nation state, citizenship and nationality became closely related. These developments highlight that citizenship is not a fixed concept, but it is developing and changing over time. As such, the concept of citizenship has recently been expanded to the supranational level and the EU citizenship has created a novel form of citizenship beyond the nation state. EU citizens are not homogenous, but a group of heterogeneous individuals with different origins, languages etc. In this sense, the notion European citizenship also reproduces the structure of the EU, which consists of diverse member states.

The EU citizenship is also a political measure that officially added a political element to the European integration process that had until then mainly been limited to the economy. The EU citizenship thus implies that the EU is no longer merely a community of states, but a political community as well. And citizens are the ultimate source of legitimacy in democratic societies. Since decision-making powers have been transferred to the European level, there has been a need for the establishment of an EU citizen that can hold governance accountable. EU citizenship, therefore, also postulates the demand of accountability of EU governance. As mentioned previously, governance in democracies is based on self-determination and legitimate if political decisions reflect the will of the people. Governance should, therefore, be responsive to citizen's demands. This is equally true for the EU level.

The theoretical framework of the concept of the EU citizenship provides the basis for further discussion on how EU citizens can become visible in the European public sphere. However, before turning to the notion of the European public sphere, the next section discusses the general theoretical framework of the public sphere as well as different public sphere theories that place varying normative requirements on the public sphere to fulfil its democratic function. Among those requirements is the role that citizens ought to play in the public sphere. Four normative public sphere theories that differ in this regard can be identified: The elitist, liberal, discursive, and participatory public sphere theory.

3. The Public Sphere

Citizenship is the basis for democratic governance at the national as well as at the European level and decision-making in democracies has to be responsive and accountable to the will of the people. As the next two chapters outline, similarly to the concept of citizenship, the idea of a public sphere also originally emerged at the national level and its scope has then been extended to the EU level in the course of the European integration. When interested in analysing the extent to which EU citizens are visible in the European public sphere, and in finding the factors that foster their visibility, first a clear conceptual understanding of the public sphere and the relevant actors within it is needed. The conceptual framework is then used as the basis for empirical analysis in the following chapters.

The public sphere is an essential element of democratic governance, because accountability and responsiveness require that democratic governance generally takes place publicly and that political institutions are subject to citizens' control (Gerhards and Neidhardt 1991; Habermas 1974; Peters 2007; Wessler et al. 2008). This understanding was already present in Aristotle's notion of *politea*, where the few govern with the consent of the many. The notion of the public sphere has a vital role in generating this consent. Very broadly, the public sphere can be defined as a *communication system that mediates between the citizens at the micro-level and the governmental system at the macro-level* (Gerhards and Neidhardt 1991, see also Price and Roberts 1987). This communication process that takes place via the intermediary system of the public sphere can flow in two directions: one the one hand, citizens gain information on the governmental system and political decision-making, on the other hand, citizens' interests are communicated and transmitted to the governmental system (cf. Rucht 1993 p.258 for a similar argument). In order to fulfil this mediating function within the political system, discussions within the public sphere need to concern governmental affairs (cf. Habermas 1974).

Normative public sphere theories propose different criteria as to what qualities the public sphere and public discussions should have in order for the public sphere to fulfil its mediating function for the democratic process. Public sphere theories address questions such as: "[W]ho should be participating and on what occasions? What should be the form and content of their contributions to public discourse? How should the actors communicate with each other?" (Ferree et al. 2002a p.289). The aim of this study is not to take all these facets into account, but to focus on one particular aspect: The role of citizens in the public sphere.

According to Althaus, normative public sphere theories are rather prescriptive than descriptive, in the sense that they "address how things ought to be rather than how things are" (Althaus 2011 p.98). As such, the elitist, liberal, discursive, and participatory public sphere theories put forward different views as to what extent ordinary citizens should participate in the public sphere. To take these different perspectives into account, this chapter first presents an analytical model of the public sphere, before turning to each one of the normative public sphere theories. The analytical model will help to "identify multiple evaluative claims that could be made" (Althaus 2011 p.97) about the visibility of ordinary citizens from the perspective of the four normative public sphere theories.

3.1. An Analytical Definition of the Public Sphere

A useful way to generally conceptualise the public sphere is the idea that it is organised in different *forums* that can be differentiated on basis of their scope (Gerhards and Neidhardt 1991). On a very specific stage, a form of the public sphere can emerge rather spontaneously in day-to-day situations, e.g., via discussions of public affairs between ordinary citizens that take place publicly. This level of the public sphere is referred to as *encounter publics* (Gerhards and Neidhardt 1991, pp. 50-52). One distinguishing characteristic is that the role of the audience and speaker is rather fluent so that every participant can embody both. The encounter level is limited with regard to its spatial, social, and time dimension. On the next level, the public sphere is more organised, namely into *issue publics* (Gerhards and Neidhardt 1991, pp. 52-54). They can take place in form of public events or demonstrations and emerge spontaneously, or possess a high organisational level. Here, the role differentiation between the audience and the speakers is more pronounced.

On the most general stage, there is the *media sphere* (Gerhards and Neidhardt 1991, pp. 54-56). It is constituted via the mass media (press, television, radio, and internet), which is seen as the primary forum of the public sphere in modern societies that is able to establish a *permanent* forum for political discussion. In democracies, the media has the function to provide citizens with information and thereby to contribute to the formation of public opinion (Beierwaltes 2002). The media not only make ongoing political events public, but also actors and their opinions and responses visible to a larger audience (Price and Roberts 1987). Through information provided via the media, citizens are able to control their governments and ensure accountability and responsiveness. Mass media have a broad reach and a high capacity to concentrate public attention on a small and highly specific set of themes and actors. The mass media have furthermore an important role in articulating public opinion. According to Gerhards and Neidhardt, public opinion that is perceived by the political system is primarily constituted via the mediated public sphere (Gerhards and Neidhardt 1991 p.55). Only if topics and opinions are picked up by the media, they gain attention of political actors.

The media sphere is the only forum of the public sphere that is in principle visible to society at large. Therefore, the media sphere is the most important forum of the public sphere for democracies and with regard to the issue of legitimacy, since mass media provide a "vision of the public sphere" (Peters 1994, p. 3) to a vast number of people. Due to this important function of the media for the democratic process, this study focuses in the following on the mediated public sphere only.

Figure 3.1 shows an analytical, structural model of the mediated public sphere and visualises the role of the public sphere for the function for the democratic process. The model broadly reflects the components of a political system that are divided into the governmental, the intermediary, and the private sphere (Rucht 1993; Fuchs 1993). The governmental sphere refers to institutions responsible for making collective decisions for a political community (Hague and Harrop 2004 p.5).[10] It is responsible for aggregating and articulating common goals, the policy making process and the implementation of collectively binding decisions. The governmental sphere consists of *governmental actors* including the executive, the legislature, the judiciary and the political administration (Fuchs 1993). The realm of the governmental sphere that does not overlap with the public sphere is the non-public polity space (Rucht 1993).

The public sphere functions as an intermediary system that connects the governmental and the private sphere through *intermediary actors* representing collective interests (Rucht 1993). As visualised in the graphic, intermediary actors can be differentiated based on how closely they are located towards the governmental or the private sphere. *Political parties* are part of both the governmental and the intermediary system; therefore, they are located at the intersection of both realms. On the one hand, political parties run in elections, aim to maximising their votes and aim to influence political decision making by the occupation of political offices (Hague and Harrop 2004). Political parties are hierarchically organised, membership and financing are formally appointed and there is a clear allocation of roles, e.g., as party chairman/chairwoman (Rucht 1993 pp.263–264). As a consequence of their formal organisation, parties are often forced to internal unity, e.g., when party members are expected to vote in accordance with the party line (Rucht 1993 p.264). On the other hand, as intermediary organisations, it is also their task to foster the formation of public opinion and to aggregate citizens' interests.

---

[10] The following discussion is mainly based on Rucht's (1993) conceptualisation of the political representation of interests.

3.1. An Analytical Definition of the Public Sphere

Figure 3.1 The public sphere as a mediating system

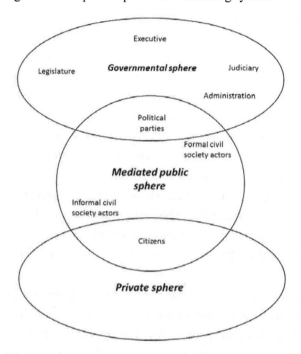

Source: Own graphic, based on Janoski 1998 (p.13)

Besides political parties, *civil society*[11] actors are part of the intermediary system. Civil society is often defined as a social space that is located between the governmental sphere, the economy and the private sphere (Kocka 2003 p.23). One important defining criterion of civil society actors is their intended actions (Rucht 2009). As such, civil society actors aim to promote and represent citizens' interests. The concept of civil society can be further divided into *formal* and *informal civil society*[12] (Habermas 1992; Rucht 1993). As the name sug-

---

[11] The term civil society is normatively loaded and derived from the public sphere theories. However, civil society here is simply used as a conceptual term without any normative value.
[12] The distinction between formal and informal civil society actors has been derived in compliance with the discursive and participatory public sphere theories that are outlined in the following section. The distinction is adopted to be able to classify and analyse civil society actors more accurately.

gests, formal civil society actors consist of more formally organised interests, such as large scale interests groups. Usually, these organisations represent specific interests of a certain groups of the population (Rucht 2005). Informal civil society actors, on the other hand, are more oriented towards the general good (Rucht 2005) and less-formally organised, such as social movements and citizen's initiatives. Therefore, they are located closer to the private sphere than formal civil society actors.

Finally, the private sphere consists of the *citizens* of the respective political community. In the previous section, a citizen was defined as individual who is a member of a democratic political community and is entitled to certain rights. Based on their citizenship rights, such as freedom of speech and freedom of assembly, citizens can become active in the public sphere, for example, by participating in intermediary organisations or by joining a protest or citizen initiative. In doing so, an individual can become an active citizen who participates in the political community.

However, citizens can also become visible in the public sphere via the news media (Janoski 1998). What distinguishes the media visibility of citizens form other forms of participation in the public sphere is that it is the only way in which ordinary citizens can become visible as individuals. When joining voluntary associations, social movements etc., citizens become part of a collective and become visible as such. The overlap between the private and the public sphere reflects this realm where *individual* citizens become visible in the public sphere. This intersection of the public and private sphere is at the heart of this study.

Differently nuanced normative theories of the public sphere have been derived originating from diverse democratic theories, stating different requirements as to how communication in the public sphere should take place and which actors should participate in public discussions. Four models of the public sphere have been identified by previous research: The elitist, liberal, discursive, and participatory public sphere (Ferree et al. 2002a; Gerhards et al. 1998; Wessler and Rinke 2013). Those public sphere theories have, *inter alia*, different conceptions of which forums of the public sphere are relevant and state different normative requirements for the actor structure of the public sphere. They can be applied to the analytical model of the public sphere discussed above, as they add expectations of the valence of public discussions. The next section discusses the four public sphere theories. It focuses on the ideal typical actor structure of the public sphere proposed by each respective theory, and pays special attention to the role of citizens.

3.2. Normative Models of the Public Sphere

Analysing the visibility of citizens in the public sphere is not straightforward as it leads to the question of when levels of visibility of ordinary citizens are satisfactory. Analysing the visibility of citizens *comparatively* to other actors in the public sphere is a useful way to determine whether the visibility of citizens can be considered as high or low. In addition, normative democratic theories propose different levels of political involvement of ordinary citizens in the democratic process as desirable (cf. Teorell 2006). Civic participation is the key focus of the following sections and whether or not citizens are seen as part of the actor constellation of the public sphere is one criterion based on which the normative public sphere theories can be distinguished. The elitist, liberal, discursive and participatory public sphere are summarised below by first providing background information on the respective democratic theory and then answering the question *how* communication in the public sphere should take place and *who* are the actors who ought to become visible in public discussions. The public sphere theories are discussed starting from the least inclusive to the most inclusive notion of the public sphere.

3.2.1. Elitist Public Sphere

The notion of the elitist public sphere is based on the elitist democratic theory.[13] The term elite generally refers to "small groups of persons who exercise disproportional power and influence in social domains" (Higley 2011 p.759). In the elitist theory of democracy, elites are perceived as those who are elected to govern. Democratic elitism is based on the assumption that political elites, compared to ordinary citizens, are more strongly devoted to democratic values (Gibson and Duch 1991). As such, elites are perceived as the "guardians of democracy" (Best and Higley 2009 p.332) and responsible for maintaining democratic institutions by serving as a "bulwark against mass intolerance" (Sniderman et al. 1991 p.349).

The idea of the elitist democratic theory limits citizens' participation to the electoral process alone, where the governing elite is elected (e.g., Schumpeter 1943; Weber 1968). In the democratic process, the only role of the citizens is to elect a government (Schumpeter 1943 p.269). Additional forms of political participation are dismissed because of citizens seen as ignorant and as lacking the capacity of judgement in political affairs (Schumpeter 1943 p.261). Schumpeter, for example, argues that despite political information being broadly available, people lack political knowledge and are not capable of rational decision-making in political matters. Schumpeter even states that "the typical citizen drops down to a lower level of mental performance as soon as [s]he enters the political field" (Schumpeter 1943 p.262). As such, ordinary citizens are not expected to hold rational opinions on policies (Held 1996 p.188). On the contrary, citizens are perceived as incapable of understanding general societal interests, but are solely driven by their own private concerns.

Once people casted a vote, their representatives are free to act based on their own judgement (Schumpeter 1943). People furthermore should refrain

---

[13] Ferree et al. (2002a) as well as Wessler and Rinke (2013) consider the elitist democratic theory as one stream of liberalism. This is because the work of elitist scholars is based on liberal values and ideals of individuality (Held 1996). However, at the same time, elitism also challenges traditional liberal ideas (Held 1996). Democratic elitism is considered as a separate democratic theory in this study since the actor structure of the political system is the main focus, which (as outlined in the following) varies considerably between the elitist and liberal democratic theory.

3.2. Normative Models of the Public Sphere

from trying to get in touch with politicians directly, e.g., by writing letters (Schumpeter 1943 p.295). "The role of ordinary citizens is not only highly delimited, but it is frequently portrayed as an unwanted infringement on the smooth functioning of 'public' decision-making" (Held 1996 p.198). Therefore, the functioning of democratic system relies on the competences and expertise of political elites. From the point of view of the elitist democratic theory, the "democratic method" (Schumpeter 1943 p.269) and only normative requirement is that political decisions are based on a competitive struggle for votes and elections are free and fair. In this sense, democracy is seen as the best way to enable effective political leadership by providing a mechanism for the selection and legitimacy of the elected elite (Held 1996 p.172). It is expected that because politicians aim to be re-elected, policies will reflect peoples' preferences. Furthermore, the elitist theory assumes that elections are not only about the candidates themselves, but also about the respective policy issues highlighted by the candidates (Sniderman et al. 1991). In this sense, by voting for a certain candidate, citizens implicitly also express their policy preferences (cf. Medding 1969 p.643).

In the elitist democratic theory, it is the political leaders themselves that "provide a feedback mechanism between the voters and governments" (Körösényi 2009 p.365). Instead of popular inclusion, the functioning of the democratic system relies on the competences of its political elite. There is no extensive intermediary system needed to facilitate between the government and the people. Instead, peoples' preferences remain latent until they are picked up and addressed by governmental actors (cf. Schumpeter 1943 p.270). In this way, accountability of governance is guaranteed. "The engine of modern democratic politics is competition between elites, characteristically organized around the electoral system" (Sniderman et al. 1991 p.349). Hence, in the elitist democratic theory, the political system is conceptualised as being divided into the governing elite and the citizens. The only exception are political parties that facilitate between citizens and elites and that are needed for election campaigns among elites (Held 1996; Ferree et al. 2002a).

The central function of the public sphere in the elitist democratic theory is to make the elites and debates among them visible to the citizens, but also to provide information on political affairs so that citizens are able to make an informed voting decision (Ferree et al. 2002a). In this sense, the public sphere is needed in the elitist democratic theory to hold the elite accountable. From a normative perspective, the public sphere contributes to transparency of the political process, but the notion of the elitist public sphere does not state any additional normative requirements concerning the style of communication.

From the point of view of the elitist public sphere, the media are the key forum of the public sphere (Best and Higley 2009). Other forums of the public sphere such as encounter and issue publics are linked to forms of political participation that are excluded from the elitist democratic theory. "If the media are doing their job (…), the media will provide enough information about the parties and candidates so that citizens can choose intelligently among them" (Ferree et al. 2002a p.291). However, it is not the role of the media to encourage political participation among the citizens, or to mirror public opinion (Baker 1998). It is argued that the role of the public sphere and public discussion is most relevant when elites are divided (Baker 1998). Such a divide might in the end result in the election of a new ruling elite. "To facilitate competition among, and timely rotation of, elites, the press should also question how well the current governmental administration responds to particular problems" (Baker 1998 p.326). This means that the role of the media is seen in a one-dimensional or top-down manner. Its function is to report from the governmental arena to the citizens, but not to give citizens a voice and report back to the governmental actors. Another stream of research argues that the public sphere is crucial for democratic elitism not only because elites become visible to citizens, but also because elites become visible to each other and provides elites themselves with information (Baker 1998; Engelstad 2009). In this sense, the media are nevertheless important for elites and might influence them in the sense that "their opinions are shaped and personal evaluations are made on basis of reports and statements that other elite actors make in the press" (Engelstad 2009 p.391).[14]

The actors ought to be visible in the elitist public sphere are mainly limited to those belonging to the governmental system. Elitist democratic theory is characterised by a strong focus on political leaders that is also reflected in the mediated public sphere (cf. Best and Higley 2009). There is no need for intermediary actors, with the only exception being political parties. Political parties are moreover considered "vehicles for leaders" (Best and Higley 2009 p.335). Political parties alone are the only relevant intermediary actor in the elitist vision of the public sphere (Ferree et al. 2002a). Political parties are primarily seen as "means for fighting and winning elections" (Held 1996 p.170) and ought to reinforce leadership since they require someone to determine the political direction. But political parties also represent citizens and thereby facilitate between citizens and the government (Ferree et al. 2002a p.290). There is no need for additional civil society actors to be present. The presence of ordinary citizens in the public sphere is altogether dismissed. "By anticipating public reactions the elite grants the citizenry a form of indirect access to public policy making, without the creation of any kind of formal institutions and even in the absence of any direct communication" (Walker 1966 p.286).

3.2.2. Liberal Public Sphere

The notion of the liberal public sphere has its roots in the liberal democratic theory. Although Hobbes' work has not always been estimated as leading in liberal democratic theory (cf. Hardin 1999 p.54), his idea that state power is needed to enforce and guarantee individuals' liberties is nevertheless the point of departure of modern liberalism (cf. Held 1996 p.77). Hobbes furthermore put forward the idea that a civil society, "a sphere free from state interference" (Held 1996 p.78), should exist. Even more than Hobbes, it was Locke who in-

---

[14] It should be mentioned here that the public sphere is an important, yet not the only channel that contributes to an exchange between elites (Engelstad 2009 p.399). For example, personal contacts might also be important.

fluences liberal thinking. Locke emphasises that individuals are free and equal, based on their consent, governments are formed and gain legitimacy (Locke 1821). The government then rules based on majority vote: "When any number of men have *so consented to make one community or government*, they are thereby presently incorporated, and make *one body politic*, wherein the *majority* have a right to act and conclude the rest" (Locke 1821 p.270, italics in original). The quote reflects the underlying idea of representative democracy put forward by Locke. Mill is often referred to as the 'father of liberalism' and can be seen as the most influential writer for contemporary liberal democratic theory (cf. e.g., Held 1996). In his essay 'On Liberty', Mill examines the role of the state, which is primarily seen as responsible for guaranteeing personal freedoms. Moreover, Mill (1989 [1859]) highlights the importance of liberty of thought and discussion and association, all vital constituents of liberalism and core values of modern democracies. Likewise, a free and independent press is regarded a precondition of democracy. Freedom of the press has been called by Mill's father one of the first "political blessings" (Mill 1997 [1811] p.17).

In liberal democracies, political participation is a central for expressing people's preferences and interests. However, similar to the elitist theory of democracy, liberal thinkers were likewise concerned with a lack of knowledge, skills and experience of the majority of citizens (Held 1996 p.108). Therefore, liberalism suggests that citizens' participation in the democratic process should mainly be limited to elections. And a direct participation of citizens in political everyday business is not needed. According to Mill, "[r]eading newspapers, and perhaps writing to them, public meetings, and solicitations of different sorts addressed to the political authorities, are the extent of the participation of private citizens in general politics" (Mill 1861 p.268) during non-election times.

Modern liberal democratic theory, however, is more open towards political participation in from of *political representation* and emphasises the importance of personal freedoms. In liberal democracies, citizens are free to decide on their religious, social, economic and political preferences (Hardin 1999; Held 1996). From a liberalism perspective, the state is seen as the central mechanism that coordinates individual interests. Liberal democracy, then, aims to organise society in a way that maximises these freedoms (Holden 1988 p.12; Steinberger 1978 p.24). Therefore, the role of the state should be limited and it is differentiated between the public and the private sphere, the latter being free of state interventions (Beetham 1992). In liberalism, limited governance ought to be constitutionally guaranteed (Hardin 2011).

Here, the notion of civil society plays an important role. Since state regulations ought to be limited, it is the function of the intermediary system to organise and articulate citizens' interests. Therefore, voluntary associations are at the heart of the liberal theory (Walzer 1990). The realm of civil society ought to be free of state interventions (Held 1996). This division emphasises that liberal democratic theory views the political system as being divided into the governmental system, the citizens and the intermediary system (cf. e.g., Beetham 1991). Citizens' political participation goes beyond the electoral process by being represented by and/or being members of political parties, trade unions and other civil society organisations (Beetham 1992 p.47). In this sense, an "active, informed and involved citizenry" (Held 1996 p.75) is desired.

The democratic process in liberal democracies allows for reconciliation between the individual interests of citizens. From the perspective of liberalism,

> [D]emocracy provides the mechanism most likely to take into account and properly weigh all interests. Interests are detectable and influence government policy primarily due to interest group pressure or representation. Political mobilization by each group creates political capital and gives each group leverage in the political bargaining that generates a democratic regime's laws and policies. Popular political participation provides a currency which assures that a group's interests are taken into account, hopefully in rough proportion to the group's size and intensity of its interests. (…) The method of properly accounting for interests provides the normative significance, the legitimizing contribution, of democracy. (Baker 1998 p.330)

The idea of proportional influence of interest groups reflects the assumption that liberalism sees the society as consisting of the total number of equal individuals (cf. Parekh 1992). Since each individual ought to be treated as equal, interest groups are in principle perceived as an aggregate of individuals (cf. Hardin 2011).

In the liberal conception, the public sphere's main function is to make different standpoints represented by intermediary actors transparent and visible to society in general and policy-makers in particular. In the liberal notion of the public sphere, public communication should reflect a variety of opinions that are present within society. Ideally, *all* relevant societal interests should be represented in the public sphere and the levels of visibility should be *proportional* to the size of the respective intermediary group (Wessler and Rinke 2013). In this sense, the liberal public sphere is also referred to as a "representative public sphere" (Gerhards 1998a p.31). The way in which different standpoints are communicated is not of interest. The only normative communicative requirement, from a liberal perspective, is that actors show mutual respect (Gerhards 1997 p.19). In terms of the mediated public sphere, the media provide information to citizens, intermediary and governmental actors alike, emphasising what interests are at stake (Baker 1998).

Regarding the visibility of different actors, the liberal public sphere merely distinguishes between the governmental and intermediary system (Gerhards and Neidhardt 1993). From the perspective of the liberal public sphere, actors who are legitimised via elections, namely governmental actors and political parties, possess distinct legitimacy to be present in public debates (see Gerhards 1997, p. 10). Besides political parties, within the public sphere, there is no requirement for a *strong* representation of intermediary actors, such as interest groups, social movements, or citizens' initiatives (cf. Ferree et al. 2002a). Yet, in terms of pluralism, it is seen as important that a broad variety of different societal interests and opinions are present in order for the public sphere to account as a democratic one. Civil society is not further divided into formal and less formal organisations. Finally, a direct form of participation of citizens is neither needed nor desired, because it is assumed that political *representation* is more efficient in holding governments accountable than individual participation (Dahrendorf 1967 p.1116). Hence, citizens are understood as the audience whose preferences and interests are articulated and represented by collective actors (cf. Gerhards 1998 p.31).

3.2.3. Discursive Public Sphere

The discursive public sphere theory originates from the deliberative democratic theory. Deliberative democratic theory sets out to criticise standard accounts of liberal democracy and is based on scholars such as Bessette (1980), Gutmann and Thompson (2009) as well as Habermas (1999). The discursive democratic theory likewise conceptualises the political system as being divided into the government, the citizens and an intermediary realm. Contrary to the liberal model, deliberative democracy does not argue for proportional representation of interests in the intermediary system, as in the liberal democratic theory, but focuses on the importance of public discussions that ought to reconcile different interests: "Deliberative policy making aims for genuine preference transformation rather than mere preference aggregation" (Hunold 2011 p.551). The underlying assumption is that aggregated interests do neither reflect public opinion nor the general interest of a society (Bohman and Rehg 1997). Only through discussions, where everyone affected by a decision participates, such a societal consensus can be reached (Bohman 1998).

To realise the potential of discussions, deliberative democracy sets high normative standards and demands for political institutions and citizens alike (Bohman 2000). While theorists of the elitist democracy argue that such a thing as a common good does not exist (Schumpeter 1943), deliberative democracy assumes that if discussions are held in a deliberative manner, it is possible for citizens to see beyond their pure self-interest and to agree on a common good (Bohman 1998). Furthermore, the elitist theory argues that voters at large are not acting rational as far as politics is concerned and therefore participation should be limited to elections, deliberative democracy holds against it that if this was the case, then also the election outcome could not be considered rational (Habermas 1997 p.57). To realise the potential of deliberative democracy, debates have to be held in a rational manner, be free in the sense that participants have no prior constraints imposed on them by norms or authorities (Cohen 2003; Habermas 1974; Habermas 2006). Furthermore, participants have to be considered as equals, they have to have even chances to participate, and information needs to be freely available (Cohen 2003). These preconditions allow that in the end, only the force of the better argument determines the outcome of deliberation (Habermas 1976 p.108). In essence, it is assumed that "the interests, aims and ideals that comprise the common good are those that survive deliberation" (Cohen 2003 p.349).

The rationale behind institutional mechanisms of deliberation is that decisions reached on basis of deliberative procedures are expected to be more broadly supported and accepted by citizens (Gutmann and Thompson 1996; Hunold 2011). In this sense, governance is considered legitimate if governmental institutions establish a framework for deliberation and if policies are a result of public discussion and reflect the general interest (Bohman 2000; Cohen 2003). With regard to the implementation of this common good, it is assumed that governmental bodies are constrained in their actions by the arguments and reasons that have been generated in the public sphere (Habermas 1997). In this way, popular sovereignty is implemented. Furthermore, governmental systems in deliberative democracies should facilitate institutions that allow for deliberation. Examples are referenda (Habermas 2006), citizen juries (Dahlgren 2002), or deliberative opinion polls (Fishkin 1991).

Regarding political participation of ordinary citizens in the democratic process, voting is considered a central mechanism for political representation in the deliberative model of democracy, however, prior to the election, there should be as much deliberation as possible in the public sphere (Bohman 1998 pp.416–417). As a consequence, it is not only assumed that discussions, but also the vote reflects a rational outcome (Rawls 1997). However, the deliberative theory argues that voting in elections or being represented by civil society organisations alone is not sufficient (Gutmann and Thompson 1996 p.4). Instead, citizens have to be granted access to deliberative discussions (ibid.). Yet, deliberative democracy would not expect that in today's society, all decision is based on deliberation and that debates are joined by every single citizen (Bohman 1998).

The idea of deliberative democracy is closely linked to the notion of the public sphere itself, since it is defined as the public space where *deliberative*

3.2. Normative Models of the Public Sphere

discussions take place and public opinion is formed (Habermas 1974). One of the first scholars who aimed to conceptualise the public sphere was Jürgen Habermas. His classic work on "The Structural Transformation of the Public Sphere" has been a major contribution to the field. According to Habermas, the original "bourgeois public sphere" (Habermas 1991, p. 401) of the 18th century consisted of private individuals who came together to publicly discuss matters of general interest. Yet, this ideal version of the public sphere is not feasible for modern mass democracies. Habermas argues that in modern societies, the democratic function of the public sphere is diminished by large-scale organisations and interest groups that strive to communicate with governments directly, rather than engaging in public discourses. As a consequence, the public sphere is excluded and thereby weakened. Habermas concludes that the former model cannot be applied to today's mass societies. The underlying normative claims of the discursive theory nevertheless remain intact. Nowadays, it is the media that is seen as the primary forum of the public sphere (Habermas 1974). Compared to other forums of the public sphere, the media have a broad societal reach:

> [D]eliberative arenas which are organized exclusively on local, sectional or issue-specific lines are unlikely to produce the open-ended deliberation required to institutionalize a deliberative procedure. Since these arenas bring together only a narrow range of interests, deliberation in them can be expected at best to produce coherent sectional interests, but no more comprehensive conceptions of the common good. (Cohen 2003 p.356)

With regard to the actors in the discursive public sphere, Habermas follows the approach of Peters (2007) who differentiates between the governmental and intermediary system, or in other words, between the *political centre* and the *periphery* (cf. Habermas 1992 p.429). The former consists of the government, the parliament, the political administration and the judiciary, but also political parties are seen as part of the governmental sphere (Gerhards 1997 p.3). As governmental actors possess the highest legitimacy to implement binding decisions, they should be in the centre of attention in the public sphere, at least during political everyday business (cf. Habermas 1992 p.459; Peters 2007 p.44). Also political parties have an important role in deliberative democracy, as they address a broad range of political issues. As such, political parties "provide arenas in which debate is not restricted in ways that it is in local, sectional or issue-specific organizations" (Cohen 2003 p.356).

The periphery refers to the intermediary system which is further spilt up into formal and informal civil society actors.[15] Formal civil society actors (output periphery) are more closely connected to the political centre. They possess official structures and are hierarchically organised, such as political parties, large scale umbrella organisations or head organisations of trade unions (Habermas 1992 p.454). According to Cohen (2003), interest organisation are important since they "provide means through which individuals and groups who lack the 'natural' advantage of wealth can overcome political disadvantage that follow on that lack" (Cohen 2003 p.356). The primary aim of those formal civil society actors is to influence the *implementation* of policies, not the decision making process of policies, e.g., by being officially or un-officially consulted in committees (Peters 2007).

Informal civil society actors (input periphery), on the other hand, mainly aim to influence public opinion, the decision making process and the formulation of policies. Informal civil society actors are more autonomous and usually possess low-scale organisational structures, such as smaller public interest groups. The discursive public sphere highlights the role of voluntary associations. Voluntary associations can be considered "nodal points" (Habermas 1997 p.57) in the public sphere as they specialise in "in discovering issues relevant for all of society, contributing possible solutions to problems, interpreting values, producing good reasons, and invalidating others" (Habermas 1997 p.58). Within the group of informal actors, Habermas furthermore pays special attention to social movements and spontaneously emerging (grassroot) organisations. Habermas assumes that newly emerging social movements, in the initial phase, have more deliberative potential since they rely largely on public support and can communicate more freely due to a lack of (bureaucratic and formal) constraints. While informal actors might receive less attention during political everyday business, their role in the public sphere becomes heightened during times

---

[15] As Habermas (1992, p.431) notes, the differentiation between the two groups is not always clear-cut.

of crisis and when normative issues are discussed; then, the visibility of actors from the input periphery should be high (cf. Gerhards et al. 1998 p.35).

Regarding the visibility of ordinary citizen, the idea of discursive democracy puts emphasis on the participation of ordinary citizens in public debates. Likewise, one defining criterion of the discursive public sphere is that the participation in discussions is, in principle, open to everyone, including citizens. Especially in earlier works, Habermas highlighted that citizens should be able to discuss in the public sphere and that access has to be guaranteed to all citizens (Habermas 1974 p.49). At the same time, Habermas favours the importance of *collective* civil society actors (Gerhards et al. 1998 p.100). Citizens themselves are not seen as an autonomous actor group, but are located at the level of informal civil society (Wessler and Rinke 2014). From the discursive public sphere theory, the inclusion of civil society and citizens is especially required when conflictual or normative issues are discussed (Ferree et al. 2002a p.300; Gerhards et al. 1998 p.35).

3.2.4. Participatory Public Sphere

Another angle on the public sphere is provided by the participatory theory of democracy. The notion of participatory democracy takes an issue with the limited forms of participation and calls for more direct channels of participation of citizens that go beyond the electoral process and being represented by political parties (Kaase 2011; Warren 2002). The participatory democratic theory has its roots in Rousseau's (1994 [1762]) work who favours direct democracy over a representative one and highlights the participation of individual citizens in the political process:

> Rousseau saw individuals as ideally involved in the direct creation of laws by which their lives are regulated, and he affirmed the notion of an active, involved citizenry: all citizens should meet together and to decide what is best for the community and enact the appropriate laws. The ruled should be the rulers. (Held 1996 p.57)

However, Rousseau was aware that the form of direct participation he had in mind, where citizens know each other and participate in assemblies, could only apply to small-scale political communities (Rousseau 1994 [1762] p.101).

Rousseau's work was rediscovered by political scientists in the 1960s (Bachrach and Botwinick 1992) and more recent accounts of the participatory democracy are based on scholars such as Barber (1984), Hirst (1994), and Warren (1992). These participatory approaches to democratic theory usually start out from a critique of elitism and liberal democracy (Barber 1984; Hirst 1994). It is argued that through elitist theorists, such as Schumpeter, democracy became equated with competitive elections (Warren 2004) and liberal democracies are not sufficiently accountable to citizens, because nowadays the scope and scale of governance has been extended and voting as the primary mechanism of political representation is not sufficient (Hirst 1994 pp.3–4). In general, in the participatory democratic theory, voting as a mean of political participation is considered "the least significant act of citizenship" (Barber 1984 p.187), because voting is seen a *private* act that does not need to be justified. Furthermore, voting alone is considered insufficient in communicating citizen's interests to the governmental system:

> At the polls, the ordinary citizen must choose from bundles of policy positions predetermined by the political parties. Some of these may reflect their own views, but others may seem more remote. (...) When taking part in other forms of political activity such as contacting officials and protest behaviour, by contrast, citizens may express their views on one issue at a time. (Teorell 2006 p.792)

Furthermore, liberalism is perceived as being too much centred around the individual and neglects the idea of a political community (Barber 1984 p.7).

Besides these general conceptions, participatory democracy scholars emphasise slightly different aspects of civic participation. Barber's (1984) concept of "strong democracy", which he himself describes as a modern version of participatory democracy (Barber 1984 p.117), puts emphasis on the idea of self-government of a political community. According to Barber (1984 p.173), "[a]t the heart of strong democracy is talk". Talk contributes to the articulation of citizens interests, allows citizens to set their own political agenda, enables them to get to know and understand each other and thereby contributes to a feeling of empathy among citizens. Eventually, in the participatory democratic theory, political talk among citizens is seen as vital for the emergence of a political community and an active citizenry.

Hirst (1994), on the other hand, puts greater emphasis on the role of civil society and makes the case that it is associationalism that is the central for participation. He argues that nowadays, new societal problems and challenges are arising, such as racism, gender and environmental issues. Traditional liberal democracies are not sufficiently able to accommodate these changes, but it is "[a]ssociationalism [that] makes accountable representative democracy possible again by limiting the scope of state administration, without diminishing social provision" (Hirst 1994 p.12). In this sense, Hirst does not see associationalism as an alternative form of democracy, but as an enhancement of liberalism (cf. Hirst 1994 p.19). Voluntary associations can function as a bottom-up mechanism in the political process and represent those who are disadvantages in society. Ideally, voluntary associations should be publicly funded and administered at the lowest level possible (Hirst 1994 p.24). It is the civil society organisations themselves, and not the governmental systems, that are "the primary means of both democratic governance and organizing social life" (Hirst 1994 p.26).

Warren (1992; 2002) likewise highlights that opportunities for participation in peoples everyday lives should be extended. According to Warren, democracy should spread out to the economic and social realm, such as peoples' workplace or local governments. This contradicts the liberal democratic theory, which demands a strict separation of the public and private sphere (Beetham 1992). Warren considered participation as *democratic*, if "every individual potentially affected by a decision has an equal opportunity to affect the decision" (Warren 2002 p.693). While it is unlikely that citizens are able to participate in all decisions, they should have the opportunity to participate in those decisions they *choose* to participate (Warren 2002 p.695).

In general, the participatory theory argues for political participation that takes place *continuous* and not only periodical (cf. Hirst 1994 p.24). This does not mean that participatory democratic theories negate the idea of representative government *per se*. According to Warren (2002 p.688), due to the size and complexity of political institutions, citizen's participation will mainly remain "limited to voting, for representatives, petitioning, influencing public opinion, participating in public hearings, and protesting". Participatory democracy does not require that all decisions at any time are made by the citizens (Fishkin 2009). But the participatory theory aims to maximise citizens' representation in the political process. Here, the "scale of decision-making" (Hirst 1994 p.36) is important and decisions should be taken at the lowest level possible.

Turning now to the public sphere, the lines between the notion of the deliberative and participatory public sphere might initially seem blurry, because direct forms of participation in the political process often involves or provide the opportunity for discussion (cf. Teorell 2006 p.791). However, contrary to the deliberative theory, the primary aim of discussions in the participatory theory is not the formation of public opinion, but collective decision making (Teorell 2006). From the point of view of deliberative democratic theory, consensus on a common good is the overall aim of public debate. Instead, participatory theorist argue that some conflicts might not be solved and plurality of opinions might even be preferable (cf. Elster 1997). Within the participatory approach to the public sphere, a tradition of "agonistic pluralism" (Mouffe 2000; see also: Wessler and Rinke 2013) can be identified that exactly picks up this point and argues that the deliberative public sphere fails to take into account antagonism that arises from a plurality of values present in societies.

A normative requirement of the participatory public sphere is that different viewpoints in society are represented. Participation should be inclusive, meaning that no societal groups (e.g., based on gender, age, or ethnicity) should be left out from participating (Fishkin 2009). The importance of the presence of ordinary citizens and civic society organisations in public debates is especially emphasised. "When individuals choose to participate, they need institutional venues that have points of access that enable participation. Ideally, individuals have equal access to the full range of organisations and institutions that affect their lives" (Warren 2002 p.695). This applied also to the public sphere or rather the media. It should be the citizens setting the agenda rather than political elites (cf. Barber 1984 pp.180–182). What is important is that civic participation takes place *continuously*. Participation during elections or at the beginning of a decision making process alone is not seen as sufficient (Ferree et al. 2002, p. 296).

Regarding the actor constellation in the public sphere, the participatory approach differentiates between the governmental system, the intermediary system and the citizens (Curran 1991 p.31). Special attention is paid to a strong representation of the intermediary system. Similar to the discursive public sphere theory, civil society is further divided into more formal and informal intermediary actors. As such, "organizations with active forms of member participation and a leadership that is accountable to members are more desirable mediators than those who are only nominally accountable" (Ferree et al. 2002a p.296), such as large scale organisations due to their rather bureaucratic nature. However, the participatory theory criticises that democratic representation nowadays refers primarily to representing organized interests and not those of individuals (Warren 1992). In the public sphere, the need for the presence of voices of ordinary citizens is emphasised to guarantee an authentic image of the will of the people (cf. Martinsen 2009). Citizens function as experts of their own living environment (ibid., p. 56) and participation that is exclusively based on representation is not accepted. The public sphere, then, is seen as responsible for giving citizens a forum to express their standpoints directly and to participate in political discussions. Citizens should be encouraged to contribute to public debates so they can take part in the political process.

3.3. Conclusion

This chapter set out to first derive an analytical, descriptive definition and model of the public sphere that leaves out any normative requirements. The public sphere has analytically been defined as a communication system that mediates between the citizens and the governmental system. While it is useful to conceptualise the public sphere as consisting of different forums, the media has been identified as the most relevant forum of the public sphere with regard to its role for legitimacy of the political process. For this reason, the empirical analysis of this study focuses on the public sphere that is constituted via the mass media only.

Furthermore, it has been differentiated between actors from the governmental system, intermediary actors including political parties, formal and informal civil society as well as the citizens of the respective political community that could potentially become visible in the public sphere. The review of the normative theories has highlighted that the elitist, liberal, discursive and participators democratic theories and the deduced normative models of the public sphere differ significantly with regard to their ideal typical actor constellation and the degree of civic participation desired.

To be able to use the actor structures derived from the normative public sphere theories for empirical analyses, standards for visibility of different actors have to be assigned criterion values (Althaus 2011). For this reason, I classify the ideal-typical levels of visibility of the different actor groups into the categories "high", "medium", and "low" (for a similar approach see Downey et al. 2012), or "none" if an actor group is not supposed to become visible in public debates. The ideal-typical levels of visibility for each theory are summarised in Table 3.1:

Table 3.1 Public sphere theories and ideal levels of visibility by actor group

Actor \ Theory	Elitist public sphere	Liberal public sphere	Discursive public sphere	Participatory public sphere
Governmental actors	High	High	High	Medium
Political parties	Medium	Medium	Medium	Medium
Formal civil society	None	Low	Medium	Medium
Informal civil society			Medium	High
Citizens	None	None		High

3.3. Conclusion

The visibility of governmental actors is labelled as "high" for the elitist, liberal, and discursive public sphere theory, because all of them acknowledge the importance of the visibility of democratically elected representatives. The participatory theory is the only model of the public sphere where the visibility of governmental actors is classified as "medium", because the governmental system in the participatory theory is seen as less relevant as it is not understood as the primary unit citizens participate in (Hirst 1994; Warren 1992). Political parties, on the other hand, ought to reach medium levels of visibility from the point of view of all four theories, as they have an important role in representing and mediating citizens' interest in the democratic process.

While the visibility of civil society actors is irrelevant for the elitist public sphere theory, they ought to reach at least low levels of visibility in the liberal version. Table 3.1 furthermore shows that in the discursive and participatory theory, the category of civil society actors is split into formal and informal civil society actors. While both should reach medium levels of visibility in the discursive vision of the public sphere[16], the visibility of informal civil society should be high in the participatory model.

Citizens themselves are not seen as part of the actor constellation in both the elitist and liberal model of the public sphere. In the discursive public sphere, on the other hand, citizens are seen as belonging to the group of informal civil society actors. Only in the participatory theory, citizens represent a *separate* actor group and their visibility in the public sphere should be high.

Despite these conceptual differences, research on the European public sphere has hardly taken the existence of different normative models of the public sphere into account. This has consequences for the debate on the existence of a European public sphere in so far as research might derive different conclusions regarding the extent to which the European public sphere is able to fulfil its role for the democratic process. That is, to facilitate between the EU and its citizens. The next chapter examines the notion of the European public sphere in

---

[16] Even though the discursive public sphere theory pays special attention to unorganized civil society actors, a high level of visibility of this actor group is only demanded when normative issues are discussed (Habermas 1992, p.460). Since this analysis does not focus on discussions of normative issues, a medium level of visibility of informal civil society actors is sufficient.

more depth and links it with the concept of the EU citizenship, forming the conceptual backbone of this study. First, an analytical definition of the European public sphere is provided and the concept of EU citizens in the European public sphere that underlies this study is presented, which is the corner stone of the empirical analysis. Afterwards, extant research on the European public sphere and the visibility of EU citizens within it is discussed.

4. The European Public Sphere

The traditional notion of the public sphere outlined in the previous chapter has initially been developed departing from the nation state as its reference framework and did not discuss the idea of a supranational or European public sphere. However, these days many politically important decisions are made at the EU level. The European integration process has led to a shift in governance from the national state to the supranational policy level and is increasingly affecting people's lives (Beetham and Lord 1998). It is in the context of legitimacy and democratic governance beyond the nation state, that the concept of the European public sphere gained importance. Even though the EU is not a state in itself, it can be considered a "functional equivalent" (Eder 2000, p. 168) to the nation state that consists of territory, political authority, the people and a public sphere that is able to control governance. Eriksen (2005, p. 342) argues: "Despite the fact that the EU neither is a state nor a nation, its development as a new kind of polity is closely connected to its development as a communicative space". As the public sphere is a requirement for democratic governance, a European public sphere is central to the legitimacy of governance at the EU level to ensure accountability and responsiveness.

The first section of this chapter provides an analytical definition of the European public sphere that is used as the basis for the empirical analyses. It then turns to definitions of the European public sphere that have been proposed and been the basis for empirical studies by previous research. The approaches, their research questions and empirical findings on the European public sphere are discussed next, guided by the question whether it can be assumed that a European public sphere exists. Finally, the chapter turns to examine studies that have taken into account the visibility of EU citizens with the European public sphere.

4.1. An Analytical Definition of the European Public Sphere

With reference to the analytical definition of the public sphere outlined in the previous chapter (Chapter 3), the European public sphere in this study is understood as a *communication system that mediates between the EU citizens at the micro-level and the EU's governmental system at the macro-level*. To have a meaningful role for the legitimacy of the EU's political system, another defining criterion of the European public sphere is that discussions need to concern EU governmental affairs. As its national counterpart, the European public sphere can be conceptualised as consisting of different forums. There are European encounter publics where EU citizens debate EU governmental affairs (Freudenberger 2013) and there are European issue publics, e.g., in form of protest events against EU policies (Rucht 2001). However, European public sphere research has nearly exclusively focused on the European media sphere (e.g., de Vreese, 2001; Eriksen, 2005; Gripsrud, 2007; Pfetsch, 2008; van de Steeg, 2002; Wessler et al., 2008), as at the national as well as at the EU level, "communication between citizens and their representatives has become essentially media-based" (Kriesi 2013a p.38).

At the EU level, the importance of the media is even heightened, as direct means of political communication are limited (Dahl 1994). For example, due to the geographic distance, protests in Brussels demand higher organisational and monetary resources (see, e.g., Rucht 2001). In the past, protests against policies of the EU have also occurred at the member state level (Imig and Tarrow 2003). In this case, despite citizens' direct action, the media are again relevant for communicating the protesters' demands to the EU decision-makers who are based in Brussels.

Regarding the actors in the mediated European public sphere, if one could simply apply actor structure of the national political system to the EU level, one would differentiate between the EU's governmental system, a European intermediary system and the EU citizens. However, the EU's political system is characterised by multi-level governance, where "decision-making competencies are shared by actors at different levels" (Hooghe and Marks 2001 p.3). Even

4.1. An Analytical Definition of the European Public Sphere

though EU institutions are independent actors, the EU is inevitably linked to the member state level. For example, it is national political parties that run in the European elections and it is the heads of state and governments of the EU member states that take part in the Council meetings. Therefore, both actors from the European, but also from the national level are relevant for the actor structure of the European public sphere.

This study argues that actors from the national level can appear in their role as European actors, by thematising EU politics, policy or politics. For example, the German chancellor Angela Merkel is a governmental actor of the German political system. However, when she is taking part in European Council meetings along with the other head of states of the EU member states, she is taking a role as an EU actor. The rationale behind this is that the European Council is an institution that is part of the EU's political system. The Council is taking decisions on general directions and priorities of EU governance. Despite the possibility that the German chancellor might primarily represent the interests of the German citizens when taking decisions in the Council, she accounts for a national-EU actor, since the decision-making process takes place within the sphere of EU governance.

Likewise, at the intermediary level, there are civil society organisations representing the aggregated interests of national citizens to the EU (e.g., the Nature and Biodiversity Conservation Union of Germany), while there are also organisations representing supranational interests. Due to this particular nature of the EU's political system, the actor structure of the European public sphere is twofold. Consequently, I distinguish between a) actors from the national arena that account for "national European actors" in the context of EU governance by thematising or deciding on EU politics, policy or polity (hereafter also referred to as *horizontal* actors) and b) European actors that are directly defined with reference to the EU level (hereafter also denoted as *vertical* actors).[17] Figure 4.1 visualises the EU's political system and the actors within the European public sphere.

---

[17] The distinction between vertical and horizontal is inferred from previous research (Koopmans and Erbe 2004; see also: Brüggemann and Kleinen-von Königslöw 2009; Peters et al. 2006; Pfetsch and Koopmans 2006; Wessler et al. 2008), which is discussed in more detail in the following sections.

Figure 4.1 The European public sphere as a mediating system

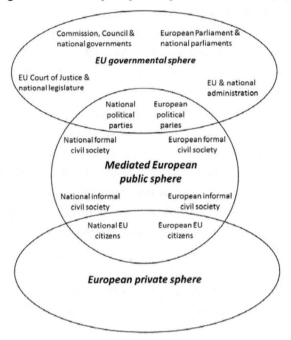

Based on this distinction, within the European public sphere, I differentiate between national and EU-level governmental actors that both *combined* constitute the actors of the *EU's governmental sphere*. Governments, the legislature, the judiciary and the political administration of the EU member states account for horizontal actors in the European public sphere when taking part in debates on EU governance. At the vertical level, European governmental actors consist of the Commission, the Council of the EU, the European Parliament and the Court of Justice, as well as the EU's administration (Hix and Høyland 2011).

The *EU's intermediary system* consists of national political parties and European political parties. Both of which are relevant for the EU's political system (von dem Berge and Poguntke 2013). On the one hand, it is the national parties of the EU member states that run in the European elections. On the other hand, within the European Parliament, transnational party groups that exceed purely

4.1. An Analytical Definition of the European Public Sphere 81

national interests have emerged (Hix et al. 2006). Here, it can be distinguished between political groups in the European Parliament, but also extra-parliamentary transnational cooperation and associations (Pedersen 1996; Hix and Lord 1997). Whether these European parties can be considered equivalents to political parties at the national level is still an ongoing debate (cf. Lightfoot 2006).

Furthermore, civil society actors based at the national and EU level representing either national or supranational interests of the citizens of the EU member states (e.g., Eising 2012; Pollack 1997; Wonka et al. 2010) are part of the EU's intermediary system. I consider national civil society as consisting of organisations that represent the interests of citizens of a certain member state to the EU. If such a civil society organisation, such as the Nature and Biodiversity Conservation Union of Germany, would join an umbrella organisation representing environmental organisations from other EU member states as well, I would refer to this organisation as a European civil society actor, because it represents not only national interests of one EU member state, but supranational interests. One example of this actor category is the European Youth Forum that is a platform for youth organisations in Europe. Its aim is to bring "together tens of millions of young people from all over Europe, organised in order to represent their common interests" (European Youth Forum 2015). However, at the EU level, also organisations have emerged that represent pan-European interests without having sub-organisations at the member states as its base. These organisations I account likewise as belonging to the group of European civil society. All of these forms of civil society in the European public sphere can again be divided into more formal civil society actors that are located closer to the governmental sphere and informal civil society actors, located closer to the private sphere.

I conceptualise the *European private sphere* as comprising the EU citizens that are, by definition (Chapter 2), members of the EU's political community. The overlap between the European private and the European public sphere reflects this realm where individual EU citizens become visible in the European public sphere. To account for the twofold structure of the European public sphere and for the purpose of this study, I consider it as important to also distinguish between a national and a European dimension of the EU citizenry. In the European public sphere, *national EU citizens* account for citizens of the individual EU member states. As the information about the EU member state a citizen comes from is known, the EU citizenry that becomes visible via the European public sphere appears as separated by nationality. An example for this group would be the news media reporting about French citizens that vote in the European Parliament election. They can be identified as EU (not national) citizens because they participate in the European (not national) political community by voting in the European election, while it is simultaneously known from which EU member state they are, namely France.

European EU citizens, on the other hand, simultaneously represent the citizens of all EU member states. Contrary to national EU citizens, which link back to the national level, European EU citizens represent a truly European and supranational form of citizenship that goes beyond the nation state. Therefore, from a normative perspective, I consider European EU citizens representing a more advanced and integrated European citizenry, because the citizens of all EU member states are represented at once, while references to national EU citizens simultaneously link back to national sentiments and only account for a fragment of the EU citizens. An example of European EU citizens in the mediated European public sphere is a news report on the "European voters" who cast a vote in the European election.

4.2. Extant Research on the European Public Sphere

After having provided an analytical definition of the European public sphere that is the basis empirical for analyses in the next chapters, in the following, definitions of the European public sphere by previous research are discussed. This literature review is guided by the questions: *How has previous research defined the notion of a European public sphere? What are the empirical measures applied to measure whether a European public sphere has come into being?* Based on the empirical findings, *can we actually assume that a European public sphere exists?*

As discussed below, even though there is a growing number of studies on the European public sphere, research has not yet developed a common definition. However, one can identify two strands of research, one focussing on a) a pan-European public sphere (also referred to as cross-national or transnational European public sphere) and the other one concentrating on b) the Europeanisation of public spheres of the EU member states.

4.2.1. A Pan-European European Public Sphere

The idea of a pan- European public sphere, in essence, applies the national concept of the public sphere to the EU level. It postulates the existence of a *single, supra-national* public sphere that covers all member states at once. This means that communication between the EU citizens and the European governmental actors takes place in a setting whose scope exceeds the one of national public spheres of the EU member states. Some argue that such a transnational European public sphere requires a shared language, culture and the existence of a European identity among the EU citizens (Grimm 1995; Gripsrud 2007; Lingenberg 2006; Lingenberg 2010; Kielmansegg 2003). These requirements are closely linked to Habermas' notion of the discursive public sphere (Schlesinger and Kevin 2000; Gripsrud 2007; cf. also Habermas 2004).

The majority of studies, however, simply equate the transnational European public sphere with a European media system and/or pan-European media (Gerhards 1993b; Brüggemann and Schulz-Forberg 2008; van de Steeg 2002). This approach basically transfers the idea of national mass media systems to the European level. It is assumed that pan-European public sphere requires "that there would be newspapers and periodicals, radio and television programmes, offered and demanded on a European market and thus creating a nation-transcending communicative context" (Grimm 1995 p.295). Instead of a common language, for the existence of a pan-European media system, news content would have to be translated into the languages of the EU member states, which is a costly venture for media businesses (Gerhards 1993b).

Hence, EU-wide media that report on the same content and that are available in all EU member states would be needed. Research is unclear about whether this media content has to necessarily concern EU governance or not. Gerhards (1993b), for example, states that a pan-European public sphere refers to a uniform media system, where citizens of the EU member states are able to consume the same media content. In Gerhards' definition, it is not explicitly stated that this media content necessarily has to include EU affairs. Contrary, Brüggemann and Schulz-Forberg (2008; 2009) argue that pan-European media focus on the EU and aim to address an "audience constituted by the EU citizenry" (Brüggemann and Schulz-Forberg 2008 p.86). These criteria allow that based on their scope and intention, pan-European media can be differentiated from other forms of transnational media.

There is relatively little empirical research on the transnational European public sphere. Those studies commonly examine the emergence of pan-European media outlets (Brüggemann and Schulz-Forberg 2008) and their news coverage (Firmstone 2008; Garcia-Blanco and Cushion 2010). Beyond this, there is also some research that examined the impact of the EU's media policy on the development of pan-European media (Ward 2004). Scholars have observed that "a multitude of transnational media have evolved over the last 20 years and that they have a small, but significant and growing audience" (Brüggemann and Schulz-Forberg 2009b). Some EU-wide media, such as *Euronews*, even provide news in various (yet not all) European languages. However, research has also shown that the news coverage of transnational media is not necessarily about the EU. In a study on transnational press, Firmstone concludes: "Although the transnational press represents a departure from the internal member state perspective where media coverage is structured by national concerns, it does not provide EU citizens with an opportunity to access information about the EU presented from a truly transnational perspective" (Firmstone 2008 pp.438–439). This is supported by a study of Garcia-Blanco and Cushion (2010) examining the news coverage of *Euronews*. The results show that the vast majority of news items do not concern the EU.

A second concern is the audience of pan-European media, which is seen as elitist and non-representative of the average population of EU member states (Firmstone 2008; Schlesinger 1999). In fact, most Europeans might not even be aware of the existence these transnational news outlets (Garcia-Blanco and Cushion 2010 p.406). In this sense, a transnational European public sphere currently only exists among a minority of politically interested actors and does not reach a broader number of people (Neidhardt et al. 2000 p.265).

The requirements of a shared language, culture and identity are even more difficult (if not impossible) to fulfil. The EU is a heterogeneous polity with a heterogeneous citizenry. One central problem for the emergence of such a European communicative space is the language diversity within the EU. Some authors argue that language is inevitably related to cultural values, or rather a specific way of seeing the world (Kielmansegg 2003; cf. also Machill et al. 2006; Strohmeier 2007; van de Steeg 2002). In the past, it has even been doubted that democracy at the EU level is possible, because EU citizens speak different languages and are therefore unable to communicate with each other (Grimm 1995).

Overall, the notion of a pan-European public sphere is seen as utopian (de Vreese 2007; van de Steeg 2002) and the majority of scholars derive the conclusion that a pan-European public sphere does currently not exist and is unlikely to emerge in the near future (Grimm 1995; de Vreese 2003; Koopmans and Erbe 2004; Schlesinger 1999; van de Steeg 2002).

4.2.2. The Europeanisation of National Public Spheres

Previous studies mostly claim that the emergence of a European public sphere can more realistically be expected to result from a Europeanisation of national public spheres (Commission of the European Communities 2006, p. 4; de Vreese et al. 2006, p. 479; Gerhards 2000, p. 293; Machill et al. 2006, p. 63). In the broadest sense, Europeanisation refers to a process where debates in the national public spheres of the EU member states become more "European" by discussing EU affairs to a greater extent. Gerhards (1993b), who systematically introduced the distinction between a transnational European public sphere and the Europeanisation of national public spheres, defines the latter as discussions of EU governance in the national media.

Later on, the notion of Europeanisations of national public spheres has been developed further. Research has broadened the definition of Europeanisation of the national public spheres by introducing the distinction of vertical and horizontal Europeanisation (Koopmans and Erbe 2004; see also: Brüggemann and Kleinen-von Königslöw 2009; Peters et al. 2006; Pfetsch and Koopmans 2006; Wessler et al. 2008). *Vertical Europeanisation* refers to a connection between the national and EU level, in the sense that EU affairs are discussed and actors from the EU level become visible in the national public spheres (Brüggemann and Kleinen-von Königslöw 2009 p.29). *Horizontal Europeanisation*, on the other hand, refers to a linkage between the member states in the form of an increased focus on actors and events taking place in fellow EU member states (Brüggemann and Kleinen-von Königslöw 2009 p.29). The rationale behind it is that "[i]n an intergovernmental polity, the other member states can no longer be treated as foreign countries whose internal politics are not really relevant for one's own country" (Koopmans and Erbe 2004 p.101). However, when thinking about the role of the public sphere for facilitating accountability and responsiveness of governance, it is the vertical dimension of the European public sphere that is of importance for the legitimacy of EU governance.

Departing from this minimal-definition that the European public sphere is established by public discussions on EU governance, scholars have defined several *additional* criteria, the European public sphere has to fulfil. As a second criterion stated in Gerhards' definition suggests that discussions on EU governance also need to be *evaluated* from a European perspective. The idea behind it is that purely national interests are overcome in favour of European ones (Meyer 2005). In a similar way, Eder and Kantner (2000) define simultaneous discus-

4.2. Extant Research on the European Public Sphere

sions on European topics with similar aspects of relevancy as the main criterion for a European public sphere (see also: Peters et al. 2006; Wessler et al. 2008). In other words, discussions of EU governance have to take place at the same time in the EU member states and arguments have to be defined in a similar manner, with a European "frame of reference" (Koopmans 2007). However, this approach has been criticised and rejected for two reasons: First, it is argued that a unified European perspective should not be a pre-condition for the European public sphere, because EU member states might have different perspectives on different issues. This disagreement between EU member states might result in intra-EU conflict, which is seen as an important element for discussions (Meyer 2005 p.123). Different national views can then be reconciled via discussion in the European public sphere. Second, a European perspective is considered as utopian, since EU-specific policy issues have not yet developed clear cleavages (Mittag and Wessels 2003 p.419).

There is also a line of research that demands the "Europeanisation of collective identities" as part of the Europeanisation of the national public spheres (e.g., Wessler et al. 2008; Hepp et al. 2012). This aspect addresses the question whether the actors in the European public sphere are defined or define themselves by a national or European reference (e.g., the French vs. we Europeans) and develop a European identity that distinguishes them from out-groups (such as the US). The identity-related aspect is closely linked to the notion of the discursive public sphere (cf. e.g., Wessler et al. 2008 pp.16–19).

Since this study is interested in a comparison of different normative public sphere theories in the context of the European public sphere, criteria derived from those theories cannot be part of the initial analytical definition of the European public sphere. This study proposes a minimal definition, in which the European public sphere is constituted by public discussions on EU governance in the national media. The thematic focus on governance has also been a defining criterion for the public sphere in the nation state context (cf. Habermas 1974). Hence, *a European public sphere exists and can fulfil its mediating function for the EU's political system and enhance democratic legitimacy at the EU level, if discussions on EU affairs take place in the national media of EU member states.*

The horizontal dimension of the European public sphere might likewise be important for an exchange between the EU member states; however, it is not directly relevant with regard to the legitimacy function of the European public sphere.

4.2.3. Empirical Observations: Does a European Public Sphere Exist?

When interested in analysing the visibility of EU citizens within the European public sphere, it is first of all important to establish that a European public sphere exists. Numerous studies and several large-scale empirical research projects have investigated the European public sphere from a Europeanisation perspective (e.g., Boomgaarden et al. 2013; Peter and de Vreese 2004; Wessler et al. 2008; Koopmans et al. 2010). As discussed above, these studies vary with regard to the theoretical conceptualisation of the European public sphere, but also in their approaches to *measure* its existence. Generally, one can identify five (sometimes overlapping) approaches: a) studies that examine the reporting of EU news and EU level actors in the national media *in comparison* to national news and actors, b) studies that examine the existence of the European public sphere during certain *time periods or events* only, c) studies that analyse whether a European public sphere might have emerged in some *member states* and/or d) in some *media outlets*, but not in others, and finally, e) there is a stream of research that concentrates on whether a European public sphere might not have always existed but have emerged over *time*. In the following, each line of research is examined and main conclusions about the state of the art are drawn.

a) The first line of research is not concerned with the question of whether EU news is reported in the national media, but to what *extent*. In this context, a number of studies have investigated the visibility of EU news and EU governmental actors *in comparison* to national governmental affairs and actors. For example, Hepp et al. (2012) carried out a content analysis of the newspaper coverage of six EU member states (Austria, Denmark, France, Germany, Poland

4.2. Extant Research on the European Public Sphere

and the UK) during the years 1982, 1989, 1996, 2003 and 2008.[18] Since the theoretical framework is heavily influenced by the discursive public sphere theory (cf. e.g., Sifft et al. 2007 p.302), their sample only includes "discursive articles", such as editorials, commentaries or interviews. The results by Hepp et al. show that it is mainly national politics that is discussed as a major topic in discursive news. The visibility of EU politics is considered very low; in 2008, on average, only 4% of the articles had EU governance as its major topic. With regard to the visibility of EU actors, the share of articles reporting on EU institutions was contrasted with the share of national institutions. The results show that while more than 60% of the news refers to national institutions, EU institutions are only visible in 14% of the articles.

Trenz (2004), on the other hand, examined the news coverage of two broadsheets from Austria, France, Germany, Italy, Spain as well as the UK in the year 2000. The study differentiated between three types of EU news: (1) "European articles" that discuss EU governance as dominant topic, (2) "Europeanised articles" that dominantly discuss national topics, but with a simultaneous reference to at least one EU sub-issue and (3) articles with a European referential frame which are not about EU governance, but make rhetorical reference, such as the use of the word "Europe". The study finds a "considerable degree of European political communication" (Trenz 2004 p.297): Overall, about 35% of the total political news coverage show one out of the three forms of European political communication.

In the context of the EUROPUB-Project, Koopmans et al. carried out a claim-making analysis, which is a form of "content analyses of public statements and demands" (Koopmans and Statham 2010a p.32), and examined the degree of Europeanisation of the news coverage across six EU member states (Germany, France, the UK, Italy, Spain and the Netherlands) and one non-EU country (Switzerland) and across seven different policy domains.[19] The time

---

[18] For each year, two constructed weeks for one broadsheet and tabloid newspaper per country were coded.
[19] The policy domains that were selected are: monetary politics, agriculture, immigration, military troops deployment, pensions/retirement and education. In addition, articles that covered the European integration process itself were included in the sample.

frame covers the years 1990, 1995 and 2000-2002.[20] Within those policy fields, the EU has varying decision-making competences and the news stories included in the sample do not necessarily have to concern EU governance (see Koopmans and Statham 2010 p.53). The analysis focuses on the visibility of different actor groups that make claims within the different policy issues. Their understanding of European actors refers mainly to EU institutions, but it is defined broader by also including supranational and intergovernmental institutions that are located at the European level (e.g., the Council of Europe). Their results show that European level actors make up to 30% of the claims in the news media where the EU has considerable decision-making power, while they are nearly invisible in policy areas (such as education) where the EU has limited competences. In contrast, the visibility of national actors in terms of claims making varies between 90% and 34% (Koopmans et al. 2010). Nevertheless, this study derives the conclusion that "actors from the European polity level were highly visible participants in public debates in those issue fields where the European Union has gained strong supranational competencies" (Koopmans et al. 2010 p.93) and that there is no empirical basis for the claim that there is too little attention to EU actors.

In short, based on different study designs and media samples, there is no consensus as to what extent EU governance is reported in the national media of the EU member states. Yet, all studies confirm at least a minimum of media attention to EU news.

b) The second line of research has investigated the existence of a European public sphere during certain time periods or events. The rational here is that these key events "are essential in shaping public opinion about European integration because they constitute some of the few moments when the EU is visible in mainstream news that attracts a large audience" (de Vreese 2001 pp.286–287). A number of studies have investigated the EU news coverage during European Parliament elections (Schuck et al. 2013; Peter et al. 2004; Michailidou

---

[20] For 1990 and 1995, one issue per two weeks and for 2000-2002 one issue per week were coded. The media sample includes two quality newspapers (one more left-oriented, and one more right-oriented) per country. In addition, for the year 2000, a regional and a tabloid newspaper were coded. To analyse the data, a claim-making analysis was conducted.

4.2. Extant Research on the European Public Sphere

and Trenz 2010; Boomgaarden et al. 2013; Wilke and Reinemann 2007). In the framework of the PIREDEU project, a large scale content analysis was carried out during the European Parliament elections.[21] The study includes content analysis data from TV channels and newspapers and covers quality and commercial media outlets of all 27 EU member states that took part in the 2009 elections. The results for the 2009 election show that the 16.3% of the total news coverage on TV and 12.1% of newspapers' front page stories are about the EU and/or the European Parliament election (Schuck et al. 2011b).

Besides European elections, there are additional factors at the EU level that can impact the amount of EU news reported. As such, events that are related to the EU as a polity, i.e., Council summits or a change in the Council Presidency, but also plenary sessions of the European Parliament, lead to an increase in EU news (Boomgaarden et al. 2010; Meyer 2005; de Vreese 2001). Some evidence has been found that the amount of EU news is also influenced by policy-related events, such as enlargements or the signing of new treaties (Boomgaarden et al. 2010; Hepp et al. 2012; de Vreese and Boomgaarden 2006; Semetko and Valkenburg 2000). In addition, EU news is likely to increase alongside certain national events that are related to the EU, e.g., referenda on EU affairs (De Vreese and Semetko 2004).

With regards to the visibility of EU level actors, previous research has indicated that the visibility of EU officials is higher during routine periods compared to EU summits (Peter and de Vreese 2004). The share of EU officials among all actors during routine periods is on average 20%, compared to 7.2% during EU summits. However, this finding is arguably due to the operationalisation of EU actors as "EU officials", which are "members of EU institutions or persons appointed by the EU" (Peter and de Vreese 2004 p.11). Hence, the head of states and governments of the EU member states, the most important actors during these meetings, are not seen as partially also belonging to the group of EU actors, but are included in the category of "non-EU actors".

---

[21] EU news was coded on two national television channels and three newspapers for all states that were members of the EU in the respective year of the election. For further details see Chapter 6 of this book.

Summarising this stream of research, it can be said that media attention to EU governance is not stable, but fluctuates is the course of certain events. Yet, there is no evidence that there are periods where EU news is completely absent from the news agenda.

c) Research has also taken the possibility into account that a European public sphere might exist or be more developed in some EU member states, but not in others. Studies have compared the Europeanisation of national public spheres across different EU member states and have observed strong differences in the degree of Europeanisation (Boomgaarden et al. 2010; Kleinen-von Königslöw 2012; Peters et al. 2005; Pfetsch 2008; Sifft et al. 2007; Statham 2007; Trenz 2004; de Vreese 2003). The PIREDEU project is until today the only study that takes into account the news coverage of all EU member states. The study finds likewise sharp cross-country differences in the level of visibility of EU news, or rather news about the European Parliament election (de Vreese et al. 2006; Schuck et al. 2011a; 2011b). In the 2009 election, the EU news coverage on television varied between 8.5% and 57.1% and was highest in Greece and lowest in Belgium (Schuck et al. 2011 p.46). The visibility of EU news on newspaper front-pages also varied strongly and was highest in Malta (42.3%) and lowest in Portugal (2.9%) (Schuck et al. 2011 p.46). While the results of the 2004 election indicated that EU news was more visible in the new EU member states (de Vreese et al., 2006), no clear East-West or North-South divide could be identified for the 2009 election, suggesting that the higher visibility was rather a result of the novel character of the election in the Eastern states, rather than a country pattern (Schuck et al. 2011a).

The majority of these comparative studies have remained descriptive in scope. The few studies that have aimed to *explain* these differences further studies found some evidence that the length of the EU membership is positively related to the amount of EU news reported in the national press (Wessler et al. 2008; Kleinen-von Königslöw 2012). It is argued that older member states report more EU news, because "[n]ewspapers in countries that have long been assimilated in the EU tend to discuss EU politics more often, as both journalists and readers have become more accustomed to this subject" (Brüggemann and

Kleinen-von Königslöw 2009 pp.40–41). Furthermore, there is some evidence suggesting that holding the EU presidency increases the amount of EU news reported in respective member state (Boomgaarden et al. 2010).

In conclusion, news media attention to EU governance varies across countries. Despite different intensity in EU news reporting, there is no evidence that the EU is completely absent from the news agenda of certain EU member states.

d) Several studies have taken into account that whether and to what extent a European public sphere exists might vary depending on the media outlet. Based on the PIREDEU election studies, Boomgaarden et al. (2013) examined variation in the EU news coverage (for a similar study see also Schuck et al. 2011) and the findings show that public broadcaster report significantly more EU news compared to commercial broadcaster and broadsheets more than tabloids. However, for the visibility of EU actors[22], no significant relationship was found for media outlets. This indicates that the two empirical dimensions of vertical Europeanisation do not necessarily go hand in hand: Reporting more EU news does not automatically lead to an increase on actors from the EU level (this finding is also supported by Kleinen-von Königslöw (2012)). For discursive articles, however, EU institutions are significantly more visible in the quality than tabloid press (Kleinen-von Königslöw 2012). This trend is stable across time and EU member states. Even though the visibility of EU governance varies across different media outlets, there is no evidence that EU affairs are not completely in some news outlets.

e) Finally, some studies have analysed the amount of EU news and actors reported over time to account for the possibility that a European public sphere might not have existed in the early stage of the European integration, but might have emerged as Europeanisation processes have deepened. Studies have generally observed an increase in EU news and EU level actors that are reported in the national media (Boomgaarden et al. 2010; Hepp et al. 2012; Koopmans et al. 2010). For discursive news stories across Austria, Denmark, France, Germany, Poland and the UK, Hepp et al. (2012) find that the amount of news that had EU governance as a main topic increased slightly from only 1% in 1982 to 4% in

---

[22] For technical reasons, only the main actors of the news story were taken into account.

2003 and then stagnated. For the visibility of EU institutions, a stronger increase was observed: The share of articles that included references to EU institutions increased from 6% in the 1980s up to 16% in 2003 and then slightly decreased by 2% in 2008. Koopmans et al. (2010) observed a similar increase in the share of European level actors from 9% in 1990 up to 15% in 2002 in newspaper articles published in Germany, France, the UK, Italy, Spain, the Netherlands as well as Switzerland. The increase in visibility also applies for EU news that are reported during European Parliament elections (de Vreese et al. 2006; Schuck et al. 2011a; 2011b) and for the visibility of EU level actors in the election news coverage (de Vreese et al. 2006). It is argued that this "overall positive trend in EU news visibility (…) reflects the process of a deepening and widening Union with increasing and increasingly relevant competencies" (Boomgaarden et al. 2010 p.515).

What conclusions about the existence or rather the stage of development of a European public sphere can be derived from these streams of research? Studies that examine the EU from the first angle, often conclude that the amount of EU news covered by the media is (too) low compared to the news coverage on national governance (Peters et al. 2005) and that therefore, there is a publicity or communication deficit of the EU (Gerhards 2002; Wessler 2008). Other scholars, such as Trenz (2004), observe a considerable degree of Europeanisation of national public spheres. If one excludes any normative criteria about the quality or style of discussions and applies a minimal definition of the European public sphere that has been proposed by this study, namely that a European public sphere comes into being by discussions on EU governance in the national media, then there is good reason to believe that a European public sphere exists. The empirical findings of all studies discussed above support that EU news is discussed in the national media of the EU member states. Hence, there is a minimum of discussion on EU governance, even though the frequency of EU news reported might vary in the course of certain events, across the EU member states, and in different media outlets. Furthermore, there is evidence that reporting of EU news is stable or rather increasing over time. No study has so far detected a complete absence of EU news in the national media of EU member states. Therefore, it can be concluded that a European public sphere exists, even though it might currently still be a rather weak phenomenon. Yet, what is the role of ordinary EU citizens within the European public sphere? This question is addressed in the following section.

4.3. Extant Research on EU Citizens in the European Public Sphere

The notion of citizenship and the public sphere are closely interrelated. In democracies, citizens rely on a public sphere that allows for political-decisions to be accountable and responsive to the will of the people and thereby legitimises governance. This understanding is based on the assumption that the public sphere is a communication system that allows for a *reciprocal* observation of citizens and actors of the governmental system. The media ought to provide information on political events and actors to citizens, but for some public sphere theories, they are also "expected to give voice to public opinion, that is, to keep the elected representatives informed about public opinion so that the elected representatives can be responsive to the public's demands" (Kriesi 2013a p.38). From this perspective, the media ought to be a forum for debate that is not only open to actors from the governmental and intermediary sphere, but also to individual citizens. As a consequence, through the public sphere, citizens and governmental actors are able to communicate with *each other* (Gerhards 1998b p.269). However, there is generally little research on the visibility of ordinary citizens in public debates.

In the traditional nation state context of the public sphere (see Chapter 3), only a limited number of studies have taken the visibility of ordinary citizens into account. These have often been carried out in the field of journalism studies, and have examined different ways in which citizens can become visible in the news coverage (Lewis et al. 2004; Brookes et al. 2004), and analysed as journalistic news sources (Dimitrova and Strömbäck 2009; Hopmann and Shehata 2011; Lefevere et al. 2011). Overall, based on these studies, it can be concluded that citizens do become visible in the news coverage, yet, their visibility seems relatively low, though there is some evidence that there is variance across countries and topics (Dimitrova and Strömbäck 2009; van Aelst and de Swert 2009). However, empirical evidence on the visibility of citizens in the news coverage is still limited as previous research is either based on single-country studies, or compared only a limited number of states.

In the context of the European public sphere, many theoretical works, but also empirical studies have highlighted the importance of EU citizens and the role of communication between the EU and its citizens in their theoretical framework (e.g., Meyer 1999; Kleinen-von Königslöw 2010; Gripsrud 2007; Trenz and Eder 2004a; Maier and Rittberger 2008b; Statham 2008). For example, Meyer (1999 p.622) writes on input legitimacy that "political communication contributes to the legitimacy of governance if it helps to increase citizens' influence on decision-making and to hold political actors accountable for their actions in between electoral procedures". Likewise, Trenz argues that a "European public sphere has come into existence and that it has evolved through the *mutual* observation of institutional actors and their audiences" (Trenz 2004 p.291, italics added). Despite these theoretical considerations, there is a lack of empirical research investigating the role of citizens with the European public sphere. Instead, studies have paid attention to the importance of political communication for output legitimacy by focussing primarily on the visibility of EU news and EU governmental actors in the media. This approach resembles a top-down communication process that exclusively highlights the importance of information the EU governmental system provides to citizens (Brüggemann 2008). Little is known about communication processes that take place from the bottom up. To my knowledge, there are only four empirical projects that partially address the way in which (EU) citizens are represented in the European public sphere.[23] However, as outlined in the following, based on previous research, no conclusive evidence about the visibility of EU citizens in the European public spheres of the EU member states can be derived.

First of all, there are some studies that did not *directly* aim at analysing the visibility of EU citizens, but their results nevertheless allow to a certain extent

---

[23] Studies that merely mention EU citizens among other civil society actors are not included.

for inferences about the visibility of EU citizens in the European public sphere. For example, in the context of the 2009 European Parliament election, Schuck et al. (2011) examine the media's use of frames that establish a reference to the EU and its citizens in newspaper and TV news of all 27 EU member states. The study considers to what extent the media reports negative reference to a gap between the EU and its citizens or positive references concerning the responsiveness of the EU towards it citizens. In most member states, both frames are present in news about the European election. On average, 5% of the news stories include a negative reference to the gap between the EU and its citizens, while positive references regarding the responsiveness of the EU towards its citizens are only included in 2% of the news. Even though based on the results of this study we can infer that citizens are visible in the EU news coverage, the focus of this study is more on the frame itself, rather than on EU citizens and their role in the European public sphere.

A number of publications based on *The Transnationalization of Public Spheres in the EU* project explored the visibility of references to a European collective in the news coverage of broadsheets and tabloids in Austria, Denmark, France, Germany, Poland and the UK during the years 1982, 1989, 1996, 2003 and 2008 (Hepp et al. 2012; Sifft et al. 2007; Kleinen-von Königslöw 2010). The study starts out from the assumption that for the existence of a European public sphere, a shared European identity is needed. It is argued that references to "the Europeans" and "we Europeans" in media discourses can be seen as a sign of a collective European identity. As mentioned previously (Chapter 2), citizenship and identity are two related concepts, however, the existence of a shared identity is not a precondition of citizenship. Nevertheless, the study provides some insights on the visibility of EU citizens in the European public sphere, because of the way a collective European identity is measured, which includes references to the European population and the European citizens (in addition to we-references in form of the use of the phrase "we Europeans") in the news media (Hepp et al. 2012 p.55).

The media sample consists of broadsheets and tabloid newspapers from five EU states and focuses exclusively on discursive newspaper articles (e.g., comments).[24] First of all, their results show that references to the European population and EU citizens exist in the news coverage; however, their share is relatively low: While in 1982 the share of references to the Europeans was 2.6%, it increased slightly over time and reached 5.7% in 2003 and then remained rather stable. In comparison, the share of references to a country's own nation is much higher (approximately 30%). This is partially also caused by the sample, which is based on the overall and not only EU-related news coverage. With regard to cross country-differences, references to the Europeans vary rather strongly across the five countries. The news coverage of Germany shows most references to this European collective (14%), followed by France (13%), the UK (9%), Austria (5%), Denmark (3%), and Poland (2%). The results furthermore show that the share of references to "the Europeans" is higher in broadsheets than tabloids across all countries included in the sample.

Overall, based on this project, it is difficult to make inferences about the visibility of EU citizens in the European public sphere in general, because the media sample includes only discursive news articles that are not necessarily about the EU. Furthermore, there are additional forms of references to EU citizens or European collective it can be thought of.[25] One example are opinion polls that can likewise account for a way of representing "the Europeans".

Based on the same project, Wessler (2007) compared different actor types that become visible in the coverage of national, European and foreign policy news in broadsheets. European topics are defined as news stories that either concern the EU or other EU member states as such. Actors were coded if they were directly or indirectly quoted in at least two sentences in the respective news story. Among the different actor groups, the visibility of "ordinary citizens" was descriptively examined. The results indicate that citizens are nearly invisible in European news: less than 3% of news stories include citizens as actors. In contrast, citizens become visible in the context of national governance in approximately 10% of news. Overall, and especially for European topics, it is

---

[24] See also pages 64-65 for further details.
[25] Sifft et al. (2007, p. 133) also mention that there are additional forms of identification with a European public, such as a common European history or values, but these rather abstract forms are not referred to here.

governmental actors that dominate the news coverage. The definition of European topics has two consequences: It does not account for a European public sphere as defined in this study since non-EU topics are included, and it cannot be differentiated whether references to citizens are made in the context of EU governance or foreign affairs. Furthermore, the generalisability of the results is limited due to an exclusive focus on discursive news articles published in broadsheets.

Second, there are studies that focused on the visibility of citizens not in the context of the Europeanisation of national public spheres, but from a *pan-European public sphere perspective*. A study by Garcia-Blanco and Cushion (2010) focuses on the presence of citizens in the *transnational* European public sphere. The study is based on a television news content analysis which examines the role of "citizens of Europe" (ibid., p. 404). Topical contexts in which citizens make an appearance on screen in addition to journalistic practices used to represent citizens are analysed. However, the study lacks a clear definition of what exactly constitutes the "citizens of Europe". It focuses on the representations of citizens in the transnational European public sphere overall and it is not distinguished whether EU or national citizens from the EU member states, or non-European countries are represented in the news.[26] This is because it is not differentiated between citizens that appear in the context of EU affairs, news about EU member states, or within news from non-EU member states. The study accounts for the general visibility of citizens in the transnational European public sphere, which are not necessarily EU citizens. It is further limited as it only takes into account a very short time period and is exclusively focused on one European medium which has only a limited reach and can therefore hardly function as a European public sphere *per se*. Furthermore, as mentioned previously (Chapter 4.2.1), scholars have raised doubts that a transnational European public sphere exists.

Third, there are studies that do not examine EU citizens within the EU news coverage, but focus on their role as an audience. Michailidou and Trenz

---

[26] It should be mentioned here that citizens that do not have a legal status as EU citizens might also play a role for the development of the EU citizenship (cf. Saward 2012). Yet, analytically, it should be distinguished between these different concepts.

(2010) examine the *online* European public sphere during the 2009 European election and the participation of citizens in discussions on journalism websites and blogs from 12 EU member states by analysing posts made by readers. Indeed, this is a way in which EU citizens are able to directly participate in the European public sphere. However, Michailidou and Trenz's approach does not provide information on the visibility of EU citizens *within* debates on EU governance, but focuses on citizens' responses to journalistic output.[27] In sum, this section has highlighted that there are only very few studies that have taken EU citizens in the European public sphere into account. Some allow inferences about the visibility of EU citizens, but they do not *directly* analyse the visibility of EU citizens as such. Other studies focus on a pan-European public sphere that is unlikely to emerge, or focus on EU citizens' role as an audience and not actors *within* debates on EU governance. Based on previous research, there is reason to believe that EU citizens become visible in the European public sphere; however, conclusive evidence is limited, mainly because clear definitions of what constitute an EU citizen in the European public sphere are absent. Crucially, even less is known about the variation of visibility of EU citizens across media outlets and EU member states. Research has not yet aimed at *explaining* different levels of visibility of EU citizens. As Peter and de Vreese (2004) outline, it is important that research on the European public sphere does not exclusively remain at the level of descriptive results:

> To emphasize, descriptions of the coverage are important, especially in an understudied area such as the coverage of the EU. However, particularly in cross-national content analyses, merely descriptive accounts of the coverage may run the risk of increasing confusion instead of reducing complexity. Content analytic research cannot do without description, and cross-national content analytic research cannot do without establishing and describing country differences. However, research must not stop here. If content analytic research aims at the general and generalizable, then it cannot do without explaining, either. (Peter and de Vreese 2004 p.4)

---

[27] One exception are letters to the editor which are responses of EU citizens as an audience, but they have likewise been selected by journalists in the first place. Furthermore, only a limited number of letters to the editor are included in the sample of this study and they are not the main focus of this paper.

4.4. Conclusion

This chapter started out by defining the European public sphere as a communication system that facilitates between the EU citizens and the EU's governmental system. To fulfil a meaningful role in the EU's governmental system, discussions in the European public sphere need to address EU governance and actors from the EU's governmental sphere, in addition to EU level intermediary actors and EU citizens ought to be visible. Previous research has discussed the possibility of an emergence of a single, pan-European public sphere or the Europeanisation of national public spheres of the member states. As studies pointed out, a pan-European public sphere does not currently exist and is unlikely to emerge in the near future. Hence, the present study follows the Europeanisation approach, where debates in the national public spheres become more European by including EU affairs and EU level actors to a greater extent. Based on the minimal definition, that a European public sphere is constituted by discussions on EU governance in the national media, empirical findings show that such a European public sphere has emerged.

So far, studies have predominantly focused on the visibility of EU news and EU governmental actors in the national news coverage. Most of those studies have exclusively focused on quality media and broadsheet newspapers in particular. With only a few exceptions (Brüggemann and Kleinen-von Königslöw 2009; Boomgaarden et al. 2013; Boomgaarden et al. 2010; Schuck et al. 2011), research in this field has remained descriptive in scope and did not aim to *explain* different levels of Europeanisation of the national public spheres.

In short, although extensive research has been carried out on the European public sphere, little is known about the visibility of EU citizens. By focusing on this neglected actor group, this study extents the scope of actors in the European public sphere thus far taken into account by past research. The approach is also more inclusive compared to other studies, as it is not *a priori* limited to a single normative theory, but it investigates the visibility of EU citizens in light of different public sphere theories. This study makes a theoretical and an empirical contribution by providing a clear definition of EU citizens in the European public sphere and by deriving explanatory factors that foster their visibility. The research questions this study addresses are presented next.

5. Research Questions

Previous research has mainly considered the extent to which a European public sphere has developed by analysing reporting on EU news and EU actors in the media of EU member states. Overall, these studies have been rather elite driven in a twofold way: a) by being predominantly focused on quality media (and broadsheets in particular) and b) by nearly exclusively taking into account the presence of national and EU level *governmental* actors (see, e.g., Boomgaarden et al. 2013; Brüggemann and Kleinen-von Königslöw 2009; de Vreese 2004). The visibility of EU citizen has been neglected in the European public sphere research. Even if a theoretical argument is developed that calls for democratic representation of EU citizens in the European public sphere, their role is solely understood as an audience who respond to the media coverage (cf. Michailidou and Trenz 2013; Vetters et al. 2009), but not as actors who participate in debates on EU governance. It seems that EU citizens have so far not been understood as visible participants in political communication at the European level.

If democracy is understood as government of the people, by the people and for the people, citizens are a central element of democratic political systems such as the EU. This study argues that as such, EU citizens should likewise be visible actors in the European public sphere. Since nowadays politics is primarily mediated, news media are not only relevant for providing information to citizens, but it is also a mean of representing citizens and making them visible to policy makers (Gattermann 2013; Kriesi 2013a). Mediated political communication between governmental actors and citizens is even more important for supranational and multi-level systems such as the EU (Kriesi 2013c). However, so far, research on the European public sphere has predominantly considered European political communication as a one-way street: Studies have analysed the information function of the media, by examining the extent to which EU news and European governmental actors become visible to citizens via the news media. Of course, the provision of information on current events at the EU level is vital. In order to approve or disapprove of decision-making at the EU level and to be eventually able to make an informed voting decision, citizens need information on EU affairs. It is furthermore important to allocate responsibility for certain actions; hence, also the visibility of EU governmental actors is a necessity. Based on empirical analyses of the news coverage, some scholars derived the conclusion that the visibility of EU governance and EU level actors is rather low and that these shortcomings lead to a communication deficit of the EU (Brüggemann 2008).

However, there is also the possibility that there is a communication deficit that is located at the bottom-up side of European political communication. For legitimacy of EU governance, policies implemented at the EU level need to be accountable and responsive to the will of the European people. Especially given the decline in support for the European integration (e.g., Eichenberg and Dalton 2007; Armingeon and Ceka 2013), it is important that politicians at the EU level take citizens' preferences into account when making decisions. One way for governmental actors to gain information on public opinion and citizens' views is the news media (Gattermann 2013; Kriesi 2013a). This dual role of the public sphere is reflected in the following quotation by Statham:

> First, a necessary condition for a public sphere to exist at all in a meaningful sense is that the decision-making process is made sufficiently and adequately visible to citizens. This occurs primarily through mass media communication. Second, the public legitimacy of decision making depends on whether citizens (...) are adequately included and empowered to voice their preferences in the policy process. At stake here are the channels of access between the polity and citizens to represent and include the popular will. (Statham 2010 p.278)

The European public sphere constitutes such a "channel of access" through which citizens can become visible by being included in mediated public debates on EU governance. As mentioned previously, so far, only a limited number of studies have paid attention to EU citizens in the European public sphere. In those studies, citizens have been perceived as one group out of many actors, but never been in the centre of attention. Furthermore, clear definitions of what constitute an EU citizen and how EU citizens can become visible in the European public sphere have so far been missing. This might result in conceptual problems when measuring the visibility of EU citizens. To investigate the visibility of EU citizen in the European public sphere, a clear conceptualisation of EU citizens is needed.

In this study, an EU citizen has been defined as a citizen of the EU member states that is a member of the EU's political community. Furthermore, the conceptual distinction between *national* and *European EU citizens* was introduced. In the European public sphere, national EU citizens account for citizens of the EU member states. As information is known about the EU member state a citizen comes from, the EU citizenry that becomes visible via the European public sphere appears as separated by nationality. European EU citizens, on the other hand, simultaneously refer to the citizens of all EU member states and therefore represent a more advanced and integrated form of the EU citizenry in the European public sphere. How visible are these, however? The first question addressed by this study is:

RQ1: *To what extent are EU citizens in general, but also national and European EU citizens visible in the European public sphere?*

Yet, the EU is a diverse polity consisting currently of 28 member states. By looking only at the aggregate level of visibility of EU citizens, crucial differences might remain hidden. This study examines the European public sphere from a Europeanisation perspective, which assumes that the national public spheres of the EU member states become more "European" by including EU governance to a greater extent into public discussions (see Chapter 4.2.2). Contrary to the idea of a pan-European public sphere, this approach does not assume that there is one overarching European public sphere that covers all EU member states at once, but argues that the national public spheres of the EU member states remain and become more European by including EU news and EU actors into public debates at the member state level (Gerhards 2000). Empirical findings have indicated that the degree of Europeanisation of the national public spheres varies across countries. Studies have observed that the amount of EU news reported in the national media, but also the visibility of EU actors varies across EU member states (e.g., Boomgaarden et al. 2013; Hepp et al. 2012).

Therefore, it is likely also EU citizens are not equally visible across the EU member states. Analysing whether the visibility of EU citizens varies across countries is important, as citizens of the EU member states might get a different impression as to what extent ordinary EU citizens are able to participate in debates in the European public sphere. As a consequence, citizens of member states with high levels of visibility of EU citizens might perceive the European public sphere as more participatory and have the impression that their opinions are taken into account in the decision making process at the EU level. Citizens of EU member states with low levels of visibility of EU citizens, on the other hand, are more likely to perceive debates in the European public sphere as elitist, which might contribute to perceiving the EU as an elitist institution. Here, the question is:

RQ2: *Does the visibility of EU citizens vary across the EU member states and if so, to what extent?*

After the general visibility of EU citizens in the European public sphere has been addressed, the question remains whether their level of visibility can be considered sufficient. Here, normative public sphere theories provide guidance to what extent citizens *should* be visible in mediated debate on EU governance (cf. Chapter 3.2). Yet, research has so far hardly taken the existence of different public sphere theories in the context of the European public sphere into account (for exceptions see: Gerhards 2002; Latzer and Saurwein 2006; Wimmel 2005). Instead, the underlying normative conceptions of the European public sphere are most often based on Habermas' deliberative theory (e.g., Eriksen 2004; Brüggemann and Kleinen-von Königslöw 2009; Peters et al. 2006; Kleinen-von Königslöw 2012), largely neglecting normative assessment (cf. Althaus 2011).

By analysing the visibility of EU citizens in light of different normative public sphere theories, this study aims to emphasise that multiple evaluative claims could be made about their level of visibility in the European public sphere (for a similar argument see: Althaus 2011 p.97). Applying different normative public sphere theories to the European level provides an opportunity for research to question existing conceptualisations based on empirically findings, but also to develop theories further (Hepp et al. 2012). The aim of the comparison of different normative theories is to clarify "the implications that empirical findings have for normative theories about the ends and means of democratic politics" (Althaus 2011 p.104).

Regarding the visibility of EU citizens in the European public sphere, the underlying normative conception of the public sphere itself is crucial, since each theory states different requirements for the visibility of citizens in public debates. While the elitist theory rejects that citizens should take part in public discussion, the participatory theory argues that citizens should be among the most visible actors. The liberal and discursive public sphere theory respectively fall somewhere between the two extremes. Depending on the underlying normative theory, research will derive different results whether EU citizens are sufficiently visible in the European public sphere. Consequently, also different conclusions will be derived as to how well the European public sphere is able to fulfil its role for the democratic process, that is to facilitate communication between citizens and those who govern.

Furthermore, analysing which normative model reflects the empirical levels of visibility of EU citizens best is important, as EU citizens hardly have any direct experience with the political system of the EU. Instead, EU affairs are primarily communicated via the forum of the mass media. Previous research has indicated that citizens perceive the EU as a distant and elitist institution (Follesdal and Hix 2006). This perception might be shaped by discussions on EU governance in the mediated European public sphere that reflect an elitist actor structure. As the news media are the primary source to learn about EU affairs, citizens might use the characteristics of debates on EU governance to make inferences about the characteristics of the EU's political system as such. The fact that citizens have the feeling that they have little to say in EU affairs (Commission of the European Communities 2006a p.2) might not least be a result of elitist public discussions and low levels of visibility of EU citizens. The third question addressed by this study is therefore:

RQ3: *To which normative model of the public sphere do the empirical levels of visibility of EU citizens correspond best?*

When starting from the premise that the visibility of EU citizens in the European public sphere is important for the legitimacy of the EU, it is not sufficient to investigate the levels of visibility, but also to understand what factors influence their visibility. If the empirical results show that the levels of visibility of EU citizens vary, the follow-up question is what makes the European public sphere of certain member states more penetrable to citizens than others. Identifying what factors influence the visibility of EU citizens allows detecting the factors that can stimulate higher levels of visibility. This is especially important, since potentially low levels of visibility of EU citizens are related to the EU's communication deficit. Understanding the factors that lead to an increased visibility of EU citizens is a first step towards opposing this deficit and in the long run, might improve the EU's overall legitimacy. The explanatory part of this study, then, aims to answer the following question:

RQ4: *How can potential differences in the visibility of EU citizens be explained and what are the factors that foster the visibility of EU citizens?*

These are the primary and overarching research questions this study aims to address in the following empirical chapters. However, before turning to the results of this study, the next section discusses the data and methodology that is applied to answer these questions.

6. Methodology

The aim of this study is to examine to what extent EU citizens are visible in the European public sphere and to detect factors that foster their visibility. The implicit assumption behind the analysis of the visibility of EU citizens in the European public sphere is that visibility is a measure for their opinions being reported by the media (for a similar argument see Bosch 2014). As political communication is mediated, it is via the European public sphere that the opinions of EU citizens become visible to policy makers and can consequently been taken into account when making decisions at the EU level. The visibility of ordinary EU citizens in the news coverage on EU governance can be seen as a necessary, yet not sufficient condition for opinions being present in the European public sphere. This chapter discusses the data and general methodological approach adopted for examining and explaining the visibility of EU citizens. More specific research strategies and methods are discussed in the respective empirical chapters. After an introduction to the data set, the concepts, measures and operationalisations of EU citizens are discussed.

6.1. Data

The concept of an EU citizen that underlies this study refers to an individual who is a member of the political community of the EU. Even though some public sphere theories argue that citizens and their interests ought to be represented by intermediary organisations (cf. e.g., Peters 2007, Janoski 1998), the present study is exclusively interested in the visibility of *individual* EU citizens in the European public sphere and not, for example, in organisations representing *collective* interests of EU citizens. To analyse and explain the visibility of EU citizens across the European public spheres of the EU member states, this study carries out a secondary analysis of the news media coverage of the 2009 European Parliament election. The content analysis data is made available by the Providing an Infrastructure for Research on Electoral Democracy in the European Union (PIREDEU) project at the University of Amsterdam and the University of Exeter (EES 2009).

European Parliament elections are an ideal setting for comparative research on the visibility of EU citizens in European public sphere, since European elections provide citizens with the opportunity to *directly* participate in EU governance. In 2009, 375 million citizens of the EU member states were entitled to cast a vote. The European Parliament is the only directly elected institution at the EU level and its members ought to represent and act in line with the interests of the EU citizens. This is very likely to also impact the visibility of EU citizens in the European public sphere during this particular time period. Since it is the EU citizens who determine the outcome of an election, their visibility in the news coverage is arguably higher compared to non-election times. Hence, this study is unlikely to underestimate the visibility of EU citizens; rather it measures the upper-bound of their visibility. During routine periods of the EU news coverage, it is probable that EU citizens are *less* visible. Hence, if even under these favourable circumstances this study finds that the visibility of citizens in the European public sphere is low, it is likely that their visibility is extremely low or that citizens are even invisible during non-election times. This means that this study is carried out under favourable conditions which probably increase the visibility of EU citizens in the European public sphere. Findings based on analyses of news media coverage during election campaigns do not automatically apply to non-election and routine periods (van Aelst and de Swert 2009 p.151). This must be kept in mind when interpreting the results, especially with regard to generalised statements on the visibility of EU citizens in the European public sphere, as the effects found by this study might be less strong during routine periods of the EU news coverage.

The 2009 PIREDEU media study includes content analysis data of news media reports from all 27 member states that took part in the election. This

6.1. Data

means, in terms of the countries included, this research is able to provide a complete image of the mediated European public sphere during the 2009 election. For each country, two broadsheets and one tabloid newspaper (N=84), in addition to two television news programmes from the most widely watched public and private TV stations (N=59) were coded.[28] These news outlets were selected in order to provide a comprehensive image of the news coverage in the EU member states. Furthermore, for EU citizens, both newspapers and television are regularly listed among the most important sources of information on EU governance (European Commission 2007). The time frame of the media study covers three weeks prior to the European Parliament elections. Depending on the date of the election in the respective country, the sample period covers the time span of three weeks between May 14 to June 4 and May 17 to June 7. The coding of the news content was conducted by 58 coders, who were native speakers of the respective languages. Regarding the reliability of the data, the inter-coder reliability was tested, using Krippendorff's alpha. For the dependent variables used in this study, Krippendorff's alpha varies between 0.65 and 0.81 (Schuck et al. 2011). The PIREDEU team itself considers a Krippendorff's alpha of 0.60 as an acceptable lower limit of reliability for their study (Schuck et al. 2010 p.21) and one has to keep in mind that for the reliability test, the coding was additionally aggravated as the coders had to code English-language articles, which is not the native language of most coders.

The population of the data set includes all news stories broadcasted on television, and the title page and one randomly selected page (within the Political/News, Editorial/Opinion/Comment, and Business/Economy sections) for newspapers. In addition, all news articles concerning the EU and/or the European election were included. This leads to a total of 48,962 news stories, for which only formal variables (e.g., date, page/story number) were coded (see also Figure 6.1). Further content-related variables were only coded for EU related news (see Figure 6.1, Filter 1), which are defined as news stories that mention either the EU, its institutions or policies or the European Parliament elections or the

---

[28] One exception is Belgium, which was treated as consisting of two media system, one for Flanders and one for Wallonia. Furthermore, four TV programmes for Germany; one programme Luxembourg; three TV programmes for Malta and three programmes for Spain were coded.

election campaign. This leads to 19,107 EU-related news stories that are included in the PIREDEU data set. However, for the purpose of this study, further adjustments to the data had to be made that are discussed below.

6.2. Dependent Variables

6.2.1. Concepts and Measurement

EU citizens are citizens from the EU member states, but citizens of the EU member states are national and EU citizens simultaneously. Therefore, an operational criterion is needed to distinguish between these two roles. To identify EU citizens, I use references to citizens from the EU member states in news with a thematic focus of EU (not national) governance (i.e., EU polity, policy or politics). Hence, in a first step, it would be important to identify whether references to citizens from EU member states in the news coverage are unambiguously related to EU governance. Ideally, the coders would have been instructed to code EU citizens only if their appearance is unambiguously related to the thematic context of EU polity, policy or politics. Yet, this is not the case as this study draws on a pre-defined data set that was not initially designed for an analysis of the visibility of EU citizens. Despite not ideal, the PIREDEU data set is still suitable for analysing the conceptual distinctions this study is interested in, and it is the most valuable source available as it has the main advantage of including content analysis data from all 27 EU member states, which is crucial since this study is interested in exploring cross-country differences in the visibility of EU citizens.

6.2. Dependent Variables

Figure 6.1 Sample selection process

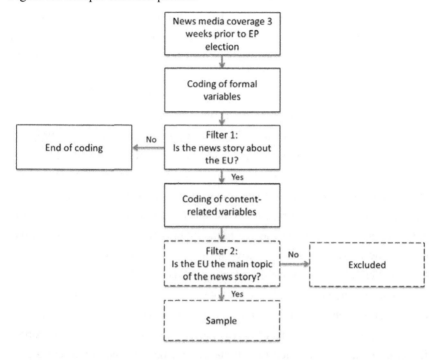

Figure 6.1 shows how the sample for this study was selected. Solid lines indicate selection procedures implemented by the PIREDEU team, dashed lines indicate selection procedures implemented for the purpose of the present research project.

Based on the data at hand, it is only known that citizens from the EU member states are mentioned within a news story that reports on EU governance, but whether the exact context in which citizens are mentioned is about the EU or not cannot unambiguously be clarified. To maximise the likelihood that EU citizens appear in the context of EU governance, I limited the data set to EU news stories whose main topic is EU governance. For this purpose I used a filter variable of the PIREDEU data set (cf. Figure 6.1, Filter 2) and only included news stories that report *extensively*, or whose *main focus* is on EU policy, its polity or politics.[29] This leaves a total of 12,850 news stories (10,811 newspaper articles and 2,039 TV news items) that are included in the sample of this study. However, through this approach, some references to EU citizens in the news coverage might be missed, while some wrongly classified cases might be included in the data.

Furthermore, this study makes the case that the concept of EU citizens in the European public sphere consists of two sub-categories: National and European EU citizens. References to national EU citizens represent a less Europeanised version of the EU citizenship in the European public sphere. Here, only citizens from specific EU member states become visible. As the information about the EU member state a citizen comes from is known, the EU citizenry that becomes visible via the European public sphere appears as separated by nationality and only subgroups of the EU citizenry become visible. These can either refer to the citizens of the respective member state or originate from a fellow EU member states. Examples of reporting on national EU citizens would be a news story by the German TV channel *ARD* reporting on the German or Greek citizens in the context of the European election. *European EU citizens* simultaneously represent the citizens of all EU member states. References to European EU citizens do not link back to national sentiments, but they represent a truly European and supranational form of citizenship that goes beyond the nation state. An example is a news report by the French newspaper *Le Monde* on the 375 million European citizens who are entitled to cast a vote in the 2009 European Parliament election.

In the PIREDEU data set, three manifestations of citizens in the news coverage can be found that can be used to measure the visibility of citizens in the EU-related news coverage. These three forms are (1) citizens being coded as *actors* in the news coverage, (2) the use of *vox pops*, or (3) references to *polls and surveys*. First of all, ordinary citizens can appear as *actors* in the EU news coverage. In general, the visibility of actors from the political system in the

---

[29] This was operationalised based on the variables V22a-e of the PIREDEU data set. It should be mentioned here, that arguably due to the sampling procedures, there is only a very small number of news stories where the EU is only mentioned briefly. Predominantly, cases were left out where no clear classification was possible, due to missing values.

news coverage is an integral part of the news reporting and some have even argued that it is a precondition for the functioning of democracy at the European levels (cf. de Vreese, 2003). For the functioning of the democratic process, citizens need to gain information on political affairs, but also on governmental actors to be able to identify who is responsible for which actions. Journalists report on different actors "to get access to information, to provide different viewpoints, to offer context and interpretations, and to validate news" (Dimitrova and Strömbäck 2009 p.75).

In general, the visibility of citizens as actors in the news coverage is a rare phenomenon, even though there is some evidence that journalists themselves consider it as important to provide citizens, to a certain extent, with the opportunity to express their views in the news coverage (Deuze 2002; Raeymaeckers et al. 2012). Sometimes, citizens are included as actors in the news coverage to provide accounts as eyewitnesses (de Keyser and Raeymaeckers 2012). For example, during the election campaign, *The Guardian* writes: "Concerned citizens in the south-west (...) tell us of voting forms that did not arrive on time and officials close to breaking point" (Muir 2009 p.27). More importantly, journalists use references to citizens in news reports to provide an account of their opinions (e.g., on political issues and events), which might not be, but are often perceived as, being representative of public opinion (Bosch 2014). For example, in a commentary, it is inferred that: "The only uncertainty about the European elections this week is whether people are so angry that they don't bother to vote or so angry that they cast a protest vote" (Bunting 2009 p.23). In another article, a politician is cited, giving his account on public opinion in the Netherlands: "'The Dutch have become very cantankerous. It's very sad,' said a senior EU official. 'They've gone from being the most pro-European country to one of the most anti-European'" (Traynor 2009 p.14).

A stylistic device report on citizens' opinions and to give them a voice in the news coverage is the use of the so-called vox pops (vox populi, or interviews with the "man/woman on the street"). Lefevere et al define vox pops as short interviews in the news with "people without any specific representative function or expertise who appear to be randomly picked" (Lefevere et al. 2011 p.103).

Vox pops are a direct, though less formal way to include citizens in the news coverage and are often used to exemplify the issue discussed (Daschmann 2000). As such, vox pops may or may not be representative for the citizens or parts of the population. An example of a vox pop in the context of the election coverage is an interview with an allegedly unemployed man asked for his opinion: "Slouched against the job centre's wall, Nicholas Boag, 23, was blunt in his assessment of the local MP and prime minister. 'I think he's doing a crap job', Boag said" (Carrell 2009 p.6). Because vox pops, by definition, give ordinary citizens the opportunity to express themselves *directly* (in form of quotations), they are more likely to measure the visibility of citizens' own *opinions* in the news coverage, compared to references to citizens in their capacity as actors.

EU citizens cannot only appear as individual actors in news stories, but there are additional ways in which citizens can be represented in the news coverage. Reporting opinion polls and surveys is another way to include citizens and their opinions in the news coverage. Contrary to vox pops that allow citizens to voice their opinions directly in the news coverage, polls do not refer to the opinions of individual citizens, but represent aggregated opinions. Therefore, polls are an important form in which citizens can become visible in the public sphere since they provide information on and represent the opinion of the people. A typical example of a poll from the 2009 European Parliament election is: "The lack of interest in the election, or protesting by abstaining, could spell a crisis of legitimacy for the parliament and of credibility for the EU more broadly. (…) A Eurobarometer poll predicts a turnout of 34% (…). A poll-tracking study being run by the London School of Economics and Trinity College Dublin predicts a turnout of around 30%, meaning that more than two out of three voters across the EU will boycott the ballot" (Traynor 2009 p.14). For this example, the source of the poll as well as the survey result is known. However, there are also references to polls in the news media that are less specific. For example: "As recently as March Ukip was flatlining in the polls and being written off as a political force. But since then the party's fortunes have been transformed and analysts believe it may even push Labour into fourth place in this week's European elections" (Taylor 2009 p.7).

6.2.2. Operationalisations

Actors

In the data set, for each news story, up to six actors[30] were coded if they were a) mentioned at least twice in two different sentences, b) mentioned at least once and directly or indirectly quoted, or c) mentioned at least once and depicted (Krippendorff's alpha= 0.65). An actor can be persons, but also groups, institutions or organisations. The first actor coded is the main actor of the news story, which was identified by the number of mentions and general importance in the story. The remaining actors were coded in order of their appearance. The actors were either classified as "EU-wide actors" (e.g., the European Parliament), or they were coded on the member state level, that is for each EU member state separately.[31] I use the actor category of "non-organized ordinary citizen(s), non-organized population groups or the population of a country as a whole (e.g., voters, people or the public; for television, e.g. country's ordinary citizens being interviewed)" that were coded from each EU member state separately to operationalise national EU citizens. European EU citizen are operationalised as "non-organized ordinary citizen(s), non-organized population groups or the EU population as a whole (e.g., Europeans, European voters, European citizens, European population or European public)" coded at the level of EU-wide actors. Both national and European EU citizens combined then measure the visibility of EU citizens as actors.

Vox pops

In the PIREDEU data set, vox pops are likely to appear along with EU citizens being coded as actors. Yet, the criteria for the actor coding outlined above as well as a specific style of vox pops might result in additional references to EU

---

[30] The PIREDEU codebook, actors were coded as either belonging to the EU-level, or they were coded for each of the EU member state separately. In addition, actors from the supranational level (e.g., NATO), from EU applicant countries, or other states were coded; however, these actors are not relevant for the purpose of the present study. For further details see also Chapter 8.

[31] The data set furthermore includes actors from the supranational level, EU applicant, and non-EU countries. As these actors are not of interest for this particular study, they have been excluded from the analysis.

citizens via vox pops. Vox pops might not have been coded simultaneously as citizens being coded as actors, if a) six actors were already coded and citizens were mentioned afterwards, or b) vox pops did not match the criteria of the actor coding (i.e., citizens being mentioned at least twice in two different sentences, being mentioned at least once and directly or indirectly quoted, or being mentioned at least once and depicted). In the data set, vox pops were only coded for news stories that are explicitly about the European Parliament election and/or the election campaign. Hence, vox pops cannot be used as a measure for the overall visibility of EU citizens in the EU news, but only account for the visibility of EU citizens in European election news, which is likely to lead to lower levels of visibility of vox pops in the sample (i.e., in comparison to the visibility of citizens as actors). Vox pop is a categorical variable, indicating whether the respective news story includes a vox pop or not (reference to vox pop=1; no reference=0) (Krippendorff's alpha = 0.81).[32]

The way vox pops were coded, they cannot be used to operationalise the visibility of national and EU citizens. First, it cannot unambiguously clarified whether a vox pop measures the visibility of national or European EU citizens. However, it can be argued that because of their reporting style, these interviews with persons on the street most likely represent national EU citizens. For example, if an interview is carried out with Ms Müller after she left a pooling station in Berlin and is asked by a journalist why it is important for her to vote in the European election, she is most likely interviewed to exemplify the opinion of a German voter. Due to the settings in which vox pops are carried out, it is unlikely that a single person who is interviewed is able to represent a supranational notion of the EU citizenship (though the content of their statement might, however, this is a different aspect which is not the focus of this study). Even though it is possible that a news story reports interviews with European voters from several EU member states without providing any reference to their nationality, such cases seem to be rather the exception than the rule. As it is not possible, based on a data set, to differentiate vox pops into the categories of national and European EU citizens, it is nevertheless safe to argue that vox pops can general-

---

[32] Based on variable V50 in the PIREDEU data set.

ly be seen as belonging to the category national EU citizens. However, they are not able to account for the visibility of European EU citizens. Therefore, I only use vox pops as part of the operationalisation of the general visibility of EU citizens in the EU news coverage.

Polls

In the data set, a filter variable was applied and polls[33] were only coded for news stories that explicitly mentioned the European Parliament elections and/or the election campaign. More specifically, opinion polls were only coded if the results reported in the respective poll predict the *outcome* of the European election in the member state where the respective news outlet is based. It was then differentiated whether a) public opinion polls were mentioned in general, b) specific poll results without sources were reported, or c) specific poll results were reported and a source (e.g., polling organisation) was mentioned (Krippendorff's alpha=0.66). I created a categorical variable, indicating whether or not the respective news story includes one of the three forms of reference to opinion polls (reference to poll =1; otherwise=0). Due to the coding procedure, polls cannot be used as a measure for the general visibility of EU citizens in the EU news coverage, but only account for the visibility of EU citizens in European election news, which is likely to lead to lower levels of visibility of polls (i.e., in comparison to the visibility of citizens as actors). However, given the time frame of this study, it can be argued that polls are most likely to be reported in the context of the European election, rather than in non-election news and that therefore the share of polls that are not included in the data set is rather low. Furthermore, as polls were only coded if they predict the outcome of the election, they cannot be seen as a general measure of citizens' preferences on the EU or its policies, but only as a measure of their electoral preferences.

Polls are in principle likely to be used by the media to represent both national and European EU citizens in the news coverage, e.g., by reporting on the 35% of the British citizens (national EU citizens) or by reporting on the 43% of the European citizens (European EU citizens) that voted in the 2009 European

---

[33] Variable V47 in the PIREDEU data set.

Parliament election. However, the way polls were coded in the data set, they only account for national EU citizens, because polls were only coded as such if they were conducted in the country in which the respective news outlet is based. Hence, based on the data, polls can only be used as a measure for the visibility of national EU citizens, and more specifically, only for the visibility of citizens from the respective EU member state where the news outlets is based. But there is no equivalent measure for European EU citizens. Therefore, I only use polls as part of the operationalisation of the general visibility of EU citizens in the EU news coverage.

Figure 6.2 Overview of dependent variables

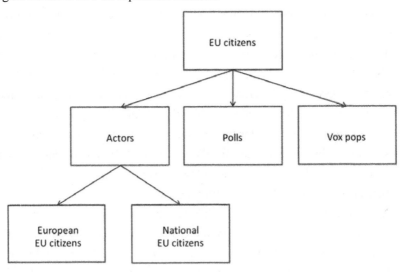

Figure 6.2 provides an overview of the dependent variables used in this study. EU citizens is a superordinate category consisting of three measures of visibility of EU citizens in the EU news coverage: EU citizens as actors, vox pops, and polls. This study is not only interested in analysing the general visibility of EU citizens, but also in comparing the levels of visibility of national and European EU citizens. Therefore, a measure is needed that is able to measure both dimensions in a comparative perspective. As discussed above, as a result of the coding

procedure, (allegedly) vox pops and polls only measure the visibility of national EU citizens and there is no equivalent measure for European EU citizens that is captured by the data. Vox pops and polls can nevertheless be seen and interpreted as measures of the visibility of national EU citizens, but should not be included in the category of national EU citizens itself. Based on the data at hand, only for EU citizens that become visible as *actors* in the EU news coverage, it is possible to measure both the visibility of European and national EU citizens.

After the PIREDEU data set, the different measures, and operationalisations have been discussed that are the basis for the empirical analyses of this study, the next chapter provides a first glance at the extent to which EU citizens are visible in the news coverage during the 2009 European elections.

7. To What Extent are EU Citizens Visible in the European Public Sphere?

A number of studies and several large-scale empirical research projects have focused on the European public sphere and analysed the visibility of EU news and EU governmental actors in the news coverage (e.g., Boomgaarden et al. 2013; Peter and de Vreese 2004; Wessler et al. 2008; Koopmans et al. 2010) (see also Chapter 4.2.3). While some of these studies have highlighted the importance of EU citizens and the role of communication between the EU and its citizens in their theoretical framework (e.g., Meyer 1999; Kleinen-von Königslöw 2010; Gripsrud 2007; Trenz and Eder 2004a; Maier and Rittberger 2008b; Statham 2008), there is hardly any systematic empirical evidence on the visibility of EU citizens in the news coverage on EU governance (see Chapter 4.3. for more details). The aim of this short introductory chapter to the empirical part of this study is to answer the first research question that constitutes the basis for further analyses: *To what extent are EU citizens, but also European and national EU citizens visible in the European public sphere* (RQ1)?

The underlying concept of the European public sphere in this study is based on the idea of a Europeanisation of the national public spheres of the EU member states. From this perspective, the national public spheres of the EU member states become more "European" by including news on EU governance and EU-level actors to a greater extent into national debates (see Chapter 4.2.2). Since the EU is a diverse polity consisting today of 28 states, it is likely that EU member states do not report on EU affairs to the same extent. While some countries might pay more attention to events taking place at the EU level, debates in other countries might remain predominantly centred around national governance. Empirical studies have observed that the amount of EU news reported in the national media, but also the visibility of EU actors varies across EU member states (e.g., Boomgaarden et al. 2013; Hepp et al. 2012). Therefore, it is likely that there is also variation in the visibility of EU citizens. Here, the question is: *Does the visibility of EU citizens vary across the EU member states and if so, to what extent* (RQ2)?

7.1. The Visibility of EU Citizens in EU News

As discussed in the Chapter 6, which has provided information on the data and the operationalisations of dependent variables, this study takes three measures of the visibility of EU citizens in the EU news coverage into account: EU citizens being mentioned in EU news as actors, as vox pops, or references to polls. Table 7.1 shows the percentage of EU news stories with extensive or main focus on EU governance where one of the measures of visibility of EU citizens is mentioned (the percentages do not add up, as in some news stories more than one measure is included). Using actors, vox pops and polls as a combined measure for the visibility, EU citizens are visible in a total of 30% of the EU news. The by far most frequent form in which EU citizens become visible in the EU news coverage is as *actors* (circa 24%).

Table 7.1 Visibility of EU citizens in EU news

Operationalisation as...	EU news (%)	SD	N = 12850
Actors	23.9	0.4	3068
National EU citizens (actors)	19.8	0.4	2546
European EU citizens (actors)	4.8	0.2	620
Polls	7.6	0.3	444
Vox pops	3.5	0.2	981
Total EU citizens	30.4	0.5	3905

Table 7.1 shows the percentage of EU news stores with extensive or main focus on EU governance that includes a reference to EU citizens. The percentages and cases do not add up, as in some news stories more than one form of visibility of EU citizens is included (see also Table 7.2).

7.1. The Visibility of EU Citizens in EU News

Conceptually, I have distinguished a more nationalised and more Europeanised form of the EU citizenry that can become visible in the European public sphere. The former, which I refer to as national EU citizens, accounts for the citizens of the individual EU member states. As the information about the EU member state a citizen comes from is known, the EU citizenry that becomes visible via the European public sphere appears as separated by nationality. European EU citizens, on the other hand, simultaneously represent the citizens of all EU member states. Contrary to national EU citizens, which link back to the national level, European EU citizens represent a truly European and supranational form of citizenship that goes beyond the nation state. Both concepts are measured based on the actor coding. The results show stark contrasts in the levels of visibility of European and national EU citizens: While European EU citizens are only visible in about 5% of EU news with extensive or main focus on EU governance, references to national EU citizens are far more prominent and are included in about 20% of the EU news.[34] Hence, national EU citizens clearly dominate the image of the EU citizenry that becomes visible via the news media.

While reporting on, and including actors in, the news coverage is an integral part of news reporting, there are two more stylistic devices journalists can use to report on citizens: *Vox pops* and *polls*, which are also used to measure the visibility of EU citizens in this study. As previously mentioned, while actors were coded for the entire EU news coverage, vox pops and polls were only coded if the respective news story explicitly thematised the European elections or the election campaign. Vox pops are used in only 3% of EU news stories with extensive or main focus on EU governance, while polls are reported in 8% of EU news.

In principle, one could expect that vox pops and polls overlap with citizens becoming visible as actors in the news coverage, as vox pops and polls are different stylistic devices used by journalists to include citizens in the news coverage. Hence, actors, vox pops, and polls all measure the same construct of EU citizens. However, as can be seen in Table 7.1, this is not the case and by in-

---

[34] As EU citizens as actors are visible in 20% of EU news, in approximately 1% of the cases both national and European EU citizens become visible simultaneously.

cluding vox pops and polls, the visibility of EU citizens increases by 6%. The reason why there is no complete overlap between the three forms of visibility can be explianed by the coding procedures (see Chapter 6.2.2.). Table 7.2 shows the percentage of EU news where exclusively one measure of the visibility of EU citizens is included (i.e., actors (only), vox pops (only), polls (only)), as well as the percentage of cases where there is an overlap with one of the other forms of visibility.

Table 7.2 Exclusive and overlapping forms of visibility of EU citizens

Operationalisation as…	EU news (%)	SD	N = 12850
Actors (only)	19.8	0.4	2541
Actors & vox pops	2.4	0.2	308
Actors & polls	2.0	0.1	256
Vox pops (only)	0.9	0.1	112
Vox pops & polls	0.5	0.1	61
Polls (only)	5.5	0.3	701

Table 7.2 shows the percentage of EU news with extensively or main focus on EU governance where only one measure of EU citizens is included, as well as the percentage of news where there is an overlap with one of the other forms of visibility.

While the visibility of vox pops is generally low, they furthermore overlap, as expected, to a large extent with citizens being coded as actors. In less than 1% of the cases, vox pops are the only form in which EU citizens become visible in EU news. For polls, on the other hand, the overlap with citizens being coded as actors (2%), or becoming visible as vox pops (0.5%) is somewhat lower. There is about 5% of EU news where polls are the only form of visibility of EU citizens in the EU news coverage.

In short, this section provided an answer to the first research question of this study, the extent to which EU citizens are visible in the European public sphere. Based on the empirical results, EU citizens are visible in a total of 30% of the EU news during the 2009 European elections.

7.2. The Visibility of EU Citizens Across EU Member States

After the general levels of visibility of EU citizens have been discussed, the question remains whether their visibility is equally distributed across EU member states, or there is cross-country variance (RQ2). Figure 7.1 shows the total visibility of EU citizens that measures the combined visibility of EU citizens as actors, vox pops, and polls, as well as the percentage of EU news including the individual measures by EU member state. In Finland, the visibility of EU citizens is the highest and exceeds the average of 30% by 19 percentage points, followed by Estonia and Romania, where EU citizens are visible in 42% of EU news. EU citizens are the least visible in Malta, Germany, and Lithuania, where the share of EU news stories with references to EU citizens is below 20%.

In the vast majority of EU member states, the most prominent form in which EU citizens appear in the EU news coverage is as actors. Therefore, the figures for the total visibility of EU citizens and the visibility of EU citizens as actors look rather similar. EU citizens as actors are most visible in Finland, Romania, and Latvia, where they are mentioned as actors in more than 40% of the EU news stories, while Germany, Lithuania, and Italy show the lowest levels of visibility (< 13%).

Again, while actors were coded for the entire EU news coverage, vox pops and polls were only coded for EU news stories thematising the European election or the election campaign. Nevertheless, in two member states, Italy and Ireland, the percentage of EU news reporting on polls is higher than the share of news mentioning EU citizens as actors. Ireland is at the same time the country with the highest visibility of polls (21%). The Irish news media report more than double the amount of EU news including polls compared to the average.

In some states, such as Lithuania and Luxembourg, polls are nearly invisible in the European election news coverage (< 1%). In the majority of EU member states, the share of polls is higher than the share of vox pops. Yet, there are some countries where vox pops are used more frequently than polls by the news media. Among them are Portugal and the Czech Republic, where the share of vox pops is above 12% and thereby three times higher than average.

Figure 7.1 Visibility across EU states

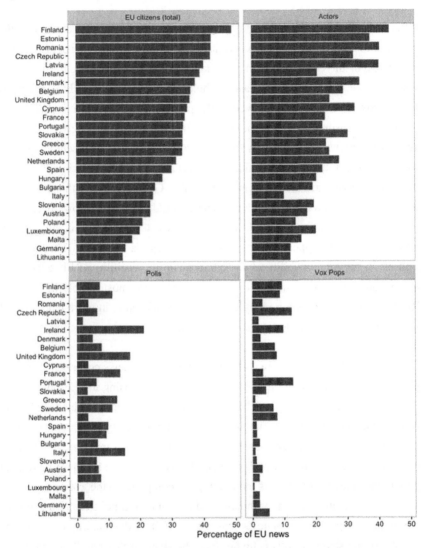

Figure 7.2 shows the percentage of EU news with main or extensive focus on EU governance including national and European EU citizens as actors by EU member state. Vox pops and polls had to be excluded, as they do not allow for a

7.2. The Visibility of EU Citizens Across EU Member States

comparative analysis of both groups. The visibility of national EU citizens varies between a maximum 39% of EU news with extensively or main focus on EU governance and a minimum of 8%. National EU citizens are most present in the news coverage of Finland, Latvia and Estonia, while their visibility is the lowest in Italy, Germany and Lithuania.

Figure 7.2 Visibility of national and European EU citizens across EU states

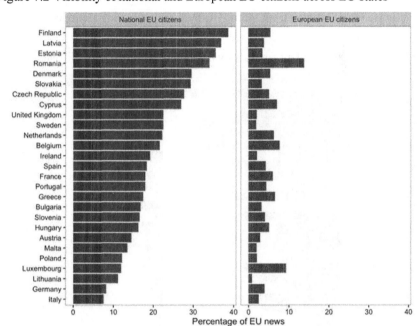

As mentioned above, national EU citizens have the largest share of the actor category. This finding is consistent across all member states, as the visibility of European EU citizens is lower in the EU news coverage of all states than the one of national EU citizens. European EU citizens are most visible in in Romania, where their visibility is with 14% nearly three times higher than the average, followed by Luxembourg with 9%. The visibility of European EU citizens is lowest in Lithuania, where they are visible in only about 1% of the EU news.

The category of national EU citizens includes both references to a member state's own citizens as well as to national citizens of fellow EU member states in news stories with a thematic focus on EU governance. For further analyses, it is of interest to investigate the composition of the category of national EU citizens in more depth. For this purpose, Figure 7.3 shows in column 1 the percentage of EU news with an extensive or main focus on EU governance where a country's own national citizens are mentioned, while column 2 shows the percentage of EU news where citizens from fellow EU member states are mentioned.

Figure 7.3 Visibility of a country's own and citizens from fellow EU states

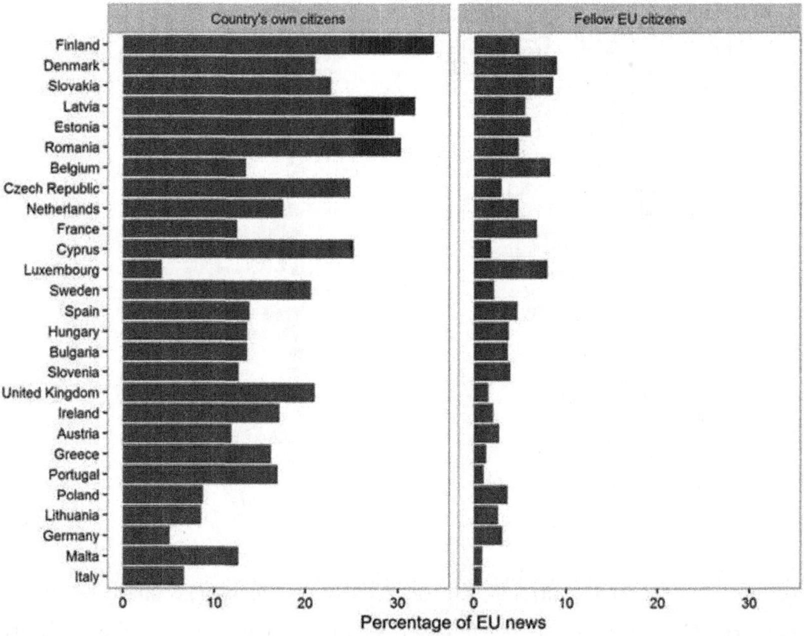

The results show that the levels of visibility of a country's own citizens clearly prevail in the EU news coverage. The only exception is Luxembourg, where the visibility of citizens from the fellow EU member states is higher than the visibility of the Luxembourgers. Overall, the visibility of citizens from fellow EU member states in the news coverage is low and, on average, they are only included in about 4% of the EU news. Yet, their visibility varies across countries and is highest in Denmark with 9% and lowest in Malta and Italy (< 1%). Based on these findings, it can be concluded that it is mainly a country's own citizens who contribute to the visibility of national EU citizens, while the visibility of citizens from other EU member states has only a small share of their total visibility.

Summarising the results of this section, the answer to RQ2 is that the visibility of EU citizens varies considerably across the EU member states. This does not only apply to their general visibility, but also to the visibility of national and European EU citizens in the EU news coverage.

7.3. Conclusion

The aim of this first chapter was to analyse to what extent EU citizens, but also national and European EU citizens are visible in the European public sphere. The findings show that overall EU citizens are visible in a total of 30% of the EU news coverage during the 2009 European Parliament elections and that it is predominantly national EU citizens rather than European EU citizens that prevail in the EU news coverage. Yet, there is notable variance in the visibility across the EU member states.

EU citizens become mainly visible as actors in EU news, and to a certain extent also via vox pops and polls. As vox pops conceptually and empirically overlap with EU citizens being coded as actors at the same time, analysing vox pops separately does not have any added value. Polls, on the other hand, exclusively measure national and not European EU citizens. Furthermore, there is no equivalent measure for polls for actors other than citizens. As this study is also interested in a comparison of the visibility of national and European EU citizens as well as an analysis of the visibility of EU citizens in contrast to other actor groups, polls and vox pops are dropped from further analyses. Hence, the following chapters only take the visibility of EU citizens as actors into account, as it is the only form of visibility that can unambiguously be used as a measure for *both* the visibility of national and European EU citizens and that was furthermore coded for the entire EU news coverage and not exclusively for news about the European election. However, focussing only on actors as a measure for the visibility of EU citizens means to underestimate their visibility. This is one of the limitations of this study that is caused by the use of secondary data that was not initially intended for an analysis of the visibility of EU citizens.

After this chapter has established the extent to which national and European EU citizens are visible in the EU news coverage, several questions remain: Are these levels of citizen visibility high or low? What factors explain different levels of visibility? The former question is addressed in the following chapter, which focuses on different normative public sphere theories that have diverging expectations as to whether and what extent ordinary citizens ought to participate in public debates. Analysing the visibility of EU citizens in comparison to other actors as well as in light of the elitist, liberal, discursive, and participatory public sphere theory is the aim of the next chapter.

8. EU Citizens in the Light of Normative Public Sphere Theories

The previous chapter presented initial results on the visibility of EU citizens in the European public sphere. However, in order to derive conclusions on whether the visibility of citizens is high or low, it is necessary to compare and examine the level of visibility of EU citizens in *relation* to other actors that become visible in the European public sphere. Here, the question "Who should participate in the public sphere?" is crucial. The extent to which citizens ought to participate in public debates is addressed by normative public sphere theories that have been derived from democratic theories. Even though participation is not the only normative criterion addressed by the theories it is the most important one for this study, as it focuses on the visibility of EU citizens. The aim of this chapter is to discuss theoretically how those theories can be applied to the EU level, and to examine which public sphere theory matches best the empirical reality of EU news.

While democratic theories revolve around accountability and responsiveness of governance, public sphere theories focus on public communication and its role in facilitating accountability and responsiveness of the decision making process (Ferree et al. 2002a p.289). Since both accountability and responsiveness are key elements of democratic legitimacy, the public sphere plays a vital role in enabling legitimacy and is considered a necessary element of democracies (Habermas 1990). The aim of the present chapter is to compare the desired levels of visibility of citizens in the European public sphere that have been derived from the normative public sphere theories with the observable levels of visibility of EU citizens in the news coverage about the EU during the 2009 European Parliament election campaign.

8.1. Aim and Research Questions

As outlined in Chapter 3, previous research has differentiated between four main public sphere theories, namely the elitist, liberal, discursive and participatory theory (Ferree et al. 2002a; Downey et al. 2012), that put forward different views on whether and to what extent citizens (but also other actors) ought to be visible in the public sphere. The starting point of the present chapter is that the requirements for the visibility of EU citizens in the European public sphere vary depending on the lens of the normative public sphere theory one is looking through. While the elitist and liberal theory reject that citizens should take part in public discussion, the participatory theory argues that citizens should be among the most visible actors (cf. Ferree et al. 2002a). The discursive public sphere theory falls somewhere between the two extremes. Gerhards (2002), who considered the EU's public sphere deficit in light of the liberal and discursive public sphere theory, argues that research will derive different conclusions about whether such a deficit exists depending on the underlying normative theory of the respective study. Likewise, assessment through different normative public sphere theories will lead to different conclusions regarding a potential "deficit" in the visibility of EU citizens in the European public sphere. The main question addressed in this chapter is: *To which normative model of the public sphere do the empirical levels of visibility of EU citizens correspond best* (RQ3)? The question is highly relevant since it helps to better understand what underlying model of democracy and political representation at the European level becomes visible to the EU citizens via the European public sphere and what role citizens play within mediated debates on EU governance.

Analysing which normative model reflects the empirical levels of visibility of EU citizens best is important, as political communication in today's societies is primarily mediated and EU citizens hardly have any direct experience with the political system of the EU. Hence, the mass media constitute their primary source go gain information on the EU's and its political system. Previous research has indicated that citizens perceive the EU as a distant and elitist institution (Follesdal and Hix 2006). This perception might be a consequence of dis-

8.1. Aim and Research Questions

cussions in the mediated European public sphere that primarily include governmental actors and do not pay attention to ordinary EU citizens. As the news media are the primary mean to learn about EU affairs, citizens might use the characteristics of debates on EU governance to infer about the characteristics of the EU's political system as such. The fact that citizens have the feeling that they have little to say in EU affairs (Commission of the European Communities 2006a p.2) might not least be a result of elitist public discussions and low levels of visibility of EU citizens.

As the notion of the public sphere itself, but also the different normative models of the public sphere have originally been developed with reference to the nation state, those theories cannot simply be transferred to the European level and careful considerations are needed. In particular, this study has argued that in the European public sphere, one can distinguish two groups of actors, namely actors that are directly linked to the EU level ("vertical actors") and actors from the EU member states that nevertheless account for European actors, if they discuss or decide on matters related to EU governance ("horizontal actors") (see Chapter 4.1). Both combined constitute the overall actor structure of the European public sphere. It can be argued that reporting on horizontal actors is more in line with traditional news media coverage on national and foreign affairs, where actors from the national arena are in the centre of attention. The novel aspect resulting from the European integration is that in addition to actors from the national level, supranational actors directly linked to the EU level have become relevant. Since the news media might take time to adjust to include these new actors from the European level into the news coverage (for a similar argument see Brüggemann and Kleinen-von Königslöw 2009), it is likely that the actor structures vary at both dimensions.

The previous chapter has already established that it is primarily national EU citizens that become visible in the European public sphere, while the visibility of European EU citizens is considerably lower. However, it is possible that this difference reflects a broader pattern. European EU citizens belong to the group of vertical actors. Their low levels of visibility might reflect that news media generally pay little attention to actors directly linked to the EU level.

Hence, when compared to other vertical actors, the initially low levels of visibility of European EU citizens might not be so low when examined in a comparative perspective. Furthermore, assessing the levels of visibility of EU citizens in comparison to other actor groups at the horizontal and vertical level helps to better understand the extent to which the mediated image of the EU citizenship remains nationally entrenched, while the governmental and intermediary realm might have become Europeanised.

By looking at the aggregated actor structure only, these differences might be overlooked. The second related research question is therefore: *Does the normative model of the public sphere that corresponds best to the visibility of EU citizens vary on the horizontal and/or vertical level of the European public sphere* (RQ3.1)? To answer this question, after examining the overall actor structure of the European public sphere, in a second step, it is considered whether this model is appropriate for the vertical and horizontal dimension of the European public sphere as well.

Furthermore, it might be possible that there is not only variance between these different levels of European public sphere, but that there are other factors impacting the visibility of EU citizens as well as the actor structure in general. The EU is a heterogeneous polity and as such, also the patterns of the news media coverage are likely to vary across countries. Studies analysing the visibility of EU governmental actors found that their visibility varies significantly across countries (Hepp et al. 2012; Koopmans et al. 2010). Chapter 7 has shown that this is also applicable to the visibility of EU citizens. Here, the question is to what extent the visibility of EU citizens, in comparison to other actor groups, varies across the EU member states. For example, there might be member states whose actor structure is more elitist, while others might reflect more participatory patterns. Depending on the respective member state, citizens' perception of the visibility of EU citizens and the overall actor structure might differ. This consequently also affects the democratic model that they might associate with governance at the EU level. Hence, the follow up question is: *Are these patterns of visibility of EU citizens consistent across the EU member states* (RQ3.2)?

8.1. Aim and Research Questions

When interested in the visibility of EU citizens in comparison to other actors, one might not only consider the mere levels of visibility, but also take indicators for the quality of visibility into account. As such, it is examined to what extent citizens are able to express themselves *directly* compared to other actors. This study argues that the visibility of EU citizens in the news coverage is important, because it functions as a feedback mechanism for policy makers at the EU level. The implicit assumption behind this is that the visibility of citizens is a measure for their opinions being reported in the news coverage (cf. Bosch 2014). However, the mere visibility of citizens in the news coverage does not necessarily imply that citizens are able to express their opinions. Direct citations by actors arguably increase the likelihood of including opinions and arguments put forward by the respective actor group (cf. Dimitrova and Strömbäck 2009). For example, it might be possible that while citizens become visible less often than other actor groups, when they do they are citied directly in most of the cases. The question is: *To which normative model of the public sphere do the empirical levels of direct citations of EU citizens in debates on EU governance correspond best* (RQ3.3)? For this reason, the analysis not only considers whether citizens become visible in the EU news coverage, but also whether they are cited directly.

By taking the particularities of the European public sphere, but also country specifics, as well as factors related to the quality of visibility into account, the aim of this chapter is to analyse the actor structure of the European public sphere from different angles to find the model of public sphere that empirically matches best to the European context. Despite conceptual differences of the normative public sphere theories, and their implications for the legitimacy function of the public sphere, research on the European public sphere has hardly taken the existence of different normative models of the public sphere into account. This has consequences for the debate on the existence of a European public sphere in so far as research might derive different conclusions as to the extent a vital European public sphere has emerged and is able to fulfil its role for the democratic process. That is, to facilitate between the EU and its citizens. By applying these existing normative public sphere theories to the EU level, future research might be able to question existing measures for the stage of development of the European public sphere and help to develop those theories in the EU context further.

8.2. State of the Art

Even though a considerable number of studies have focused on the European public sphere (e.g., Boomgaarden et al. 2013; de Vreese 2001; Koopmans and Erbe 2004; Trenz and Eder 2004), only a few have taken into account that different normative models state different requirements for the functioning of a European public sphere. The majority of studies are implicitly or explicitly based on Habermas' conception of the deliberative public sphere (Brüggemann and Schulz-Forberg 2009a; Brüggemann and Kleinen-von Königslöw 2009; Eriksen 2005b; Gripsrud 2007; Hepp et al. 2012; Kleinen-von Königslöw 2012; Koopmans 2007; Peters 2005; Peters et al. 2005; Schlesinger 1999; Splichal 2006; van de Steeg 2002; Trenz 2004; Wessler et al. 2008). These studies have often focused on the visibility of different actor groups in the EU news coverage, as the visibility of EU level actors is seen as a measure for the degree to which public spheres of the EU member states are Europeanised. However, as outlined in the following, research has nearly exclusively focused on the visibility of governmental actors.

For Germany, France, the UK, Italy, Spain, and the Netherlands, Koopmans et al. (2010) examined the visibility of "European actors" across seven different policy domains, where the EU has varying decision-making competences.[35] Their understanding of European actors refers mainly to EU institutions, but it is defined broader and includes "not just the European Union and its component institutions but also non-EU supranational and intergovernmental institutions on the European level, such as the European Council or European Free Trade Association" (Koopmans et al. 2010 p.65). Their results show that European level actors make up to 30% of the actors in fields where

---

[35] The time frame covers the years 1990, 1995, 2000, and 2002.

8.2. State of the Art

the EU has considerable decision-making power, while they are nearly invisible in policy areas (such as education) where the EU has limited competences. With regard to cross-country differences, the study finds that it is Spain that has the highest share of European actors (20%), followed by France (ca. 18%), Italy (ca. 16%), the Netherlands (13%), Germany (ca. 13%), and the UK (7%).

In a similar study based on the same data, the actors within the EU news coverage are investigated in greater depth (Koopmans 2007). The question addressed is: "which actors profit from and which actors stand to lose from the Europeanisation of political communication in mass-mediated public spheres?" (Koopmans 2007 p.183). The results show that across all issues of EU news, the share of executive actors from the EU institutions is two to three times higher compared to the share of national executive actors in national news (Koopmans 2007 p.194). Likewise, European civil society actors, such as European trade unions, consumer and professional associations, are nearly invisible in the news coverage. Based on these results, Koopmans derives the conclusion that the "European integration has remained a project by elites" (Koopmans 2007 p.205), at least as far as communication in the European public sphere is concerned. Similarly, Trenz observes that the strong dominance of national and European governmental actors constitutes a "clear media bias towards institutional and governmental actors and away from civil society" (Trenz 2004 p.301). Yet, citizens have not been included as actors in any of those studies.

The *Transnationalization of Public Spheres in the EU* project content analysed discursive news articles in six EU member states (Austria, Denmark, France, Germany, Poland and the UK) during the years 1982, 1989, 1996, 2003 and 2008 (Wessler et al. 2008).[36] The study provides information on the visibility of governmental actors, and to a certain extent also on the visibility of EU citizens.[37] Yet, the main focus of the study is a comparison of actors from the national and EU level, not a comparison of different actor groups. Their results

---

[36] For each year, two constructed weeks for one broadsheet and tabloid newspaper per country were coded.

[37] As discussed in Chapter 4.3, the study measures the visibility of a European identity in the news coverage, which includes references to the European population and the European citizens (Hepp et al. 2012 p.55).

show that references to the European population and EU citizens are relatively low and reach a share of maximum 5.7%. For governmental actors, the findings show that while more than 60% of the news refers to national institutions, EU institutions are only visible in 14% of the articles. Furthermore, the study indicates for both citizens and governmental actors strong variance between countries as well as between quality media (i.e., broadsheets) and commercial media (i.e., tabloids).

Based on the same project and data, Wessler (2007, p. 65-67) compared different actor groups that become visible in broadsheet news (see also Chapter 4.3.). The study differentiates between national governmental actors, EU governmental actors, civil society actors as well as citizens. The findings show that EU news is dominated by national and EU level governmental actors, follow by civil society actors. Citizens, however, are nearly invisible in the EU news coverage. The study offers some first insights into the actor structure of the European public sphere, but while governmental actors are divided into national and EU actors, this is not the case for the remaining actor groups. Hence, it cannot provide information on differences in the actor structure at the horizontal and vertical level of the European public sphere.

While the studies discussed above provide some evidence of the visibility of different actors in the European public sphere, their focus is not on a comparison of different normative public sphere theories in the context of the European public sphere. Nevertheless, some scholars have addressed the relevance of different public sphere theories in the context of the European public sphere. Latzer and Saurwein (2006) discuss the liberal, discursive and participatory public sphere theory in the context of the European public sphere. The study theoretically transfers the normative requirements of the theories to the European context and makes suggestions for research questions that aim to examine these approaches empirically. Yet, no concrete proposal for how such a comparison should look like is made, nor does the study suggest any empirical measures for comparison.

Similarly, other studies acknowledge and discuss the existence of different public sphere theories in their theoretical framework, but then neglected to take

8.2. State of the Art

these different theories into account when assessing their empirical findings. For example, an article by Wimmel (2005) compares a model of the Europeanisation of the national public spheres that is based on Luhmann's notion of the public sphere, which is closely associated with the liberal model of the public sphere (cf. Gerhards et al. 1998 p.28), and with Habermas' model of the discursive public sphere. The study argues that the core element that distinguishes the two theories is that the latter requires an exchange of opinions across the public spheres of the EU member states, while the former does not. Despite the theoretical comparison of the two theories, the empirical analysis, then, exclusively focuses on the discursive public sphere theory.

The study that is closest to the aims of this research was carried out in the national context by Ferree et al. (2002b, see also Gerhards et al. 1998), and examined normative public sphere theories in the context of the news media coverage. The study analysed the news media coverage on the topic of abortion in the US and Germany[38] from the 1960s to the mid-1990s (for a similar study with a different thematic context see also (Gerhards and Schäfer 2011). The study distinguishes between the elitist, liberal and discursive public sphere theory.[39] The classifications of the normative public sphere theories by Ferree et al. were also used to a large extent as guidelines for the present study.

Ferree et al. differentiate the theories based on a) *who* should participate in public discussion, b) about *what* and *how* discussions should take place, and c) what is the desired *outcome* of the debate. For the purpose of the present study, only the first aspect is of interest. The study by Ferree et al. derives the expectation that the media coverage should show an elite dominance from the angle of the elitist public sphere theory, while there should be some extent of popular inclusion for the remaining theories. Yet, the study does not propose more specific measures for comparison of the actor structure (cf. Ferree et al. 2002b p.229). Regarding the actors that are taken into account, the study differentiates

---

[38] The media sample consists of the following newspapers: The New York Times, The Los Angeles Times, the Frankfurter Allgemeine Zeitung, and the Süddeutsche Zeitung.
[39] The study itself differentiates between a "representative liberal theory" which is the equivalent to the elitist theory in this study and a "participatory liberal theory" which is the liberal public sphere theory in this study. In addition, a constructivist approach based on Foucault is included, which is not further discussed here.

rather broadly between collective and individual actors (Ferree et al. 2002b p.89). Collective actors are divided into state-actors (executive, legislative, and judiciary), political parties, as well as associations and movements. Individual actors, on the other hand, refer to experts or other persons that are not representatives of organisations. Citizens as such are not included as a separate actor category in study by Ferree and colleagues.

The empirical analysis examines how the total share of actors is split between these different groups of actors. Based on the distribution between these different actor groups, it is concluded that the German mediated debate on the abortion issue reflects an elitist public sphere, while the debate in the US can be better described by the liberal and discursive public sphere theory. However, there are no concrete expectations or criteria drawn from the normative theories against which these results are compared.

Another empirical paper by Downey et al. (2012) compares the models of the elitist[40], liberal and discursive public sphere in the context of the EU constitutional debate across quality newspapers and tabloids in the US, Germany, France, the UK, and Switzerland. Actors are not *per se* the main focus of the study, but it can provide some insights on the visibility of different actors. Downey et al. conducted a claim-making analysis[41] by analysing quotations made by the 30 most quoted actors in the media of four EU and two non-EU member states. The results show that it is primarily the heads of the EU member states that become visible in the news coverage on the EU constitutional debate (p. 342). Overall, the study draws the conclusion that the debates in the media of the three EU member states reflect a liberal-elitist public sphere as "public spheres are dominated by political elites" (Downey et al. 2012 p.352). However, this is also a result of their sampling strategy that excluded intermediary actors and citizens that might likewise be visible in the public sphere, but not be among the 30 most frequently quoted actors. As a result, there are nearly exclusively politicians from the national political arena included in the sample.

---

[40] More specifically, the study itself refers to a "republican" notion of the public sphere, which is the equivalent to the elitist public sphere in this study.
[41] A claim-making analysis is a form of "content analyses of public statements and demands" (Koopmans and Statham 2010a p.32).

Therefore, based on the results of this study, no conclusive assumptions about the visibility of different actor groups in the European public sphere can be drawn. Furthermore, the study was only carried out within the *thematic* context that concerns the EU, a direct link to the notion of a European public sphere, however, is missing. Instead, the main focus of the study is on differences between *national* public spheres across different states and over time.

Based on previous empirical studies that took different actor groups into account, no conclusion regarding the actor structure in EU news can be drawn. The empirical analyses of previous studies that compared different normative public sphere theories in the context of national news remain rather vague and the measures for comparison are not made explicit. In the European context, research has analysed the visibility of different actors in the EU news coverage, but one important actor group, namely EU citizens, has been neglected. Whether the levels of visibility of EU citizens can be considered as high or low varies depending on the underlying normative public sphere theory. Hence, a more precise elaboration on normative and analytical criteria of the public sphere is needed to understand whether the European public sphere is functioning and able to fulfil its democratic role. The research strategy and methodological approach of this study are outlined next.

8.3. Research Strategy

Public sphere theories state different normative requirements for the functioning and the structure of the public sphere. The theories can be used to derive ideal types that can then be utilised for empirical analyses and comparisons. As Althaus notes:

> [O]ne of the reasons for studying the characteristics of news coverage about public affairs is that we want to know whether this news coverage is fulfilling or failing the informational needs of democratic systems. But when normative concerns show up in political communication research, they often take the form of assertions rather than assessments. (...) Whereas a normative assertion advances a particular evaluative claim about an empirical finding without clarifying the basis of evaluation, a normative assessment aims to identify multiple evaluative claims that could be

made about an empirical finding while also identifying the standards underlying those value judgments. (Althaus 2011 pp.97–98)

In Chapter 3, I derived the desired levels of visibility for different actor groups from the elitist, liberal, discursive and participatory public sphere. The present chapter aims to empirically examine the visibility of EU citizens in comparison to other actor groups through the lens of the four different public sphere theories.

The actor structures deduced from the normative public sphere theories can be considered as ideal types, which are "ideal *limiting* concept[s] with which the real situation (...) is *compared*" (Weber 2011 [1949] p.93, italics in original). Ideal types can be used as benchmarks and against which the empirical reality can be compared. An empirical phenomenon often deviates from the ideal type and therefore it is likely that the empirical findings of this study are not completely in line with either of the theories. Yet, the normative theories can be used as analytical tools for analysing the visibility of EU citizens in the European public sphere. To answer the question to which normative model of the public sphere the empirical levels of visibility of EU citizens correspond best, this study compares the ideal typical actor structure proposed by the public sphere theories with the empirically observable levels of visibility of different actors in the mediated European public sphere of the EU member states (cf. also Ferree et al. 2002b; Ferree et al. 2002a; Gerhards et al. 1998).

I have differentiated between five different actor groups that can potentially become visible in the public sphere, namely actors from the *governmental system*, intermediary actors including *political parties, formal* and *informal civil society*, as well as the *citizens* of the respective political community (for more details on the actor groups listed by normative theories see Chapter 3). The public sphere theories put forward different standpoints as to whether and to what extent these actors ought to become visible in public debates. I divided these desired levels of visibility of different actors into three categories: *high, medium,* and *low* (see Chapter 3, Table 3.1). Figure 8.1 visualises the ideal typical levels of visibility by public sphere theory and actor group.

8.3. Research Strategy

What is important is that these categories are not understood in absolute numbers. Instead, the visibility of EU citizens put forward by the public sphere theories has to be seen in *comparison* to the levels of visibility of the remaining actor groups. With the exception of the participatory public sphere theory, governmental actors are seen as central in the political system and possess direct legitimacy by being elected. To communicate their activities to the citizens and gain legitimacy for their actions, governmental actors have to be visible in the public sphere. What is more important is how the visibility of other actor groups *compares* to the visibility of governmental actors. Taking the visibility of governmental actors as a benchmark, the presence of EU citizens and the remaining actor groups is measured against the visibility of governmental actors.

Figure 8.1 Ideal typical levels of visibility by theory and actor group

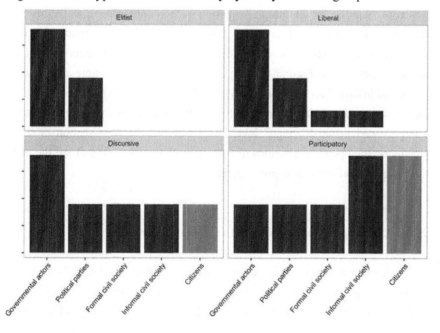

I have labelled the level of visibility of *governmental actors* as "high" for all public sphere theories with exception of the participatory public sphere theory.

For the participatory theory, I categories the visibility of governmental actors as "medium", because the elitist, liberal and discursive public sphere theory all acknowledge the importance of the visibility of democratically elected representatives, while the governmental system in the participatory theory is seen as less relevant because it is not perceived as the primary unit citizens participate in (Hirst 1994; Warren 1992). The visibility of *political parties* is characterised as "medium" for all four models, because of their importance for mediating citizens' interests. For the remaining intermediary actors, the theories diverge more strongly. While *civil society* actors are irrelevant for the elitist public sphere theory, they ought to reach a low level of visibility in the liberal public sphere (Ferree et al. 2002a). The discursive and participatory theory, on the other hand, divide civil society actors up into formal and informal groups (Ferree et al. 2002a; Peters 2007). I argue that both should reach "medium" levels of visibility for the discursive notion of the public sphere, while informal civil society actors should be highly visible in the participatory model. Similarly, *citizens* should not become visible in the elitist and liberal theory. From the point of view of the discursive theory, citizens ought to be visible and are seen as part of informal civil society (cf. Wessler and Rinke 2014). The participatory public sphere theory is the only approach that sees citizens as a separate actor category and demands "high" levels of visibility. The next section provides details on the operationalisations of the different actor groups that are the basis for the empirical analysis in this chapter.

8.4. Concepts, Measurement and Operationalisations

There are two different angles from which the visibility of EU citizens in the news coverage in comparison to other actors can be examined, the news story and the actor level. Both complement each other and together provide a more complete perspective of the phenomenon. The analysis on the *news story level* implies that it is less important how many times citizens become visible, but what is decisive is that citizens, in addition to other actors, are in fact mentioned

8.4. Concepts, Measurement and Operationalisations

in a news story. The benchmarks for the visibility of EU citizens are lower, as the news story level only takes into account whether or not (and not how many times) EU citizens are mentioned in an EU news story. Furthermore, from a methodological standpoint, an analysis at the news story level is sensible, as only up to six actors were coded per news story. It is very likely that, in some cases, more than six actors were mentioned in a news story. Yet, as only six actors were coded, those actors were not included in the data set. Hence, the data does not contain the entire population of actors in EU news and examining only at the absolute number of actors might under or overestimate the visibility of certain actors.

Nevertheless, the *actor level* complements the analysis and can be used to check the robustness of the initial findings at the news story level. Here, the total number of actors mentioned in EU news represents the population and the question is how high the share of EU citizens of the total number of actors is. Hence, instead of focusing on the relative frequency of visibility of EU citizens, the analysis at the actor level takes the absolute numbers of visibility into account. An analysis at the actor level is a stricter measure compared to the news story level as it implies the logic of a zero-sum game: References to one of the other actor groups automatically decreases the visibility of EU citizens (and the other way round). At the news story level, on the other hand, it is in principle possible that all actors can reach equally high (or low) levels of visibility.

Both units of analysis are relevant for the visibility of EU citizens, even though they take different aspects into account. Instead of focussing on only one unit of analysis and potentially missing out on important findings at the other unit, the analyses in this chapter are carried out in parallel at both units of analysis to provide a more complete picture of the visibility of EU citizens in news on EU governance. For the analysis at the news story level, for each of the actor groups, I created a categorical variable indicating whether or not a specific actor group was mentioned in a news story (mentioned=1, not mentioned=0). Based on this, I calculated the percentage of news stories including a certain actor group based on the total number of news stories (N= 12,850). For the actor level, I calculated the percentage of EU citizens and the other actor groups of the total number of actors (N= 37,990).[42]

The normative models of the public sphere mentioned above are ideal types. To operationalise the respective actor categories that were derived from the theories, this study recoded and combined different groups and individual actors from the PIREDEU media data set of the 2009 European parliament election. In the data set, actors were coded on the EU and member state level separately. Since the codebook was not constructed for a comparison of public sphere models, some compromises and approximations had to be made to measure the actor groups that were derived from the public sphere theories. These are discussed below.

In Chapter 4, based on the structure of the EU's political system, the actors of the European public sphere have been categorised into actors from the EU governmental system, the European intermediary system and the European private sphere consisting of the EU citizens. Moreover, I have argued that these actors can be further categorised into actors from the national level that appear in the context of EU governance (horizontal actors) and actors that are directly linked to the EU level (vertical actors). For the operationalisation of vertical actors, I use actors that were coded as EU level actors in the PIREDEU data set. For horizontal actors, the operationalisation is less straightforward. As for the operationalisation of EU citizens, it is important to distinguish whether horizontal actors appear in their role as purely national actors, or as part of the EU's political system. To distinguish between these two roles, I operationalise horizontal actors as actors from the EU member states in news with a thematic focus of EU (not national) governance (i.e., EU polity, policy or politics). Therefore, also for this chapter, it is important to limit the date set to EU news stories with main or extensive focus on EU governance to maximise the likelihood that actors form the national level appear in the context of EU governance.[43] While the

---

[42] As mentioned previously, for the purpose of this study, actors that could neither be classified as (a) belonging to the group of national actors from the EU member states, or (b) as actors from the EU level were excluded from the analysis (e.g., actors from non-EU member states or supranational organisations other than the EU).

[43] This was operationalised based on the variables V22a-e of the PIREDEU data set.

8.4. Concepts, Measurement and Operationalisations

operationalisations of EU citizens as actors have already been discussed (see Chapter 6.2.2), the operationalisations of the remaining actor categories are outlined in the following (an overview can be found in Table 8.1):

Governmental actors

The governmental sphere refers to the political-administrative system that is responsible for aggregating and articulating common goals, the policy making process and the implementation of collectively binding decisions. At the member state level, the governmental sphere consists of the government, the legislature, the judiciary and the political administration (Fuchs 1993). At the EU level, the governmental sphere is constituted by the Commission, the Council of the EU, the European Parliament and the Court of Justice, and the EU's administration (Hix and Høyland 2011). I have operationalised governmental actors based on various individual actors and actor groups coded in the PIREDEU data set. At the member state level, governmental actors include national executive actors (e.g., governments, head of states, ministers), legislative actors (e.g., parliaments and MPs), the political administrations (e.g., civil servants and diplomats), and the judiciary (e.g., courts, judges) of the EU member states. At the EU level, governmental actors are: EU executive actors (e.g., European Commission, Council of the EU, Council of Ministers), legislative actors (e.g., European parliament, MEPs[44]), the European political administrations (e.g., EU civil servants and diplomats), and the judiciary (e.g., Court of Justice).

The intermediary system is crucial for the political system as it is responsible for mediating between the governmental sphere and the citizens (Rucht 1993). In order to fulfil this function, *intermediary actors* aggregate and represent collective interests. This study divided intermediary actors into political parties as well as formal and informal civil society actors that can be differentiated based on how closely they are located on side of the governmental or the private sphere.

---

[44] MEPs were coded on the EU level as well as individually on the member state level. For the coding at the member state level, it is not possible to distinguish between MEPs and MEP candidates.

Political parties

Political parties are the closest to the governmental sphere. It is their task to foster the formation of public opinion and to aggregate citizens' interests. Political parties aim at maximising their votes and at influencing political decision making by the occupation of political offices (Hague and Harrop 2004). Political parties are hierarchically organised, membership and financing are formally appointed and there is a clear allocation of roles, e.g., as party chairman/chairwoman (Rucht 1993 pp.263–264). As a consequence of their formal organisation, parties are often forced to internal unity, for example, when party members are expected to vote in accordance with the party line (Rucht 1993 p.264). In the PIREDEU data set, for each EU member state a minimum of 6 and a maximum of 20 different political parties were included in the codebook, which I use as a measure for political parties at the national level. Based on individual groups of the European Parliament (e.g., the European People's Party or The Greens) coded in the data set, I measure political parties at the EU level. However, there are also extra-parliamentary cooperation of political parties at the EU level that extend beyond the institutional setting of the European Parliament, for example "transnational associations of like-minded national parties" (Pedersen 1996 p.16). Unfortunately, these extra-institutional associations cannot be captured on basis of the data set. Hence, the vertical measure for European political parties is not ideal and might somewhat reduce the visibility of European political parties.

Formal/informal civil society

Civil society refers to organisations that are located between the governmental sphere and the private sphere and that aim to promote or represent citizens' interests (Rucht 2009). The concept of civil society can be further divided into formal and informal civil society. The two can be differentiated based on their degree of organisation (cf. Rucht 1993 p.263). Formal civil society actors consist of more formally organised interests, such as large scale interests groups (e.g., Greenpeace) and trade unions. Usually, these organisations represent specific interests of certain groups of the population (cf. Rucht 2005). Informal civil society refers to organisations such as social movements and citizen's initiatives that are more oriented towards the general good (cf. Rucht 2005) and often represent interests that are not (yet) sufficiently represented by political parties and formal civil society organisations. Informal civil society actors are less-formally organised and lack official rules about hierarchies, membership, financing etc. Therefore, informal civil society organisations are considered more flexible organisations, but are also perceived as more unstable (Rucht 1993 pp.263–264). As people can more easily join or quit their membership, informal civil society organisations have a higher and continuous need to generate support of their members. Therefore, there is often a high need of discussion within informal civil society organisations (cf. Rucht 1993 p.264).

Ideally, formal civil society actors would include trade unions, professional organisations and head organisations and leading interest groups, while informal civil society would consists of smaller interest groups, social movements, citizens' initiatives and grassroot organisations (cf. Peters 2007). Unfortunately, since the PIREDEU codebook was not constructed for a comparison of public sphere models, civil society actors were not coded in this fashion. To approximate the concept of *formal civil society actors*, I draw on two actor categories of the PIREDEU codebook, namely "professional groups" (representing e.g., the interests of teachers, framers etc.) and "interest organisations" that have been coded on the member state and EU level. The code for interest organisations is a rather broad category and while it would be desirable to be able to differentiate what particular interests are represented and whether those organisations are highly or less organised, this is not directly possible based on the data set.

To measure *informal civil society actors*, this study draws on the actor categories of "activists" and "experts" that were coded in the PREDEU study at the national and EU level respectively. Activists can be seen as an approximation to measure social movement actors. An expert is "credited in public with special knowledge or expertise in some area. He or she often belongs to a profession or academic discipline and has often (but not necessarily) achieved a professional reputation among the members of his or her field" (Peters 2008 p.97). Even though one might argue that experts may represent and/or speak on behalf of organised interests, they are included in the category of informal civil society in this study because I argue that their primary role in public debates is not to represent interests, but to impart knowledge (for a similar argument see Peters 2008 pp.94–97). Previous research has shown that even though experts might be affiliated with organisations, they often make clear that they speak for themselves (Ferree et al. 2002b p.98). Following a similar line of reasoning, experts have also been included as a measure of informal civil society by previous research (see Wessler and Rinke 2014). As the measures for formal and informal civil society are not ideal, the results for their level of visibility should be interpreted more cautiously, since their visibility might vary, if more nuanced measures were to be applied.

The empirical analysis in this chapter first focuses on the overall actor structure of the European public sphere that includes both national and EU level actors (first column Table 8.1). In a next step, the horizontal (second column) and vertical (third column) actor structures are analysed separately.

For the investigation of cross-country differences in the actor structure, the analyses are carried out for each of the 27 EU member state separately. To examine the quality of the visibility of EU citizens, it is furthermore taken into account whether EU citizens are able to participate *directly*. In the data set, for each of the six actors, it was coded how many times the actor was quoted directly.[45] For newspapers, direct quotations are identified by quotation marks, for TV, sound-bites were coded. For the analysis, I differentiated between actors that where quoted directly (N=6,693) in news stories and those who were not.[46] At the news story level, I calculated the share of EU news stories where each actor group is quoted directly. At the actor level, the share of each actor group of the total number of quotations was calculated.

---

[45] This was calculated based on the variables V18 a-f in the PIREDEU codebook.
[46] I decided to recode quotations into a categorical variable as the distribution of the variable is skewed. This might be caused by a high number of quotations in some news stories that might be caused my formats such as interviews. As interviews are in the vast majority of cases not conducted with ordinary citizens, but more prominent actors such as politicians, I think that the categorical variable is more insightful.

8.4. Concepts, Measurement and Operationalisations

Table 8.1 Overview of actor coding

Overall	Horizontal (national)	Vertical (European)
Governmental actors	National executive actors (e.g., governments, head of states, ministers), legislative actors (e.g., parliaments, MPs), the political administrations (e.g., civil servants and diplomats) and the judiciary (e.g., courts, judges) of the EU member states	EU executive actors (e.g., Commission, Council of the EU, Council of Ministers), legislative actors (e.g., European Parliament, MEPs), the European political administrations (e.g., EU civil servants and diplomats) and the judiciary (e.g., Court of Justice)
Political parties	National political parties of the EU member states	Political groups of the European Parliament
Formal civil society	National "professional groups" (representing e.g., the interest teachers, framers etc.) and "interest organisations" of the member states	EU level "professional groups" (representing e.g., the interest teachers, framers etc.) and "interest organisations"
Informal civil society	National "activists" and "experts"	EU level "activists" and "experts
EU citizens	National "non-organized ordinary citizen(s), non-organized population groups or the population of a country as a whole" (e.g., voters, people or the public; for television, e.g., country's ordinary citizens being interviewed) of the EU member states	EU-level "non-organized ordinary citizen(s), non-organized population groups or the population of a country as a whole" (e.g., Europeans, European voters, European citizens, European population, European public)

However, this measure is influenced by the general visibility of each actor group. Therefore, in a second step, I consider the relative number of quotations. Here, it is taken into account if an actor group is quoted directly when mentioned in a news story. For this purpose, for the news story level, taking the number of news stories where an actor group is visible as a baseline, the percentage of EU news where this actor group is visible and quoted directly was calculated. For the actor level, taking the absolute number of visibility of each actor group as a benchmark, the percentage of cases where the respective actor group is visible and quoted directly was calculated.

To analyse whether the actor structures deviate significantly from the grand means (i.e., the overall actor structure), t-tests (for the news story level) as well as chi²-tests (for the actor level) were calculated.[47]

8.5. Results: The Actor Structure in EU News

In order to derive conclusions on whether the visibility of citizens is high or low, it is necessary to compare and examine the level of visibility of EU citizens in *relation* to other actors that become visible in the European public sphere. Yet, this alone is not sufficient, as different normative public sphere theories put varying emphasis on whether and to what extent the visibility of citizens is required in public discussions. The aim of this section is to analyse the desired levels of visibility of EU citizens from point of view of different normative public sphere theories, and to compare their theoretical expectations with the observable levels of visibility of EU citizens in the news coverage about the European Union during the 2009 European Parliament election campaign.

The news story level takes the relative visibility of EU citizens into account and analyses whether or not citizens are included as actors in EU news stories with main or extensive focus on EU governance. Figure 8.2 shows the overall actor structure at the news story level in the mediated European public sphere during the 2009 European Parliament election campaign. As can be seen in the figure, EU citizens are visible in 24% of the EU news. The visibility of political parties, who are arguably important actors during election campaigns, is only 10% higher (34%). More importantly, EU citizens are more visible in the EU news coverage than formal and informal civil society actors combined, who are included in only 13% of EU news. Yet, it is governmental actors that domi-

---

[47] I used chi²-tests for the actor level, as the population of actors is not constant, but changes depending on the analysis. For the news story level, however, the population remains constant and hence t-tests can be used.

8.5. Results: The Actor Structure in EU News

nate the news coverage. Governmental actors are visible in 85% of the EU related news coverage. Their visibility clearly prevails compared to all other actor groups.

Figure 8.2 Overall actor structure (news story level)[48]

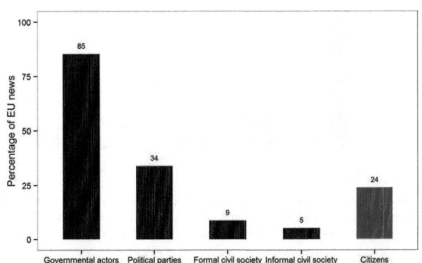

Figure 8.2 shows the overall actor structure in EU news measured as the combined visibility of national (horizontal) and EU level (vertical) actors, calculated based on the percentage of EU news stories where the respective actor group is mentioned.

Contrary to an analysis at the news story level, the actor level takes the absolute visibility of EU citizens into account. As mentioned previously, the actor level can be considered a stricter measure for the visibility of EU citizens, as it implies the logic of a zero-sum game: References to one of the other actor groups automatically decreases the visibility of EU citizens.

---

[48] Governmental actors: N= 10970, political parties: N=4364, formal civil society: N=1114, informal civil society: N=665, citizens: N=3068.

Figure 8.3 Actor structure (actor level)[49]

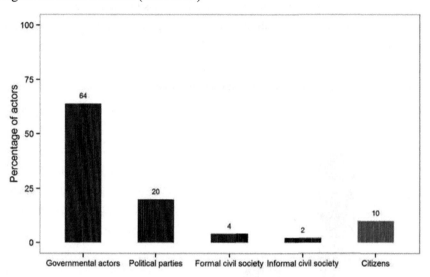

Figure 8.3 shows the overall actor structure in EU news measured as the combined visibility of national (horizontal) and EU level (vertical) actors, calculated based on the share each actor group of the total number of actors.

At first glance, the actor structure of the European public sphere at the actor level (Figure 8.3) looks very similar to the actor structure at the news story level. Yet, the visibility of EU citizens is lower: Out of the total population of actors, the share of citizens is 10%. Even though this number seems initially very low, the visibility of political parties is only two times higher (20%). Civil society actors are again the least visible actor group and the share of EU citizens is higher than the share of formal and informal civil society actors combined, who respectively make up 4% and 2% of the actors. While EU citizens and the other intermediary actors jointly make up 36% of the total actors, it is governmental actors whose share is the largest (64%) and are clearly the predominant actor group in the EU news coverage.

---

[49] Governmental actors: N=24221, political parties: N=7565, formal civil society: N=1557, informal civil society: N=816, citizens: N=3831.

8.5. Results: The Actor Structure in EU News

When comparing the results obtained at both units of analysis, the findings are relatively similar. This was to some extent expected and supports the robustness of the findings, as the actor level is a similar, but stricter measure than the news story level. The percentage difference between the visibility of citizens and governmental actors is -61% at the news story, and -54% at the actor level. Political parties are at both levels 10% more visible than citizens. EU citizens exceed the visibility of formal civil society actors by 15% at the news story level, while the visibility of citizens in comparison to formal civil society actors is 6% higher at the actor level. Citizens are even more prominent actors when compared to informal civil society: At the news story level, citizens are 19% more visible than informal civil society actors, while it is 8% at the actor level.

Yet, what do these results regarding the visibility of EU citizens mean when addressed through the lens of the different normative public sphere theories? For this purpose, the empirical results are compared to the ideal levels of visibility that are visualised in Figure 8.1. From the elitist perspective, citizens should not be visible in public debates on governance. Instead, political parties ought to represent citizens' interest and parties have the highest share among the intermediary actors in EU news. In the elitist model, besides governmental actors, who should dominate the news coverage, there is no need for the presence of additional actor groups, including citizens. However, citizens are not invisible in mediated debates on EU governance and their levels of visibility are only 10% below the visibility of political parties. The liberal theory likewise rejects the visibility of citizens, but requires low levels of visibility of civil society actors. However, the visibility of citizens in the EU news coverage exceeds the levels of visibility of civil society. Therefore, citizens are not an irrelevant actor group and it can be concluded that the overall actor structure of the European public sphere is neither the one of an elitist nor a liberal public sphere. Yet, it is neither participatory, because the model would require a high levels of visibility of ordinary citizens that furthermore exceed the visibility of governmental actors as well as of political parties. This is clearly not the case as governmental actors are six times more visible than citizens at the actor level and 3.5 times more visible at the news story level. Likewise, the visibility of political parties exceeds the visibility of EU citizens.

This leaves the discursive public sphere theory. In the actor structure of the discursive public sphere theory, citizens are not seen as a separate actor category, but citizens belong to the group of informal civil society. When defined in this way, EU citizens as part of informal civil society actors are visible in 28% of EU news, and their share of the total number of actors is 12%. Especially at the actor level, the visibility of informal civil society actors is still significantly lower compared to governmental actors. As the distance to governmental actors is smaller at the news story level, the actor structure at the news story level gets somewhat closer to the discursive ideal. Summarising the results and answering the third research question of this study (RQ3), the discursive public sphere is the ideal type that is the closest match to the empirical levels of visibility of EU citizens.

8.5.1. Horizontal and Vertical Actor Structure

As mentioned previously, a typical characteristic of the European public sphere is that it possesses a vertical and horizontal dimension and it is possible that the results vary on these different levels. In this study, the *horizontal* actor structure takes actors from the national level into account who appear in EU news with main or extensive focus on EU governance. At the news story level, the visibility of horizontal and vertical actors is inevitably lower compared to the overall actor structure: As the actors are split into two groups, vertical and horizontal, the number of cases where an actor can appear is ultimately reduced for all actor groups, while the total number of news stories remains the same. Hence, the levels of visibility of all actor groups are inevitably lower compared to the overall actor structure. Therefore, calculating significance tests to answer the question whether the patterns at the vertical and horizontal level significantly differ from the overall actor structure would not lead to meaningful results. Instead, for the purpose of comparison, Figure 8.4 includes the grand means of the over-

8.5. Results: The Actor Structure in EU News

all actor structure (cf. Figure 8.2) (tables for all following results can be found in Appendix II).

Figure 8.4 Horizontal and vertical actor structure (news story level)[50]

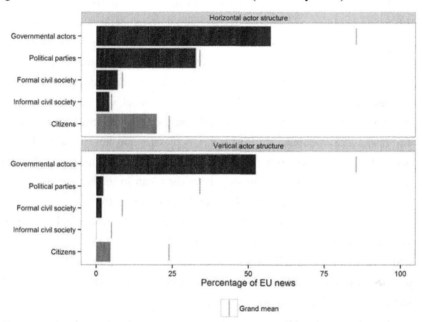

Figure 8.4 shows a) the visibility of national actors (horizontal actor structure), and b) the visibility of EU level actors (vertical actor structure) as the percentage of EU news where the respective actor group is mentioned. Lines indicate the means of the overall actor structure (Figure 8.2).

The image of the horizontal actor structure seems, at first glance, relatively similar to the overall actor structure. National EU citizens are visible in 20% of EU news, which is approximately twice as high as the visibility of civil society actors. The percentage difference in the visibility of citizens and political parties

---

[50] Horizontal level: Governmental actors: N=7377, political parties: N=4191, formal civil society: N=914, informal civil society: N=566, citizens: N=2546. Vertical level: Governmental actors: N=6740, political parties: N=306, formal civil society: N=233, informal civil society: N=107, citizens: N=620.

is, with 13 percentage points, slightly higher compared to the overall actor structure, as national political parties are mentioned in 33% of EU news. At the same time, the gap in visibility between citizens and governmental actors narrows. National governmental actors are included in 57% of the EU news. While governmental actors are overall visible in 61% more news stories than citizens, the difference is only 37% when analysing the horizontal actor structure. As a consequence, the visibility of citizens and intermediary actors in comparison to governmental actors is higher at the horizontal than at the overall level.

For the analysis of the actor level, the share of each actor group of the total number of actors at the vertical and horizontal level was calculated. To see whether the actor structures differ significantly from the overall actor structure, chi^2-tests were calculated. In Figure 8.5, both stars and lines indicate the position of the grand mean of the overall actor structure (cf. Figure 8.3), which differs in the case of stars significantly from the mean in the horizontal / vertical level, while lines indicate that it does not differ significantly.

At the actor level, the share of citizens among the total number of actors from the national level is slightly higher (+2%) compared to the overall actor structure, more specifically, the share of national EU citizens is 12%. The visibility of citizens in comparison to civil society actor remains unchanged, as the share of national civil society actors is likewise 2% higher. The difference in visibility compared to political parties is more pronounced, as their share gains 8%. Yet, similar to the analysis at the news story level, when compared to governmental actors, the visibility of citizens is higher at the horizontal level, as the share of governmental actors is with 53% 11 percentage points below the average at the overall actor structure.

8.5. Results: The Actor Structure in EU News

Figure 8.5 Horizontal and vertical actor structure (actor level)[51]

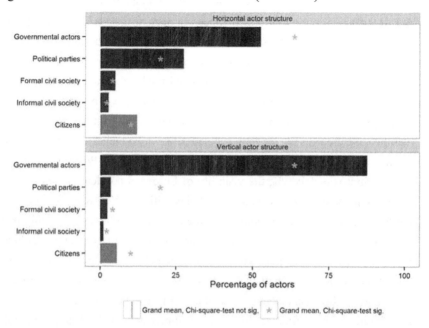

Figure 8.5 shows a) the visibility of national actors (horizontal actor structure), and b) the visibility of EU level actors (vertical actor structure) as the total number of actors in EU news. Stars and lines indicate the position of the grand mean in the overall actor structure (Figure 8.3). Stars show significant chi^2-test results, indicating that the value differs significantly from the overall actor structure, while lines indicate that it does not differ significantly.

Based on these findings, it can be concluded that the horizontal dimension of the European public sphere is generally more participatory than the overall actor structure when it comes to the visibility of citizens. However, the visibility of national EU citizens can still by no means considered as high when compared to governmental actors and hence the empirical reality regarding the actor structure in EU news is still best described by the discursive public sphere theory when it

---

[51] Horizontal level: Governmental actors: N=13702, political parties: N=7153, formal civil society: N=1278, informal civil society: N=694, citizens: N=3166. Vertical level: Governmental actors: N=10519, political parties: N=412, formal civil society: N=279, informal civil society: N=122, citizens: N=665.

comes to the visibility of ordinary citizens. Therefore, the first part of the answer to RQ3.1 is that the normative model of the public sphere that corresponds best to the visibility of EU citizens does not vary at the horizontal level compared to the overall actor structure of the European public sphere.

Finally, the *vertical* actor dimension of the European public sphere refers to attention to EU level actors in the national media coverage on EU governance. When looking at these EU-level actors separately, the picture changes radically compared to the overall actor structure. At both units of analysis, the visibility of European EU citizens is below 6%, which makes citizens nevertheless the most visible actor group after governmental actors. With levels of visibility of approximately 3%, the visibility of European political parties and European civil society actors is somewhat below citizens. Yet, what is decisive is that the visibility of citizens compared to EU governmental actors is only marginal. At the vertical level, governmental actors from the EU level are included in 52% of the EU related news coverage and their share among the total actors is 88%. This means that at the news story level, governmental actors are about 11 times more visible than citizens, while it is 16 times at the actor level.

Based on these findings, the vertical dimension of the European public sphere is clearly elitist, where only governmental actors are visible and citizens and civil society actors are nearly completely absent in public debates. One could even argue that it is too elitist, even from the perspective of the elitist public sphere theory, since political parties are nearly invisible as well. Therefore, the answer to RQ3.1 is that the normative model of the public sphere that corresponds best to the visibility of EU citizens varies significantly at the vertical, but not at the horizontal level of the European public sphere compared to the overall actor structure.

8.5.2. *Country Level Differences*

The results discussed above represent the actor structure of the European public sphere form a Europeanisation perspective, where the national public spheres of

8.5. Results: The Actor Structure in EU News

the EU member states become more "European" by including debates on EU affairs to a greater extent (e.g., Gerhards 2000). As the previous results are aggregated, it is possible that the actor structure varies across the EU member states. If this is the case, citizens might get a different impression to what extent EU citizens become visible in the European public sphere. This might consequently also impact their perception of how elitist or participatory debates on EU governance in the media are. Therefore, after the general patterns have been discussed, the question is addressed whether the actor structure is similar across EU member states or there are country-specific differences. Are the patterns of visibility of EU citizens at the overall, horizontal, and vertical level consistent across countries?

Figure 8.6 shows the overall actor structure in EU news across the 27 EU member states at the news story level, while Figure 8.7 shows the same for the actor level. At first glance, the actor structures seem very similar compared to the grand mean (cf. Figure 8.2 and Figure 8.3), as the rank order of the actors is the same in the majority of the countries. In all member state, governmental actors are by far the most visible actor group in EU news. Overall, the second most visible group are political parties, followed by citizens, formal[52], and informal civil society actors.[53] Yet, on closer inspection, some differences can be revealed.

At the news story level, in 9 member states (Belgium, Denmark, Estonia, Finland, Latvia, Lithuania, the Netherlands, Romania, and Slovakia), citizens, not political parties, are the second most visible actor group. This finding holds for 5 states (Finland, Latvia, Lithuania, Romania, and Slovakia) at the actor level. Only in Germany and Poland, citizens are neither the third nor second most visible actor group, but the visibility of formal and informal civil society actors respectively exceeds the actor share of citizens (at the news story level this only applies to Germany).

---

[52] At both levels of analysis, only in Lithuania, the share of formal civil society is higher than the share of political parties.
[53] At both levels of analysis, only in the Czech Republic, Denmark, Estonia, Poland, and Slovakia, informal civil society actors are more visible than formal civil society actors.

Figure 8.6 Overall actor structure by EU member state (news story level)

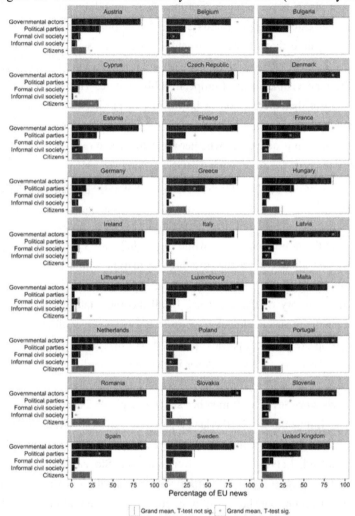

Figure 8.6 shows the percentage of EU news where the respective actor group is mentioned by EU member state. Stars and lines indicate the position of the grand mean in the overall actor structure (Figure 8.2). Stars show significant t-test results, indicating that the country value differs significantly from the overall actor structure, while lines indicate that it does not differ significantly.

8.5. Results: The Actor Structure in EU News

Figure 8.7 Overall actor structure by EU member state (actor level)

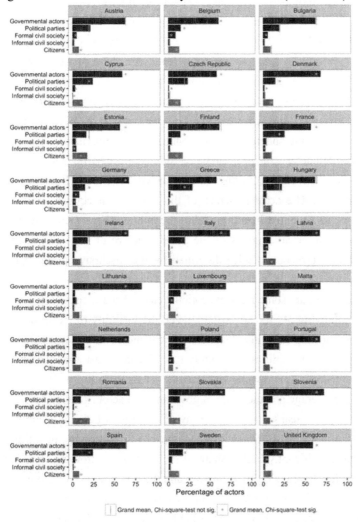

Figure 8.7 shows the percentage share of each actor group in EU news of the total number of actors by EU member state. Stars and lines indicate the position of the grand mean in the overall actor structure (Figure 8.3). Stars show significant chi^2-test results, indicating that the country value differs significantly from the overall actor structure, lines indicate that it does not differ significantly.

Besides these differences in the rank order, the visibility of EU citizens generally varies rather strongly across counties. At the news story level, EU citizens are most visible in the EU related news coverage in Finland, where citizens are visible as actors in 44% of EU news and lowest in Italy where citizens are only included in 10% of EU news. At the actor level, the share of EU citizens is highest in Romania with 20% and again lowest in Italy with only 4%. The t-tests and chi^2-tests furthermore reveal that citizens are significantly more visible in 10 EU member states at the actor level, and in nine states at the news story level. The European public spheres of those countries, in comparison to the grand mean of the overall actor structure, can be considered more participatory. On the other hand, there are eight countries where the visibility of EU citizens lies below the average. The actor structure of those states, in comparison, leans somewhat more to the elitist-liberal model of the public sphere. Generally it can be said that the empirical findings of the actor structure of EU news in most countries are best (yet not ideally) described by the discursive public sphere theory.

However, there are some more exceptional cases that are discussed in more detail in the following. At the news story level, the visibility of EU citizens in Lithuania does not significantly deviate from the mean. It is nevertheless an interesting case, as Lithuania is the country that diverges most strongly when it comes to the visibility of governmental actors: Their visibility is 19% higher compared to the average and the share of governmental actors goes up to 83% at the actor level. This means that the visibility of citizens in Lithuania compared to governmental actors is 10 times lower (compared to an average of 6 times). Because of the significantly higher share of governmental actors and the comparatively low levels of visibility of citizens and the remaining actor groups, the actor structure in EU news in Lithuania rather reflects the structure of an elitist-liberal public sphere, even though these theories would ideally require higher levels of visibility of political parties and the complete absents of citizens, who despite their comparatively low level of visibility are the second most visible actor group in Lithuania. Italy is a case that gets closest to the ideal type of an elitist public sphere. In Italy, the share of citizens among the total number of actors is only 4%, while the share of governmental actors is with 74% 18 times higher. At the same time, the share of political parties is 20%, while the civil society actors are nearly invisible (2%).

Horizontal

The horizontal level of the European public sphere takes the visibility of actors from national level who appear in the context of EU news into account. Again, in the majority of EU member states, the results show the same rank order of visibility, with a predominance of national governmental actors, followed by national political parties, national EU citizens, as well as national formal and informal civil society (Figure 8.8 and 8.9). With regard to cross country differences, it is mainly the same countries that show exceptions in the rank order as in the overall actor structure.[54]

Furthermore, at the horizontal level, the visibility of national EU citizens varies even more strongly across countries. At both units of analysis, the visibility of citizens is highest in Finland (39% at the news story level, 28% at the actor level) and again lowest in Italy (8% news story level, 4% actor level). The visibility of citizens in comparison to governmental actors is generally higher across countries, as the share of national governmental actors is lower across all member states, which is consistent with the trend found for the pooled analysis. Consequently, the share national EU citizens, but also civil society actors and political parties are higher, which means that the actor structure at the horizontal level generally gets closer to the ideal type of the discursive public sphere.

---

[54] At the actor level, in Lithuania, the share of formal civil society is higher than the share of political parties, while in the Czech Republic, Denmark, Estonia, Poland, and Slovakia, informal civil society actors are more visible than formal civil society actors. In Finland, Latvia, Lithuania, Romania, and Slovakia, national EU citizens, not national political parties, are the second most visible actor group. In Germany, national formal civil society actors are more visible than national EU citizens, while it is national informal civil society actors in Poland. At the news story level, a higher percentage of informal than formal civil society actors was found in the Czech Republic, Denmark, France, Estonia, Lithuania, Poland, and Slovakia. It is mainly the same countries where citizens (not political parties) are the second most visible actor group as in the overall structure, i.e., Belgium, Estonia, Finland, Latvia, Lithuania, Romania, Slovakia, but now also Poland.

Figure 8.8 Horizontal actor structure by EU member state (news story level)

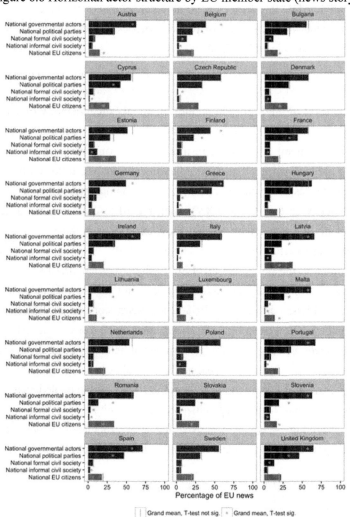

Figure 8.8 shows the percentage of EU news where the respective actor group is mentioned by EU member state. Stars and lines indicate the position of the grand mean in the horizontal actor structure (Figure 8.4). Stars show significant t-test results, indicating that the country value differs significantly from the overall actor structure, lines indicate that it does not differ significantly.

8.5. Results: The Actor Structure in EU News

Figure 8.9 Horizontal actor structure by EU member state (actor level)

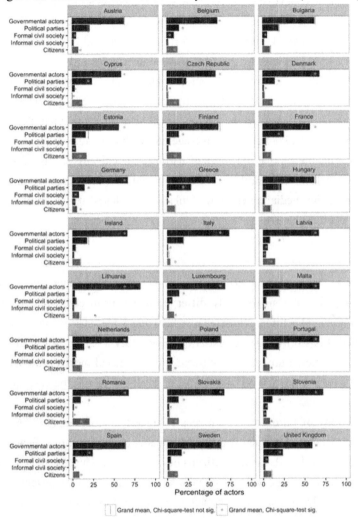

Figure 8.9 shows the percentage share of each actor group in EU news of the total number of actors by EU member state. Stars and lines indicate the position of the grand mean in the horizontal actor structure (Figure 8.5). Stars show significant chi^2-test results, indicating that the country value differs significantly from the overall actor structure, lines indicate that it does not differ significantly.

Yet, for some countries, some noteworthy changes in the actor structure are observed. At the actor level, the share of national EU citizens in Finland is significantly higher. The visibility of citizens is with 28% 16 percentage points above the average. While the visibility of formal and informal civil society actors does not vary significantly, political parties are significantly less visible. Thus, in Finland, the visibility of citizens is higher than the share of political parties (25%). While the portion of governmental actors in Finland does not significantly differ from the average in the overall actor structure, their share at the horizontal level is 13% below the average and with only 40% the lowest in the 27 states. This means that the share of national EU citizens is only 12 percentage points below the visibility of governmental actors. Therefore, at the horizontal level, the media coverage of Finland gets closest to the ideal of a participatory public sphere.

Vertical

Turning now to the vertical actor structure, across all actor groups, there are generally less cases that significantly differ from the mean compared to the overall and horizontal actor structure (Figure 8.10 and 8.11). Starting again with the rank order, it is worth noticing that at the news story level, in 24 out of the 27 EU member states, European EU citizens are the second most visible actor group after governmental actors.[55] At the actor level, this is still the case in 20 countries.[56]

The visibility of European EU citizens is highest in Romania (14% news story level, 12% actor level) and lowest in Lithuania (approximately 1% at the news story and actor level). Besides citizens being the second most visible actor group, and the clear dominance of EU governmental actors, no consistent pattern in the rank order of the remaining actors at the vertical level can be determined that prevails in the majority of EU member states.

---

[55] In Italy, Lithuania and Poland citizens are not the second most visible actor group.
[56] Citizens are not the second most visible actor group in the following countries: Bulgaria, Estonia, Germany, Hungary, Italy, Malta, and Poland.

8.5. Results: The Actor Structure in EU News

Figure 8.10 Vertical actor structure by EU member state (news story level)

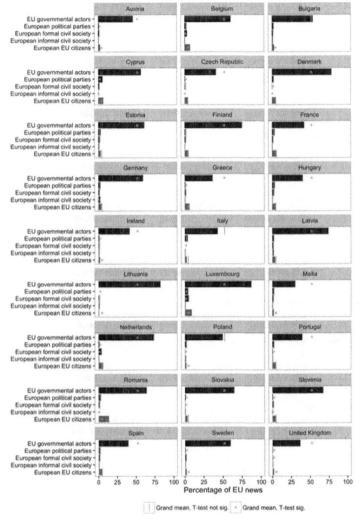

Figure 8.10 shows the percentage of EU news where the respective actor group is mentioned by EU member state. Stars and lines indicate the position of the grand mean in the vertical actor structure (Figure 8.4). Stars show significant t-test results, indicating that the country value differs significantly from the overall actor structure, while lines indicate that it does not differ significantly.

Figure 8.11 Vertical actor structure by EU member state (actor level)

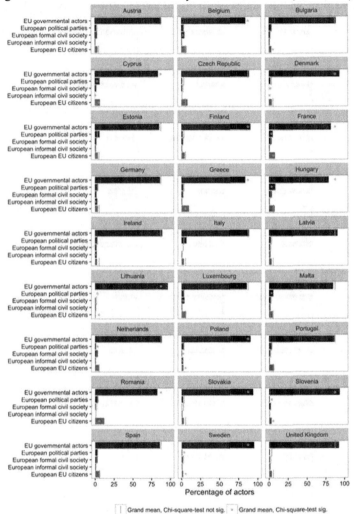

Figure 8.11 shows the percentage share of each actor group in EU news of the total number of actors by EU member state. Stars and lines indicate the position of the grand mean in the horizontal actor structure (Figure 8.5). Stars show significant chi^2-test results, indicating that the country value differs significantly from the overall actor structure, lines indicate that it does not differ significantly.

In several countries, some actor groups are even completely absent at the vertical level, namely European political parties in Lithuania, formal civil society actors in Italy and informal civil society actors in the Czech Republic, Denmark, and Romania. Even though citizens are more visible than European political parties and European civil society actors, in comparison to EU governmental actors, the visibility of European EU citizens is marginal. Despite small cross-country differences, it can be concluded that without any exception, the vertical actor structure in all 27 EU member states is the one of an elitist public sphere.

For the country-by-country analysis, it can concluded that even though the levels of visibility in most of the countries deviate significantly from the mean and there is considerable variation in the visibility of EU citizens, overall, the results in most EU member states are best described as a discursive actor structure at the overall and horizontal level, while across all EU member states, the actor structure at the vertical level resembles the one of an elitist public sphere. Hence, the answer to RQ3.2, which asked if the normative model of the public sphere that corresponds best to the visibility of EU citizens varies across countries, is that the patterns of visibility of EU citizens are overall consistent across the EU member states.

8.5.3. Quality of Visibility

The indicator for the quality of actors' visibility in discussions on EU governance that is applied by this study is that of quotations. Here, the question that has been raised is to which normative model of the public sphere do the empirical levels of direct citations of EU citizens in debates on EU governance correspond best. The underlying assumption is that the visibility of citizens is a measure for their opinions being reported in the news coverage (cf. Bosch 2014). Direct citations arguably increase the likelihood of including opinions and arguments put forward by the respective actor group (cf. Dimitrova and Strömbäck 2009). To measure this aspect of the quality of participation in European public debates, direct quotations are taken into account.

Figure 8.12 shows the percentage of EU news stories where an actor group is visible and quoted directly (news story level), while Figure 8.13 shows how the total number of actors that are quoted in EU news is distributed between the five different actor groups (actor level).

Figure 8.12 Actor structure based on quotations, absolute (news story level)[57]

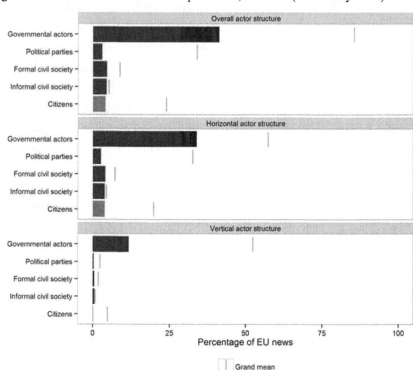

Figure 8.12 shows the percentage of EU news where the respective actor group is mentioned and quoted directly. Lines indicate the means of the overall (Figure 8.2), horizontal, or vertical actor structure (Figure 8.4).

---

[57] By only taking the share of news where actors are quoted into account, the number of cases where an actor group can appear is reduced, while the total number of news stories remains the same. This leads to a decrease in visibility of all actor groups. Calculating significance tests does not lead to meaningful results. Instead, Figure 8.12 reports the overall means to be better able to compare the actor structures.

8.5. Results: The Actor Structure in EU News

Figure 8.13 Actor structure based on quotations, absolute (actor level)

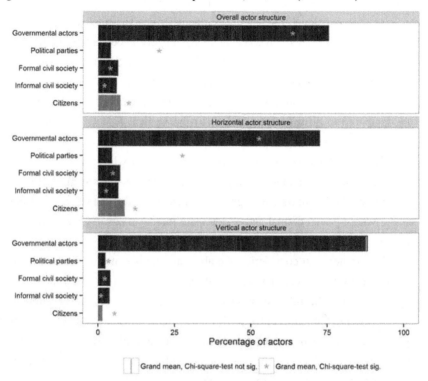

Figure 8.13 shows the percentage share of each actor group of the total number of actors quoted in EU news. Stars and lines indicate the position of the grand mean in the overall (Figure 8.3), horizontal, or vertical actor structure (Figure 8.5). Stars show significant chi^2-test results, indicating that the value differs significantly from the overall, horizontal, or vertical actor structure, while lines indicate that it does not differ significantly.

The results based on both units of analysis show that the actor structure based on quotations varies strongly compared to the grand means. In the overall and horizontal actor structure at the news story level, citizens are quoted more frequently in news stories than political parties, but slightly less often than formal and informal civil society actors. At the vertical level, European EU citizens are the least quoted actor group. It is governmental actors that clearly dominate the actor structure based on quotations at all three levels.

At the actor level, the share of citizens among the total number of actors quoted in the EU news coverage is approximately 3 percentage points below their level of visibility. In the overall and horizontal actor structure, citizens are nevertheless the second most quoted actor group. Yet, the dominance of governmental actors is more pronounced and citizens are about ten times less visible compared to governmental actors. At the vertical level, European EU citizens are even the actor group that is quoted the least.

Based on those results, it can be concluded that when taking the distributions of quotations among the different actor groups into account, the actor structure of the EU news coverage clearly resembles the one of an elitist public sphere where governmental actors dominate the news coverage and all remaining actor groups are nearly invisible.

Yet, rather than considering the absolute number of quotations, which are influenced by the levels of visibility of each actor group, it might be more insightful to take the relative frequency into account. Here, the question is: If citizens are mentioned in news stories, how many times are they quoted directly? For the news story level, taking the percentage of news stories where an actor group is visible as a baseline, the percentage news where this actor group is visible and quoted directly was calculated. For the actor level, taking the absolute number of visibility of each actor group as a benchmark, the percentage of cases where the respective actor group was visible and quoted was calculated. The results based on the relative number of quotations are shown in Figure 8.14 at the news story level and in Figure 8.15 for the actor level. In both cases, the picture changes radically.

8.5. Results: The Actor Structure in EU News

Figure 8.14 Actor structure based on quotations, relative (news story level)

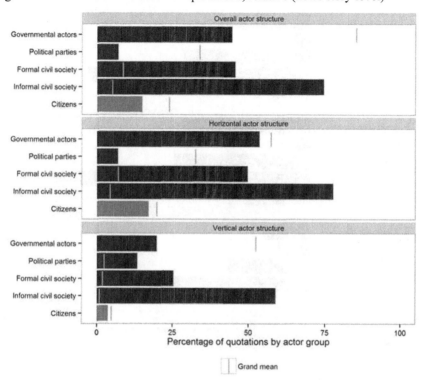

Figure 8.14 shows the percentage of EU news stories where the actor group was quoted directly, calculated based on the EU news stories where the respective actor group was mentioned. Lines indicate the means of the overall (Figure 8.2), horizontal, or vertical actor structure (Figure 8.4).

For EU citizens, the results suggest that they are less often than other actor groups able to express themselves directly. While the visibility of citizens has been more than twice as high as the visibility of formal and informal civil society, in terms of quotations, they now fall far behind not only formal, but also informal civil society. This holds for both units of analysis as well as all three levels of the European public sphere.

Figure 8.15 Actor structure based on quotations, relative (actor level)

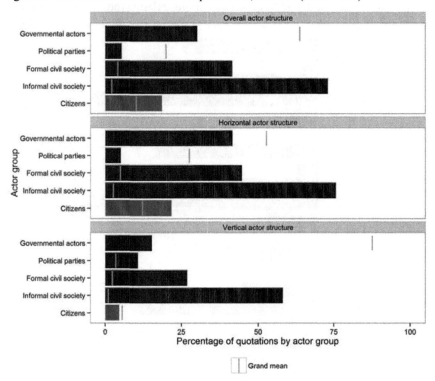

Figure 8.15 shows the percentage of direct quotations calculated based on the number of times an actor group was mentioned. Lines indicate the means of the overall (Figure 8.3), horizontal, or vertical actor structure (Figure 8.5).

If one would take the relative number of quotations as a basis for the actor structure, neither the overall, vertical, nor horizontal level resemble the actor structure of an elitist or liberal public sphere, because of a too weak role of governmental actors in comparison to citizens, but especially civil society actors. The high percentage of quotations of informal civil society actors is in line with the participatory public sphere, yet, for this model, the percentage of quotations of citizens is too low. Therefore, the results based on quotations are again to a large extent in accordance with the deliberative public sphere theory that emphasises the visibility and participation of informal civil society actors (including citizens) in public debates. However, this is mainly due to the high percentage of quotations of informal civil society actors. When assuming that direct quotations can be seen as an indicator for opinions being reported, it can be concluded that citizens are less often than other actor groups able to express their opinions directly via the news coverage.

The answer to the final research question of this chapter, to which normative model of the public sphere do the empirical levels of direct citations of EU citizens in debates on EU governance correspond best (RQ 3.3), is ambivalent. The results vary strongly depending on how the number of quotations is operationalised. When analysing the total number of actors that are quoted in EU news, at all three levels, the actor structure mirrors the one of an elitist public sphere. Hence, the findings differ strongly from the discursive pattern that was found in the previous analyses. However, when taking the absolute number of visibility of each actor group as a benchmark and calculating the number of times the respective actor was quoted directly when mentioned, the pattern changes radically and is best described by the discursive actor structure at all three levels. In this case, for the first time, the vertical actor structure does not reflect an elitist pattern.

8.6. Conclusion

Building on previous research by Ferree and colleauges (2002a), who examined to what extent the news media coverage reflects democratic ideals proposed by normative public sphere theories, this chapter has provided an account of the empirical relevance of different normative public sphere theories in the context of the European public sphere. More specifically, it has focused on one dimension of those normative theories, namely on the visibility of different actors and the visibility of citizens in particular. By deriving ideal typical actor structures from normative public sphere theories, the visibility of EU citizens was examined. Taking the characteristics of the European public sphere into account, the analysis has focused on the overall actor structure, but also analysed the horizontal and vertical dimension of the European public sphere separately. In addition, to provide details on the actor structure that is as nuanced as possible, this chapter has accounted for country specific variance, as well as indicators for the quality of visibility. Furthermore, the analyses were carried out at two units of analysis, the news story and the actor level. The findings show that the differences based on the two units of analysis are rather small; therefore, the conclusion is mainly focussing on the overall tendencies found at both levels of analysis.

The results for the overall actor structure of EU news have shown that the visibility of EU citizens is rather low when compared to governmental actors. However, EU citizens are clearly more visible than civil society actors in the EU news coverage during the 2009 European Parliament election. Furthermore, the percentage difference in visibility between citizens and political parties is never higher than 13 percentage points.

If one would leave citizens aside and would not consider them as a relevant actor group, the empirical results regarding the overall actor structure of the European public sphere correspond largely with the vision of the liberal public sphere. However, the empirical results show that citizens are not an irrelevant actor group. Therefore, the visibility of EU citizens is largely, yet not perfectly, in line with the discursive public sphere. The analysis furthermore showed that this pattern is essentially consistent across the EU member states and media outlets, as cross-country and media-related differences in the actor structure are rather small, even though the analysis revealed some exceptional cases, such as the actor structure in the Finish media, which is more participatory, or in the Lithuanian media coverage, which is more elitist.

However, the results differ strongly when analysing the visibility of horizontal/national and vertical/EU level actors in EU news separately. While the horizontal dimension is more inclusive of EU citizens and civil society, the vertical level is clearly elitist and it is nearly exclusively EU governmental actors that are in the centre of attention. As far as the Europeanisation of the news media coverage is concerned, i.e., the extent to which news media include actors from the EU level, the results show that this Europeanisation process is mainly

8.6. Conclusion

limited to EU governmental actors. In the EU news coverage, their visibility is approximately equal to the visibility of governmental actors from the national level. Yet, when comparing the visibility of political parties, civil society as well as citizens, significantly lower levels of visibility at the vertical level are observed. When contrasted with the horizontal level, the vertical actor structure shows some deficits in providing those actors equal access to debates on EU governance. For EU citizens, this means that the mediated image of the EU citizenry that becomes visible does not reflect a vision of a supranational-European citizenry, but predominantly consists of national EU citizens from the member states. Overall, based on the results of this study, one can differentiate between an *elitist-vertical* and *discursive-horizontal* dimension of the European public sphere. Again, this finding is consistent at both units of analysis as well as across countries and media outlets.

Yet, these observations change when taking measures for the quality of visibility in EU news into account: When it comes to quotations, which are seen as an indicator to what extent actors are able to express their opinions directly in the news coverage, citizens are among the least relevant actors. This raises questions about the extent to which citizens' opinions on EU governance are in fact reflected in the EU news media coverage on EU governance. If citizens are only mentioned, but not able to express their opinions on EU governance, this limits the extent to which the European public sphere is able to contribute to a meaningful exchange between EU citizens and policy makers at the EU level.

Furthermore, the elitist character of the vertical level of the European public sphere reflects some of the issues that have been raised in the context of the debate of the EU's democratic deficit, namely being driven by elites while lacking civic support. Especially the lack of European intermediary actors ought to represent the citizens is striking and since European EU citizens are not visible themselves, there is hardly anyone who is able to speak on behalf of or represent the interests of the European citizenry as a whole. As a consequence, governmental actors are hardly able to hear the voice of the European people, which impacts the ability of EU governance to be responsive to citizens' will. The higher visibility of national intermediary actors as well as national EU citizens is able to diminish this deficit to a certain extent. Yet, it might still make the EU appear as a rather elitists institution and contribute to the fact that citizens perceive the EU as distant. This (among other things) might contribute to the EU's democratic deficit, while hinder the development of a truly European citizenry at the same time.

The analysis has contributed to the field of European public sphere research by showing that public sphere theories developed at the national level can be applied and utilised for normative assessment of European political communication. Yet, it is limited in so far as it has only focused on one specific dimension of those normative theories: The visibility of different actor groups. The study provided ideal types of the actor structures of four different normative public sphere theories that can be used as a basis for further empirical analyses. While previous research has thus far primarily analysed the European public sphere from the perspective of the discursive public sphere (e.g., Brüggemann and Kleinen-von Königslöw 2009; Koopmans 2007; Peters 2005; Trenz 2004; Wessler et al. 2008), this study was able to contribute to the discussion of the European public sphere by highlighting that there is not only one normative model of the public sphere that sufficiently describes empirical reality. Depending on the respective normative ideal, the results regarding the development state and health of the European public sphere vary. Additionally, differences on the vertical and horizontal actor dimension of the European public sphere have to be taken into account. This chapter has highlighted the need to specify normative theories of the public sphere when talking about its European framework. These specifications might help to develop the theoretical concept of the European public sphere further and contribute to our understanding of the image of EU democracy that becomes visible to the EU citizens via the European public sphere. In the long run, a European public sphere that is more open for European civil society as well as EU citizens might contribute to more responsive and more democratic governance at the EU level.

9. Explaining the Visibility of EU Citizens in the European Public Sphere

The previous chapter has shown that EU citizens are visible actors in 24% of the EU-related news coverage during the 2009 European parliament election and their share of the total number of actors is 10%. Furthermore, when comparing the visibility of EU citizens to other actor groups that become visible in the EU-related news coverage, citizens are not a marginal group, but even exceed the visibility of civil society actors. The analysis showed that the actor structure of EU news in most EU member states matches best the discursive model of the public sphere. Yet, the results also show that the visibility of EU citizens varies considerably across countries. In some states, such as Finland, EU citizens are significantly more visible and thus the public sphere gets closer to the participatory ideal, while in other countries EU citizens are less visible and the actor structure rather resembles an elitist public sphere. When assuming that the presence of EU citizens in the European public sphere is crucial for the legitimacy of EU governance, understanding the factors that lead to higher levels of visibility is important. Finding these factors that foster the visibility of EU citizens in the European public sphere is the aim of this chapter.

In the European public sphere, I have distinguished between two different forms of visibility of EU citizens, one accounting for a truly European citizenry, and the other one linking back to the member state level. As discussed in the previous chapters, it is predominantly national EU citizens that become visible in the news coverage and constitute the largest share of the total visibility of EU citizens. Analysing the overall visibility of EU citizens and national EU citizens separately therefore produces very similar results. Hence, this chapter exclusively focuses on a comparison of the visibility of national and European EU citizens. The question addressed by this chapter is: *How can cross-country differ-*

ences in the visibility of national and European EU citizens be explained and what are the factors that foster their visibility (RQ4)? As levels of visibility of national and European EU citizens vary, the follow-up question is: *Are there different factors that explain the visibility of national and European EU citizens* (RQ4.1)?

9.1. State of the Art

European public sphere research commonly differentiates between a horizontal and vertical dimension of the European public sphere. Horizontal Europeanisation refers to a linkage between the member states in terms of an increased focus on actors and events taking place in fellow EU member states (Brüggemann and Kleinen-von Königslöw 2009), while vertical Europeanisation refers to a connection between the national and EU level (Koopmans and Erbe 2004). Studies focussing on vertical Europeanisation have examined the extent to which EU affairs and EU level governmental actors are reported in the national media (e.g., Boomgaarden et al. 2013). To a large extent, these studies have remained descriptive in scope and did not try to explain cross-country differences further. Those who did, have predominantly focused on explaining variation in the amount of EU news reported, while there is only a limited number of studies that aim to explain different levels of visibility of EU governmental actors (Boomgaarden et al. 2013; Brüggemann and Kleinen-von Königslöw 2009; Peter and de Vreese 2004; Schuck and de Vreese 2011). So far, no study has aimed to analyse and explain the visibility of EU citizens in the news coverage on EU governance. Nevertheless, previous research might provide information on more general patterns of reporting on actors that can explain variance in their visibility in EU news. Those results cannot be directly applied to the visibility of EU citizens, but they can provide some guidance as to what factors might influence their visibility.

Regarding variation in the visibility of EU level actors, research first of all suggests that their visibility might not be stable, but fluctuate in the course of certain events. Generally, the visibility of EU news and institutions seems to be higher during policy-related and institutional events at the EU level, such as European elections, changes in the European commission and EU presidency, EU enlargements, or the signing of new treaties (Boomgaarden et al. 2010, see also Hepp et al. 2012). A study by Peter and de Vreese (2004) found on the contrary that the visibility of EU officials is higher during routine periods compared to EU summits. The share of EU officials among all actors during routine periods is on average 20%, compared to 7.2% during EU summits. However, this finding is arguably due to the operationalisation of EU actors as 'EU officials'; which are "members of EU institutions or persons appointed by the EU" (Peter and de Vreese 2004 p.11). Hence, the head of states and governments of the EU member states, that become part of the EU's political system when taking part in EU summits of the European Council, are not seen as partially also belonging to the group of EU actors, but are included in the category of "non-EU actors". However, as I have argued previously (cf. Chapter 4), the EU's multi-level political system is inevitably linked to the member states and, as a result, also actors from the national level are part of the EU's political system.

Generally, previous research has indicated that both media and country level factors have an effect on the visibility of EU actors. Starting with the former, a study based on the PIREDEU data set found that TV news, but also commercial media outlets (i.e., tabloids) feature significantly less EU governmental actor (Schuck and de Vreese 2011). Likewise, for "discursive" articles (e.g., editorials, commentaries, or interviews), findings by Kleinen-von Königslöw (2012) suggest that EU institutions are significantly more visible in the quality than tabloid press. Brüggemann and Kleinen-von Königslöw (2009) find that for the visibility of EU institutions, also a newspaper's editorial mission plays and important role: The more European a newspaper considers its editorial mission, the more space is giving to EU actors.

At the member state level, for the news coverage during European Parliament elections, Boomgaarden et al. (2013) found that the more the EU is contested within a country by elites[58], the lower the visibility of EU governmental actors, while at the same time positive elite opinions towards the EU[59] have a positive effect on the visibility of EU governmental actors (Boomgaarden et al. 2013). Furthermore, the size of a EU member state seems to play a role for the visibility of EU governmental actors as EU member states with larger populations seem to report significantly less on EU governmental actors (Schuck and de Vreese 2011). In addition, some evidence is found that Euroscepticism among the population of a member state leads to more media attention to actors from the EU (see also Wessler et al. 2008). The length of EU membership, on the other hand, seems to have a negative effect (Kleinen-von Königslöw 2012).

In short, there is only a limited number of studies aiming to explain variation in the EU news coverage. When EU level actors have been taken into account, it has exclusively been governmental actors who have been in the centre of attention. As discussed in detail in Chapter 4.3, only a limited number of studies have included EU citizens in their analysis of actors in the European public sphere. There is only very little evidence on cross-country variation, but most importantly, research has not yet aimed at *explaining* different levels of visibility of EU citizens or citizens in general. Taking previous research on the European public sphere into account, the next section presents the hypotheses of this study.

9.2. Hypotheses

The aim of this chapter is to analyse and explain the visibility of national and European EU citizens in the news coverage on EU affairs. The following hypotheses are formulated for both forms of visibility. Some hypotheses expect the

---

[58] Elite dispersion is operationalised based on the party manifesto component of the European Election Study the standard deviation per country from the mean score on EU issues that is weighted by party size (Boomgaarden et al. 2013 p.616).
[59] Elite positivity towards the EU is operationalised based on the party manifesto component of the European Election Study and measures the "mean score of all parties' position towards the EU, within a particular country for each of the three elections weighted by party size, yielding a country-level by election campaign aggregate score on party positions towards the EU" (Boomgaarden et al. 2013 p.616).

same directions of effects, if they apply to the visibility of citizens in the (EU) news coverage more generally, while others have diverging expectations. When thinking about the visibility of EU citizens in the EU news coverage, different sets of factors that could potentially influence their visibility in the news can be identified, (1) factors at the news story level, (2) media related factors, (3) factors that concern a member states relation to the EU, and (4) factors at the country level independent of EU governance. The respective hypotheses are discussed in the following. (An overview of the hypotheses can be found in Table 9.1.)

9.2.1. News Story Related Factors

The general visibility of citizens in the news media coverage might be influenced by certain characteristics of news stories and/or certain circumstances of reporting that make it more likely that citizens are included in a news story (cf. Hopmann and Shehata 2011; van Aelst and de Swert 2009). As such, this study takes the thematic context as well as prominence into account. The arguments and hypotheses are outlined below.

Topic: European elections
News media coverage during election campaigns differs from routine periods (van Aelst and de Swert 2009). According to van Aelst and de Swert, election campaigns impact the working conditions of journalists, as they are "confronted with more active political actors and a more attentive public. These changes create a different news environment, and ultimately daily news broadcasts that differ significantly from the news broadcasts in non-campaign periods" (van Aelst and de Swert 2009 p.153). Similarly, I have previously argued that the visibility of EU citizens in the news coverage is arguably heightened during European elections, compared to the media coverage during non-election times (see Chapter 6). Even though one might argue that political communication during election times takes place in a top down manner where political parties

and candidates, rather than citizens are the main actors, election campaigns also possess a bottom-up component (Schmitt-Beck and Farrell 2002). Elections function as a feedback mechanism and ensure the responsiveness of representatives, and election campaigns facilitate institutionalised communication between citizens and their representatives (Asp and Esaiasson 1996 p.93). Politicians need to know what their electorate wants in order to be able to act according to the interests of their voters and to be responsive to them (cf. Pitkin, 1967). Therefore communication is crucial, especially during elections.

The mass media play an important role in maintaining communication flows between politicians and citizens, since they "keep citizens informed of what public officials are doing and public officials informed of what citizens want" (Milbrath 1972 p.144). In the end, it is the citizens that decide on the outcome of an election and it can be expected that journalists "honor this high level of importance [of citizens] by offering regular people a voice in the political news" (van Aelst and de Swert 2009 p.157). In general, there is some (survey) evidence supporting that journalists themselves consider it as important to provide citizens with the opportunity to express their views in the news coverage (Deuze 2002; Raeymaeckers et al. 2012). As European elections are one of the few instances where citizens are able to directly participate in EU governance, European elections call for a more direct representation of EU citizens in EU news. Therefore, I expect that the thematic context of the European Parliament elections impacts the general visibility of EU citizens in the news coverage. Therefore, my hypothesis for both national and European EU citizens is that:

H1.1: *National EU citizens are more visible in EU new stories covering the European election compared to non-election news.*

H1.2: *European EU citizens are more visible in EU new stories covering the European election compared to non-election news.*

Dynamics of the news coverage

Similarly, during the course of an election, the campaign itself, but also its media coverage intensifies (Just 1996). Hence, the closer the election day gets, the more news media coverage on the election is taking place. According to Hopmann and Shehata, the visibility of citizens in the news coverage is "all the more important close to elections where the people will decide on their future government which ideally will execute what the citizenry asks for" (Hopmann and Shehata 2011 p.657). Although their study was not able to identify a clear linear trend for the election coverage in Sweden, their results show that the visibility of citizens increases once the election has been called. If it is correct that journalists see citizens as important actors, since it is them who decide on the election outcome, the perceived importance of citizens will increase the closer the election day gets. Hence, I expect that:

H2.1: *The visibility of national EU citizens in EU news increases in the course of the election campaign.*

H2.2: *The visibility of European EU citizens in EU news increases in the course of the election campaign.*

Prominence

In general, space in news coverage is limited and actors are competing for news media attention. Journalists function as gatekeepers deciding not only upon topics covered, but also upon which actors are included in the news media coverage (Gerhards and Neidhardt 1990; Gerhards et al. 1998). During election campaigns, especially political parties and their candidates are more active than during non-election times aiming to get media attention (van Aelst and de Swert 2009). Even though it has been outlined above why citizens are important actors during election campaigns, they might not perceived as the *most important actors* by journalists during election campaigns. One reason might be that citizens are considered by journalists as less credible sources than governmental actors, which results in a lower visibility of citizens in the news (de Keyser and Raeymaeckers 2012 p.825). News value research has more generally highlighted that "news is *elite-centered*" (Galtung and Ruge 1965, italics in original) and that acts of elite actors, such as politicians, are more likely to receive media attention. Ordinary citizens lack the news value of "prominence" (Corrigan 1990; Herbert 2000). More generally, "ordinary citizens as actors (..) have less news value than elite sources such as elected and influential politicians" (Hopmann and Shehata 2011 p.659). In comparison to other actors, citizens might therefore be reported less prominently in EU news.

There are two potential factors that can be used to analyse how prominent an actor in a news story is. First of all, it is well established that news that is on the front page of a newspaper or that is the first news story on TV, is considered the most important news of the day (Behr and Iyengar 1982; Gans 1979; Reisner 1992). Given that news media coverage is generally elite-centred and that ordinary citizens lack news values, I expect that the first and most important news stories are dominated by actors who are considered as more elitist and prominent, such as politicians and political parties (Hopmann and Shehata 2011). For TV news in Sweden, there is evidence supporting that citizens are less often shown in the first news stories of a news broadcast (Hopmann and Shehata 2011). If this holds true across other EU member states, it can be expected that:

H3.1: *National EU citizens are less likely to become visible in the first news items.*

H3.2: *European EU citizens are less likely to become visible in the first news items.*

Secondly, the elite status and prominence of an actor might be reflected in the order in which actors are mentioned in a news story. Because of a lack of the news value of prominence, it is likely that journalists report first on more well-known and prominent actors and then include less prominent actors, such as citizens. Yet, the longer a news story, the more space there is for additional and less prominent actors to be mentioned. For citizens in the EU news coverage, my expectation is therefore that:

H4.1: *The longer a news story, the more likely is the visibility of national EU citizens.*

H4.2: *The longer a news story, the more likely is the visibility of European EU citizens.*

9.2.2. Media Related Factors

Beyond characteristics at the news story level, there might be explanatory factors at the media outlet level that can explain variance in reporting on EU citizens. One can generally differentiate between different types of media (newspaper and television) as well as different media outlets (quality vs. popular media). Previous studies that examined the EU news media coverage found that newspapers and quality media tend to report to a greater extent on EU topics and EU-level governmental actors than TV and commercial media (Kleinen-von Königslöw 2010; Peter and de Vreese 2004). The aim of the present study is not to analyse variation in the extent to which EU news is reported, but to explain variation in the visibility of EU citizens *within* the EU news coverage. Nevertheless, there might likewise be variance between different media types and outlets due to certain characteristics of their news coverage, namely *personalisation* of the news coverage and the use of *episodic framing*. Both arguments are outlined in the following.

Personalisation and Episodic Framing

The importance of the news media is grounded in its crucial role for the democratic process. The media provide citizens with information on governmental affairs, which enables citizens to control their governments and ensure accountability and responsiveness. However, in the last decades, important changes in the media landscape took place: Media outlets have diversified and an increase in commercialisation has been observed (Holtz-Bacha and Norris 2010; Kriesi 2013c). Commercialisation refers to a tendency of news media to adopt the news coverage to consumer demands due to an increased dependency on advertisement revenues (Kriesi 2013c). Both personalisation and episodic framing are seen as part of this phenomenon (Iyengar 1991).

Personalisation, as a stylistic device, is used by journalists to reduce complexity and enable their audience easier access to information (Bentele and Fähnrich 2010), for example., by relating news to people's everyday life. News value research argues that: "[t]he more the event can be seen in personal terms, as due to the action of specific individuals, the more probable that it will become a news item" (Galtung and Ruge 1965 p.68). Traditionally, the concept of personalisation has been applied to governmental and other elite actors. Yet, personalisation might also influence the visibility of citizens, especially during election times. In general, research has shown that compared to national affairs, the media coverage of EU news (e.g., Hepp et al. 2012), but also of European elections is relatively low (e.g., Tenscher and Maier 2009) and that the EU is perceived as a rather abstract institution by voters. To generate interest in topics related to EU governance, and to bring the European election coverage closer to their audience, media might draw on personalisation.

Episodic framing, or rather an episodic frame, "depicts public issues in terms of concrete instances or specific events – a homeless person, an unemployed worker, a victim of discrimination" (Iyengar and Simon 1993 p.369), or potentially an ordinary citizen who votes in an election. Episodic frames portray news in terms of individual incidents, rather than providing a broader picture and background information and often include reports and statements of individual persons. The EU itself argues that such frames can help to bring the EU closer to its citizens: "Citizens need help to connect with Europe, and political information has greater impact when put in a 'human interest' frame that allows citizens to understand why it is relevant to them personally" (Commission of the European Communities 2006b p.9). Therefore, it is proposed that the EU institutions should strive to put a human face to the information they provide. From the media side, there is likewise an incentive to use episodic framing and Iyengar (1991) has argued that episodic framing predominantly results from market pressure, since there is demand for this kind of news.

9.2. Hypotheses

It is suggested that if journalists adopt a self-concept as service providers, this result not only in an attempt to adjust the news coverage to audience's demands, but also in a higher presence of citizens in the news coverage itself (Hepp et al. 2012). Similarly, Lefevere et al. argue that an increased use of interviews with citizens by "journalists is rooted in media's need to attract an audience in a climate of increased commercialization and competition" (Lefevere et al. 2011 p.115).

Despite reporting generally less EU news than newspapers (Schuck and de Vreese 2011), EU citizens might be more visible on TV, because television news is generally more personalised compared to print media (Bentele and Fähnrich 2010 pp.54–56) and relies to a greater extent on episodic framing (Iyengar 1991). Even though interviews with citizens can also be found in print media (Daschmann 2000), they might be more characteristic for television news and have mainly been analysed in this context (Brookes et al. 2004; Hopmann and Shehata 2011; Lefevere et al. 2011), because television can make better use of their dynamic and visual element. Because of a more pronounced tendency towards personalisation and episodic framing, the respective hypothesis for national EU citizens is:

H5.1: *The visibility of national EU citizens in television news is higher than in the newspaper coverage.*

European EU citizens, on the other hand, measure a truly European and supranational concept of the EU citizenship that does not match the criteria of personalisation and episodic framing. The concept of European EU citizens refers to the citizens of *all* EU member states at the same time, meaning that the respective citizen or group of citizens cannot be distinguished by nationality, but accounts for the EU citizens as such. Both the idea of personalisation and episodic framing heavily rely on the idea that *individual* actors become visible and often it is their statements that are used as exemplifications. Even though it is possible that a news story, for example, reports interviews with European voters from several EU member states without providing any reference to their nationality, such cases seem rather exceptional. Hence, it is rather unlikely that a single person who is interviewed is able to represent a supranational notion of the EU citizenship. In line with this theoretical argument, the findings in Chapter 8.4.3. revealed that European EU citizens are hardly ever quoted in the EU news coverage. Therefore, the expectation is that:

> H5.2: *The visibility of European EU citizens does not vary significantly in television news and in the newspaper coverage.*

Personalisation and episodic framing are not only a characteristic of television, but also of popular media outlets. Of course, personalisation and episodic framing are not exclusively used in popular media, but those media outlets have a stronger tendency to use those stylistic devices compared to quality media (Esser 1999). Especially for television, market pressure is more relevant for private TV stations since they rely to a greater extent on advertisement revenue compared to their public counterparts. In addition, it has been argued that popular media are able to establish an *alternative public sphere* (cf. Örnebring and Jönsson 2004) that aims to address (and possibly also include) a non-elite audience by focussing to a greater extent on human interest news, also when reporting of EU affairs (Kleinen-von Königslöw 2010). A higher share of "soft news"[60] compared to quality media outlets is a typical characteristic of popular media (Sparks 2000). One aspect of the soft news coverage is a more pronounced focus on "the personal and private lives of people, both celebrities and ordinary people" (Sparks 2000 p.10). For the visibility of citizens from the EU member states, I expect therefore that:

> H6.1: *National EU citizens are more visible in popular than quality media outlets.*

European EU citizens, on the other hand, represent an image of a more integrated European citizenry. While quality media make less use of personalisation and episodic framing, their coverage is at the same time more Europeanised com-

---

[60] "Soft news" refers to news stories that provide personally relevant information or are perceived as purely entertaining, while "hard news" report on governance and public affairs (Zaller 2003).

pared to popular media: Quality media tend to report more EU news (e.g., de Vreese et al., 2006; Kleinen-von Königslöw, 2010), but also the visibility of EU level governmental actors is higher (de Vreese et al., 2006; Peter and de Vreese, 2004). This stronger European focus might also be reflected in a more European image of the European citizenship that becomes visible via the news coverage of quality media outlets. Furthermore, quality media are generally more open towards a more extensive European integration and show a "greater openness towards and interest in the arguments and opinions of European foreign speakers" (Kleinen-von Königslöw 2012 p.457). Popular media and tabloids in particular sometimes convey more Eurosceptic views (de Vreese et al., 2006). Popular media outlets are considered to try to uphold a populist appeal to gain the interest of their audience and are therefore seen as "agents of national perspectives" (Pfetsch 2008 p.30). Hence, the hypothesis for the visibility of European EU citizens is:

H6.2: *European EU citizens are more visible in quality than popular media outlets.*

Europeanisation of news coverage
Via the European public sphere, EU governmental actors and their actions become visible to citizens and a forum for debate and opinion formation on EU governance is provided. Therefore, the European public sphere contributes to accountability of governance and is linked to the democratic performance of the EU as a whole. A functioning and vital European public sphere also indicates awareness that a shift in governance from the national to the EU level has been taking place (Wessler et al. 2008). As mentioned previously, research has shown that the degree to which national public spheres are Europeanised in terms of visibility of EU news and actors varies across the EU member states (see, e.g., Brüggemann and Kleinen-von Königslöw 2009; Peters et al. 2005; Peters et al. 2006; van de Steeg 2002). If a more developed European public sphere improves the democratic performance of the EU, it might also lead to the insight that EU citizens need to be represented and included in public debates on EU governance, especially given the much-debated gap between public and elite

support for the European integration. In addition, a more extensive focus on EU affairs might go hand in hand with a larger range of EU issues that are covered, which consequently also broadens the range of actors that become visible in the European public sphere. Hence:

> H7.1: *The more EU news a media outlet reports, the higher the visibility of national EU citizens compared to media outlets that report to a lesser extent on EU governance.*
>
> H7.2: *The more EU news a media outlet reports, the higher the visibility of European EU citizens compared to media outlets that report to a lesser extent on EU governance.*

Even though I expect that there is a relationship between the degree of EU news reported and the visibility of national EU citizens as well as European EU citizens, it is likely that the relationship is stronger for the latter. I expect that the relationship should be stronger for European EU citizens, since the concept is more closely linked to this vertical dimension of the Europeanisation process. European EU citizens represent a more Europeanised and integrated image of a European citizenry that might be fostered by a higher degree of vertical Europeanisation. Therefore, I hypothesise that:

> H7.3: *If there is a relationship between Europeanisation and the visibility of EU citizens, it is stronger for the visibility of European EU citizens than for national EU citizens.*

9.2.3. Country Level Factors: Member State's Relation to the EU

After potential factors that influence the visibility of EU citizens at the news story and media level have been discussed, this section now turns to additional influence factors at *the member state level*. Here, two sub-categories are distinguished: a) factors at the country level that concern a member state's relationship with the EU, and b) country level factors that are independent of EU governance. Starting with the former, the respective hypotheses for the country level are discussed next.

European consolidation

When the European integration process started out in 1951 with the signature of the Paris Treaty establishing the Coal and Steel Community, six EU member states were part of the European project. At the time, the primary aim of the European integration was to secure peace and political stability in Europe and to foster an economic upturn and economic cooperation among the European states. Over time, more and more policy areas have been transferred to the EU level and the number of member states has increased to 28. The term Europeanisation (independent of the news coverage) is used to express that EU governance penetrates and impacts national political systems and refers to the processes of "domestic assimilation of EU policy and politics" (Radaelli 2003 p.30). As member states joined the EU at different stages, the depth to which EU member states are integrated into the political system of the EU varies across countries (Featherstone and Radaelli 2003). The length of the EU membership is thus an indicator for the extent to which member states are involved in this *European consolidation* process.

As discussed above, the process of Europeanisation has also been applied to the news media coverage and it is assumed that the media coverage of the member states becomes more European over time by including EU affairs to a greater extent into their news coverage. Regarding the relationship between the length of the EU membership and EU news, former research has provided mixed findings: While the length of EU membership has a positive impact on the number of EU news stories reported in the national media, it does not impact the frequency of references to EU actors within the coverage of EU news (Brüggemann and Kleinen-von Königslöw 2009).

However, EU citizens might nevertheless be more visible actors in the EU news coverage of old EU member states, as the implementation of the EU citizenship has been a gradual process (cf. Maas 2007) and the concept of the EC/EU citizenship as such was already discussed in the 1970s, long before the

EU citizenship was legally established (Wiener 1998, see also Chapter 2.5). In this sense, the media of old member states might be more familiar with the EU and the notion of European citizenship than new member states. This is, because "[w]orking routines of journalists take time to develop, and the audience only slowly gets used to new topics of discussion (...). Over time, audience expectations and journalistic selection criteria might converge towards accepting that the EU is a topic suited for continuous in-depth discussion in newspapers" (Brüggemann and Kleinen-von Königslöw 2009 p.31).

This process also applies to the EU citizenship, or rather the visibility of EU citizens as actors in the European public sphere. The introduction of the EU citizenship in 1993 might have had a different effect on member states that were already members of the EU for a considerable amount of time when the EU citizenship was introduced and hence observed the various steps that finally led to its legal introduction. In comparison, citizens of new member states that joined the EU after the introduction of the EU citizenship automatically became EU citizens by the time of the EU accession and are less familiar with the debate on the EU citizenship. The respective hypotheses are:

H8.1: *The visibility of national EU citizens in the EU news coverage is higher in old than in new EU member states.*

H8.2: *The visibility of European EU citizens in the EU news coverage is higher in old than in new EU member states.*

Even though I expect that the length of the EU membership influences both the visibility of national and European EU citizens, it is likely that it is even more important for the latter. The more time a state spends as a member of the EU, the more its citizens might feel as part of the European political community. As such, also the understanding of a truly European citizenship might be more advanced and visible in the news media coverage of old EU member states compared to newer members of the EU. In addition, I expect therefore that:

H8.3: *The effect of the length of the EU membership is stronger for European EU citizens than national EU citizens.*

9.2. Hypotheses

EU support

The legitimacy of a democratic system is essentially based upon citizens' support. This holds true at the national, but also at the European level. The EU itself, but also the EU citizenship and the rights of EU citizens are evolving over time. According to Mass, the EU citizenship can therefore not be seen as irreversible, but it "remains contingent on sustained political support from the member states and their populations" (Maas 2005 p.1). While in earlier phases of the European integration the EU was seen as legitimate via its policy output (Scharpf 1999), the lack support for the European integration is today a frequent topic of public and academic debate (e.g., Henjak et al. 2012; Boomgaarden et al. 2011).

McLaren argues that citizens who lack support for the EU are "ultimately concerned about problems related to the degradation of the nation-state" (McLaren 2013 p.554), one of them potentially being the EU citizenship. Even though EU and national citizenship coexist, the introduction of the EU citizenship has affected and altered the notion of national citizenship. While it has once been argued that "citizens alone enjoy an unconditional right to remain and reside in the territory of a state" (Brubaker 1992 p.24), this holds no longer true for the EU member states, since EU citizens gained the right to move and reside freely within the territory of the member states, but also gained the right to vote in local election in another member state.

Previous research has argued that a lack of support for the EU might increase the news media coverage on EU governance, because of the news value of negativity (Brüggemann and Kleinen-von Königslöw 2009). A study by Boomgaarden et al. (2013) found that in member states where the European integration is contested and seen as negative, news media attention to the EU overall increases. Hence, the EU receives more media attention in EU member states whose population is Eurosceptic. The same might apply to the visibility of national EU citizens in the news coverage. To underline and exemplify the negative attitudes of the population towards the EU, news media might more often include citizens as actors in the EU news coverage. Therefore, I expect that:

H9.1: *The lower the support for the EU in a member state, the higher the visibility of national EU citizens.*

However, for the visibility of European EU citizens, I expect the opposite effect. As European EU citizens represent a more integrated and supranational concept of the EU citizenship, they should be more visible in EU member states whose population is more pro-European and in favour of the European integration process.

H9.2: *Higher support for the EU in a member state has a positive impact on the visibility of European EU citizens.*

According to Easton (1965), one can differentiate between specific and diffuse support for a political system. While specific support refers to concrete policy outcomes and might therefore fluctuate more strongly, diffuse support accounts for "generalized attachment to political objects" (Easton 1965 p.444), i.e., the political community. According to Boomgaarden et al., also research on EU governance needs to reflect on and take into account the existence of different types of support (Boomgaarden et al. 2011 p.242). As such, *European identity* is seen as indicator to for (diffuse) support for the European integration (cf. Risse 2003). According to Risse, the "willingness to grant the EU authority requires some identification with Europe" (Risse 2003 p.489). Research has shown that there is a strong correlation between an exclusive national identity and Euroscepticism (Hooghe and Marks 2004) and that a strong national identity can lead to a decrease in support for the EU (see, e.g., Carey 2002). When assuming that a European identity measures another aspect of support for the EU and that the news media of less-supportive states report more on citizens in the context of EU news because of the news value of negativity, it can be expected that:

H10.1: *The visibility of national EU citizens is higher in the EU news coverage of EU member states where a European identity is less developed.*

Vice versa, it can be expected that the more citizens feel attached to the EU, the higher their support for the European integration. Even more than EU support, the notion of a European identity is more closely related to the concept of European EU citizens. National EU citizens refer to citizens from the EU member states that become visible in the context of EU governance. They simultaneously link back to national sentiments, as it is know from which EU member state the respective citizen or group of citizens comes from. European EU citizens, on the other hand, represent a truly European citizenry without any reference to nationality. A more European identity in a member state might also be reflected in a more European image of the EU citizenship that is conveyed via the news media.

H10.2: *The more developed the European identity in a member state, the higher the visibility of European EU citizens_in the EU news coverage.*

Civic participation in EU governance
As I have outlined earlier (Chapter 2.6), the introduction of the EU citizenship cannot merely be considered a symbolic act, since citizens are, in fact, given rights to actively participate in EU governance. Participation in the political community has traditionally been an important criterion of citizenship and the right to vote is among the most important citizenship rights (Bagchi 2000). Since decision-making powers have been transferred to the European Union level, there has been a need for a formal introduction of the EU citizen that can hold governance accountable. EU citizenship, therefore, also postulates the demand of accountability of EU governance. Governance in democracies is legitimate if political decisions reflect the will of the people. In the case that citizens derive the conclusion that their government is not sufficiently accountable, they have the option to vote them out of office in the next election.

Turnout in the European Parliament election has been extensively discussed by a body of research ever since the first election took place in 1979 (see, e.g., Reif and Schmitt 1980; Franklin 2001; Steinbrecher and Rattinger 2012). As turnout in European elections is relatively low (compared to turnout in national elections) and has additionally been declining, it has often been argued that it indicates a decline in support for the EU, its policies and the European integration in general (e.g., Steinbrecher and Rattinger 2012, for a discussion see also Franklin 2001). Here, however, turnout is seen as an indicator for an active European citizenry. The more active and involved citizens of the EU member states are in EU governance, the higher their visibility might also be in the EU news media coverage. Generally higher levels of involvement in EU governance might also foster a more European understanding of the EU citizenship that is reflected by higher levels of visibility of European EU citizens. Therefore, I hypothesise that:

H11.1: *The higher the turnout in European Parliament election, the more visible are national EU citizens in the European public sphere.*

H11.2: *The higher the turnout in European Parliament election, the more visible are European EU citizens in the European public sphere.*

Intra EU-Exchange
Beyond citizens' attitudes towards the EU, there might be factors at the national level that contribute to more exchange that takes place among the citizens of the EU member states that impact the visibility of EU citizens in the news coverage. The European integration has a profound impact on various aspects of the lives of citizens of the EU member states. For example, it became much easier to travel, study, but also to work abroad. As a consequence, more interactions are taking place among the EU citizens. These social interactions between citizens of different EU member states are "affecting how people think of themselves and others" (Fligstein 2008 p.2) and are consequently also influencing citizens' understanding and perception of the EU citizenship. As mentioned previously, the EU citizenship was introduced in a top down manner, this section concerns the question of how EU citizens can become aware of the consequences (and advantages) of being an EU citizen in their everyday lives.

An important aspect of the EU citizenship is the right to move and reside freely within the territory of the EU member states (Treaty on the Functioning on the European Union, Art. 21.1) and EU citizens are even equipped with the

9.2. Hypotheses

right to vote in European and local elections in their member state of residence (Art. 22). "As border controls between most EU countries disappeared (...) and living in other European countries became easier, Europeans have more chances than ever to interact with each other" (Sigalas 2010). One aspect that might determine the extent to which citizens are aware of the EU citizenship in the first place, but also the visibility of EU citizens in the news media is the number of fellow EU citizens living in a member state. In 2008, more than 11 million EU citizens have been living in fellow EU member states (Eurostat[61]). The higher the number of EU migrants living in another member state, the more interaction and exchange is taking place among the EU citizens. As discussed in Chapter 7, with the exception of Luxembourg, across all countries, the group of national EU citizens predominantly includes references to citizens of the country the news outlet belongs to. For example, the BBC predominantly reports about the British citizens in the context of EU governance, rather than about citizens of the other 26 EU member states. Therefore, it is likely that the number of EU migrants is less relevant for the visibility of national EU citizens, but more so for European EU citizens, which are a measure for the extent to which a supranational vision EU citizenship is reflected in the news media. The more exchange might foster awareness and a more European vision of the EU citizenship that is also reflected in the news coverage. Hence, it is expected that

H12.1: *The number of EU migrants living in an EU member state is not related to visibility of national EU citizens in the EU news coverage.*

H12.2: *The number of EU migrants living in an EU member state has a positive effect on the visibility of European EU citizens in the EU news coverage.*

Another factor that is related to the idea that interaction and exchange among the EU citizens might have positive effects for the emergence and visibility of European EU citizens in the news coverage is related to the economy and the common market more specifically. The economy is the policy field that has

---

[61] Eurostat: Population on 1 January by five year age group, sex and citizenship, Code: migr_pop1ctz, accessed: 02/02/2015.

been affected most by the European integration. "The creation of Europe-wide markets had one important but largely unintended consequence. It caused people who worked for government and business from across Europe to interact with one another on a routine basis" (Fligstein 2008 p.14). One indicator for economic interactions is intra-EU trade (imports as well as exports). Across the EU member states, trade makes up to 40% of the GDP and more than 70% of the exports from EU member states go to other states within the EU (Fligstein 2008 p.62). It has been shown that intra-EU trade has a positive impact on support for the European integration (Eichenberg and Dalton 1993; Gabel and Palmer 1995; Gabel and Whitten 1997; Hooghe and Marks 2004). Here, however, intra-EU trade concerns cross-border exchange that takes place between different EU member states. "If an economy depends strongly on trade with other European countries, it becomes more relevant to follow events in these countries, and take notice of the opinions of actors from these countries, as these may have repercussions on that particular economy"(Koopmans et al. 2010 p.70). However, a higher dependency on trade with fellow EU member states might also lead to more exchange taking place among the citizens of the EU member states and it might also foster a more European understanding of the EU citizenship and consequently lead to an increased visibility of European EU citizens. Hence, it is expected that:

H13.1: *Higher levels of trade with fellow EU states are not related to visibility of national EU citizens in the EU news coverage.*

H13.2: *Higher levels of trade with fellow EU states are positively related to the visibility of European EU citizens in the EU news coverage.*

Situational factors: Economic crisis
Furthermore, there might be temporary or rather situational elements that influence a member state's relation to the EU and have an impact on the visibility of EU citizens in the European public sphere.[62] The recent economic crisis might

---

[62] Theoretically, there might also be situational factors at the country level that are independent of EU governance, but this is not the case for the present analysis.

be such an event. In general, the EU's economic policy is an important topic of debate within the European public sphere (Meyer 2005). Already at the beginning of 2000, fiscal policy and public deficits of the member states were prominent topics on the news agenda (ibid.). The following years were marked by the global financial crisis, the economic crisis as well as the European sovereign debt crisis. Even though the economic crisis is still ongoing, it already had a severe impact on the economy of the EU member states in 2009, when the European Parliament election took place. For example, a rise in unemployment as well as a sharp drop in GDP growth has been observed (Eurostat[63]).

Recent public opinion surveys have shown that citizens' expectations regarding the EU are closely linked to economic issues such as employment in general and the economic crisis in particular (see European Commission 2012). In addition, the economy is seen as the topic that is most likely to generate a feeling of community among the EU citizens (ibid.). By entering the Eurozone, member states agree to give in parts of their national sovereignty and to transfer it to the EU level, namely their national currency and monetary policy. One of the consequences is that during times of crisis, Eurozone members are unable to act independently, e.g., by devaluing their currency (De Bardeleben and Viju 2013). The economic crisis is also linked to accountability of governance, since it became increasingly more difficult for citizens to allocate responsibilities to the national and EU level (ibid.). This impacts democratic legitimacy since people are unable to estimate who to hold accountable, the EU or their national governments.

The economic crisis and possibly depending on EU support and solidarity of fellow EU member states make the interdependency of EU member states tangible. Due to this process, citizens of EU member states that might need financial support become more aware of the consequences and depth of the European integration process. As a side effect, those citizens might become more conscious of the EU citizenship and its consequences compared to people living in EU member states who are not directly hit by the financial crisis. (One

---

[63] Eurostat: Main GDP aggregates per capita, Code: nama_10_pc, accessed: 29/09/2015, Eurostat: Unemployment rate by sex and age groups - annual average, %, Code: une_rt_a, accessed: 29/01/2015.

has to keep in mind that this expectation concerns the news coverage in 2009, where the economic crisis in Europe was only at the beginning and that the news coverage changed in the course of the crisis.) In addition, since the crisis has direct impacts on people's lives, media outlets in the member states struck more severely by the crisis might generally tend to include citizens to a larger extent, e.g., by reporting on people affected by austerity measures. The consequent hypotheses are:

> H14.1: *The visibility of national EU citizens is higher in European public spheres of member states that are severely affected by the financial crisis compared to EU member states that are less influenced by the crisis.*

> H14.2: *The visibility of European EU citizens is higher in European public spheres of member states that are severely affected by the financial crisis compared to EU member states that are less influenced by the crisis.*

9.2.4. Country Level Factors: Independent of EU Governance

Besides media and country specific factors that are related to the EU, there might be factors at the national level independent of EU governance that impact the visibility of citizens in the public sphere in general.

Active national citizenry

The extent to which citizens generally participate in the political and societal life beyond the electoral process varies across countries (e.g., Curtis et al. 2001; Howard 2002). The more participatory a society is, the more visible and better represented citizens are in the political process in terms of politicians being able to perceive citizens demands. At the same time, journalists might become more aware of citizens' actions and perceive citizens as relevant actors in the political process. Associational membership in political and social organisations[64] plays an important role as an indicator for an active citizenry at the national level. As

---

[64] Associational membership is also a common indicator used to measure social capital (see, e.g., Bekkers et al. 2008; van Deth and Kreuter 1998; Welzel et al. 2005).

intermediary organisations, such voluntary associations, facilitate communication between citizens and governments (Maloney et al. 2008; van Deth and Kreuter 1998) and play an important role for determining the degree of civic involvement of a society.

Previous research has shown that membership in voluntary associations is related to socialisation processes (Hooghe 2008). By being socialised in a society with an active citizenry, journalists might be primed to see citizen as relevant political actors that should have a say in public debates. Linking back to the visibility of EU citizens, member states with a more active citizenry that participates in the political process might include citizens to a greater extent into public debates, because journalists are generally paying more attention to citizens as political actors. The hypothesis regarding the visibility of EU citizens is:

H15.1: *The more active the national citizenry of an EU member state, the higher the visibility of national EU citizens in the news coverage on EU governance.*

References to European EU citizens, on the other hand, measure a supranational and more abstract concept of the EU citizenship that is expected to be more closely related to the presence of pro-European attitudes and other EU-related factors. An active national citizenry at the member state level should not be relevant.

H15.2: *An active national citizenry of an EU member state is not related to visibility of European EU citizens in the news coverage on EU governance.*

Importance of a member state
Finally, EU member states vary with regard to their importance and impact at the international, but also at the European level. Traditionally, scholars in the 1960s and 1970s have focused on diplomatic and military power to determine the importance of a state and "small" states were seen as those who are more vulnerable to external forces (Thorhallsson 2006). Today, a country's population as well as economic size are seen as indicators to determine the importance

of a state that also impacts their actions at the supranational level of governance (Thorhallsson 2006).

The size of a state also plays a role at the European level. For example, the number of seats in the European Parliament is not equally distributed, but varies depending on the population size of a member state. Furthermore, smaller member states are more economically as well as politically dependent on the European integration (Berkel 2006 p.64). Because smaller states have less autonomy, "[t]hey depend on external alliances to guarantee their security, and they have little potential to exert significant influence in international affairs on their own account" (Koopmans et al. 2010 p.70). As their own influence is limited, smaller member states have a higher incentive to transfer power to the EU level, as they depend to a greater extent on political and economic cooperation (c.f. Brüggemann and Kleinen-von Königslöw 2009, p. 31). Similarly, it is suggested that the benefits of being part of the European single market are higher for smaller compared to larger member states (Alesina and Wacziarg 1999). Even though the size of an EU member state and its GDP play a role for EU governance, they are first and foremost country level characteristics that are not determined by EU governance.

The importance of the member state also affects the media coverage. Wessler et al. have argued that "weaker countries depend more heavily on their neighbours both politically and economically, so that their media outlets will pay more attention to what is going on abroad (Wessler et al. 2008 p.58). For EU news, studies have analysed whether "smaller" states in terms of their population size and economy pay more attention to actors from the EU level (Koopmans et al. 2010; Schuck and de Vreese 2011). For quality newspapers, it has been shown that smaller EU member states include references to other member states and foreign speakers to a greater extent into their coverage than lager states (Brüggemann and Kleinen-von Königslöw 2009). Likewise, for the news coverage during the 2009 European Parliament election, Schuck and de Vreese (2011) find that GPD is negatively related to the visibility of EU governmental actors. In short, "[t]he characteristics of a nation matter in international communication" (Wu 1998 p.501).

9.2. Hypotheses

If smaller EU member states have higher incentives for and are more supportive of a more extensive European integration, their more pro-European stance might lead to a more European perspective and a more European understanding of the EU citizenship that is consequently reflected in a more European vision of the EU citizenship that is reflected in the EU news coverage, while it should not influence the visibility of national EU citizens.

H16.1: *Country size and economic status of an EU member state are not related to visibility of national EU citizens in the EU news coverage.*

H16.2: *European EU citizens are more visible in EU member states with a lower socio-economic status compared to EU member states with a higher socio-economic status.*

Table 9.1 Summary of hypotheses

Level	Hypothesis	National EU citizens	European EU citizens
News story	H1 Election news	Positive	Positive
	H2 Election day	Positive	Positive
	H3 1st news story	Negative	Negative
	H4 Length	Positive	Positive
Media	H5 TV (vs. newspaper)	Positive	No effect
	H6 Quality (vs. commercial)	Negative	Positive
	H7 Reporting EU news	Positive	Positive
Country	H8 Length EU membership	Positive	Positive
	H9 EU support	Negative	Positive
	H10 European identity	Negative	Positive
	H11 Turnout	Positive	Positive
	H12 EU migrants	No effect	Positive
	H13 Intra-EU trade	No effect	Positive
	H14 Economic crisis	Positive	Positive
	H15 Active citizenry	Positive	No effect
	H16 Socio-economic status	No effect	Positive

9.3. Methodology

To analyse and explain the visibility of EU citizens in the news coverage on EU governance, I use a multilevel approach, where the individual news story is the unit of analysis (N=12,850) that is nested in news outlets (N=143), which are nested in countries (N=27). When thinking about the news media coverage, it is likely that news stories that are reported by the same media outlet share common characteristics. The Guardian, for example, might have the tendency to report longer news stories than other newspapers. Similarly, even though certain types of media might show similarities in their reporting across countries, it is likely that media outlets from the same country share common characteristics and are not independent from each other. A high correlation between news stories from one media outlet as well as a high correlation between media outlets from one country potentially leads to biased estimates that could distort the results (cf. Arceneaux and Nickerson 2009). By accounting for these contextual factors in the analysis, the problem of non-independent observations can be overcome (Field et al. 2012 p.859). Therefore, I use a three level random intercept model that is able account for the clustered structure of the data set. Random effects allow for correlations within media outlets and within countries. Therefore, the multilevel model is able to simultaneously analyse factors located at the news story, media outlet and country level. Another issue is the number of the clusters, which is at the highest level limited to 27, according to the total number of EU member states that took part in the 2009 European Parliament election. In the literature, it is suggested that a minimum of 20 clusters is sufficient to derive reliable estimates (Arceneaux and Nickerson 2009).

9.3.1. Measures – Dependent Variables

The measures and operationalisations of national and European EU citizens have been discussed in detail in Chapter 6. For the purpose of the present chapter, *national EU citizens* and *European EU citizens* are operationalised as categorical variables, which take the value 1 if the respective actor group is mentioned in a news story and otherwise take the value 0.[65] As the dependent variables are categorical, I use multilevel logistic regression models to analyse their visibility.

9.3.2. Measures – Independent Variables

As the analysis takes the threefold structure of the data into account, also the independent variables are located at different levels. The first set of independent variables concerns characteristics of the individual news stories. Next, the media-specific independent variables are aggregate measures or categorical variables for the respective media outlet. The country-specific characteristics are likewise either categorical variables, or aggregated to the country level. (An overview of the operationalisations of the independent variables can be found in Table 9.2.) For the regression analyses, continuous independent variables were standardised ranging from 0 to 1.

Starting with the dependent variables that are measured at the level of the individual news story, I expect that EU citizens are more visible in EU news that is about the European elections. As an independent variable, *EP election topic* is operationalised based on a filter variable[66] of the PIREDEU data set. The filter variable measures whether or not the respective news story is about the European Parliament election and/or the campaign. EU news stories that are about the election were coded as 1 and 0 otherwise. Furthermore, the visibility of EU citizens in news stories should increase in the run up to the election. Based on the date when a news story was published or broadcasted, and based on the election day in the EU member state where the respective news outlet is based, *Days to election* measures the remaining days until the European Parliament election takes place.[67]

---

[65] Theoretically, it would also be possible to use the share of EU citizens of the total number of actors per news story as an additional dependent variable. However, it is not feasible as there is not enough variance.
[66] Variable V46 in the PIREDEU data set.
[67] In the Czech Republic, the European Parliament election too place on two days. Both election days were coded as 0.

9.3. Methodology

To analyse whether EU citizens are less visible in news stories that are more prominently placed in the news coverage, I created the variable *1st news story* that takes the value 1 if a) a news story was published on the first page of a newspaper, or b) a news story was broadcasted as the first news item in TV news and 0 otherwise.[68] Similarly, I argued that as citizens are generally no prominent actors, the likelihood of them being mentioned as actors increases with the length of the news story. For the length of newspaper articles, the PIREDEU data set measured whether an article makes up to ¼ of a page (coded as 1), makes up to ½ of a page (coded as 2), makes up ¾ of a page (coded as 3), or it makes up more than ¾ of a page (coded as 4). For TV, on the other hand, the length of a news story was measured in seconds. To gain a comparable measure for *Length*, I calculated the quartiles for the length of TV news stories. Based on the quartiles, I coded TV news that are up to 74 seconds long as 1, news between 75 and 115 seconds as 2, news stories between 116 and 158 seconds as 3, and news stories longer than 159 seconds as 4.[69]

Turning now to the independent variables at the news outlet level, I expected that national EU citizens are more visible on TV than in newspapers, because TV news has a higher tendency to use personalisation and episodic framing as stylistic devices. I recoded the individual news outlets and created a categorical variable *TV* that was coded as 1 if the respective news outlets is a TV channel and takes the value of 0 for newspapers.

Personalisation and episodic framing are not only a characteristic of TV, but also of popular media rather than quality media outlets. Quality media in this study refers to media that cover predominantly "hard news" and ought to have a rather elitist audience (cf. e.g., Esser 1999). Popular media, on the other hand, are understood as media outlets that focus to a larger extent on "soft news" and have a less elitist audience (Boykoff 2008). Public broadcasters can be considered quality media as public service broadcasting channels are traditionally characterised by "a heavy emphasis on the provision of news and current affairs at the center of prime time" (Sparks 2000 p.11). Public broadcasting

---

[68] This was operationalised based on the variables NP1 and TV2 in the PIREDEU data set.
[69] The length was operationalised based on the variables NP5 and TV1 in the PIREDEU data set.

is often (yet not exclusively) funded by licence fees and public financing. Therefore, public broadcaster, compared to their private counter parts, rely to a lesser extent on advertising revenues, which should have a positive impact on the quality of their reporting. Consequently, private television channels rely to a greater extent on advertising revenues and aim to reach a broader audience by decreasing the amount of hard news and increasing the coverage on human interests (cf. e.g., Esser 1999). For this reason, private TV channels are seen as popular media outlets in this study. In addition, I recoded broadsheet newspapers as quality media. Broadsheet newspapers predominantly cover hard news (cf. e.g., Esser 1999). Tabloids, on the other hand, were coded as popular media outlets. With regard to the content of reporting, tabloids have the tendency to devote less attention to "hard news" on politics and economics, but to report more "soft news" about sports and entertainment as well as on private lives of celebrities and ordinary people (Sparks 2000 p.10). For this reason, in this study, tabloids account for popular media. I recoded the individual news outlets and created a categorical variable *Quality media* that was coded as 1 for public broadcaster and broadsheets and takes the value of 0 for commercial TV channels and tabloids (see Appendix I for more details).[70]

The underlying concept of the European public sphere in this study is the one of a Europeanisation of the national public spheres. Previous research has shown that the European public spheres of the EU member states vary in the degree they are Europeanised, i.e., news media attention to EU affairs (e.g., Boomgaarden et al. 2010; Peters et al. 2005). I expected that the visibility of EU citizens is higher in news outlets that pay more attention to EU affairs. With regard to vertical Europeanisation, there are two important indicators, namely the amount of EU governmental actors and EU news reported in the national media. In this particular case, references to actors from the EU governmental level might be a less adequate indicator. In the European public sphere, actors are competing for visibility (Thompson 1995). As a consequence, the more the news coverage focuses on elite actors, the less space is available for references

---

[70] As mentioned previously, the relevant information for the recoding of the media outlets was provided by the PIREDEU team at the University of Amsterdam.

9.3. Methodology

to EU citizens. Hence, the indicator for Europeanisation of the national public sphere used in this study is the amount of EU news reported. The independent variable *Share EU news* is based on the PIREDEU data set and operationalized as the percentage of EU news of the total coverage[71] by media outlet.

At the country level, I expect that the length of the EU membership has a positive effect on the visibility of EU citizens. The EU citizenship was introduced in 1993 and the visibility of EU citizens in the news coverage might vary in states that joined the EU before or after the event. Hence, I created the variable *Old member state* that differentiates between "old" EU member states that were members of the EU before 1993 (coded as 1) and "new" member states that joined the EU after 1993 (coded as 0).

EU member states also differ with regard to public support for the European integration. I expect that national EU citizens receive more media attention in EU member states whose population is more Eurosceptic, while I expected the opposite for European EU citizens. Following previous research (Schuck et al. 2013; Steinbrecher and Rattinger 2012), as a general indicator for EU support, I use a Eurobarometer survey question asking respondents what they think about their country's membership in the EU. To be more explicit, based on the Eurobarometer[72] question (EB 70.1) "Generally speaking, do you think that [Country's] membership in the European Union is a good thing, a bad thing?" I calculated *EU support* as the percentage of respondents by EU member state that said the EU membership is a good thing.

European identity is another indicator for (diffuse) support for the EU. To measure the concept of European identity, this study follows previous research that has largely relied on the Eurobarometer[73] question "In the near future do

---

[71] For newspapers, sport, travel, housing, culture, motor/auto, fashion and entertainment sections were excluded from the coding, for TV weather forecast and specific sections of broadcast devoted to sports were excluded. For further details see also Chapter 6.
[72] European Commission (2012). Eurobarometer 70.1 (Oct-Nov 2008). TNS OPINION & SOCIAL, Brussels [Producer]. GESIS Data Archive, Cologne. ZA4819 Data file Version 3.0.2, doi:10.4232/1.10989. (Different waves of the Eurobarometer survey were tested that yield towards similar results.)
[73] European Commission (2012). Eurobarometer 67.1 (Feb-Mar 2007). TNS OPINION & SOCIAL, Brussels [Producer]. GESIS Data Archive, Cologne. ZA4529 Data file Version 3.0.1, doi:10.4232/1.10983. I rely on the Eurobarometer 67.1, because there is a break in the time series in 2008 and 2009. The Eurobarometer 67.1 is the earliest data available that was collected previous to

you see yourself as [NATIONALITY] only, [NATIONALITY] and European, European and [NATIONALITY] or European only?" (European Commission 2007). Commonly, the indicator is recoded into a dummy variable and used as a measure for strength of an exclusive national identity (Hooghe and Marks 2004). This is because it is, for example, assumed that the strength of national identity is negatively related to support of the European integration and increased Euroscepticism. In contrast, this study is interested in the scope of a European identity. *European identity* takes into account the percentage of respondents that see themselves as exclusively (European only) or predominantly European (European and [NATIONALITY]). What is important is that data previous to the European election is used. This is, because the hypothesis assumes that journalists are able to sense general societal trends. Yet, it might take some time until an effect on the coverage can be observed.

Regarding civic participation in EU governance, I have argued that the more active and involved citizens of the EU member states are in EU governance, the higher their visibility is in the EU news media coverage. One indicator for an active European citizenry and their participation in EU governance is turnout in European elections. I use turnout in European elections, as it is the political community EU citizens participate in. As an independent variable, *EP turnout* measures the percentage of the voting population of each EU member state that turned out to vote in the 2009 European election (Source: Eurostat[74]).

Furthermore, I expect that factors related to exchange that takes place among EU member states influence the visibility of European EU citizens in the EU news coverage. Migrants from fellow EU member states can contribute to such an exchange. As independent variable, *Share EU migrants* is operationalised as the logarithm of the share of foreign population that have the citizenship of one of the fellow EU member states of the total population in 2008 (Source: Eurostat[75]). Another measure for such a cross-border exchange between the EU

---

the 2009 European Parliament election. Yet, the strength of a European identity has been very stable over time.

[74] Eurostat: Voter turnout in national and EU parliamentary elections, Code: tsdgo310, accessed: 01/09/2014.

[75] Eurostat: Population on 1 January by five year age group, sex and citizenship, Code: migr_pop1ctz, accessed: 02/02/2015.

9.3. Methodology

member states is intra-EU trade. *Intra-EU trade* measures the percentage of the trade (imports and exports combined) an state does with other EU member states as the percentage of the total trade (imports and exports combined) in 2008 (cf. Isernia et al. 2012). I calculated intra-EU trade based on Eurostat[76] data for intra- and extra-EU trade.

The recent economic crisis has been identified as a temporary, situational factor that might influence the visibility of EU citizens. There are several potential indicators that account for economic crisis. Previously, the government deficit and debt as well as GDP growth and unemployment have been used (Inotai 2013). This study uses *Unemployment change* as a measure for economic crisis. First of all, unemployment is the best suited indicator for economic crisis when EU citizens are concerned. This is, because it is more directly related to peoples everyday lives and might have a more severe personal impact compared to more abstract economic indicators (cf. Bengtsson 2004; Lewis-Beck and Paldam 2000). Yet, unemployment is likely to be influenced by structural factors other than the economic crisis alone. To reduce the effect of additional factors, the change in unemployment that occurred between 2008 and 2009 is used as a measure (Kern et al. 2015). The data for unemployment is taken from Eurostat.[77] Unemployment change is measured as the percentage change in the annual average of the number of people unemployed of the labour force between 2008 and 2009 by EU member state.

Turning now to the factors at the country level independent of EU governance, I argued that national EU citizens are more visible in member states with a more politically active citizenry. Associational membership in social and political organisations is used as an indicator for an active national citizenry. Following previous research (cf. e.g., van Deth and Kreuter 1998 p.137; Welzel et al. 2005), *Associational membership* measures the percentage of the population of the respective EU member state that is a member of at least one voluntary asso-

---

[76] Eurostat: Intra and Extra-EU trade by Member State and by product group, Code: ext_lt_intratrd, accessed: 02/02/2015.
[77] Eurostat: Unemployment rate by sex and age groups - annual average, %, Code: une_rt_a, accessed: 29/01/2015.

ciation. The data is drawn from the European Value Study[78] of 2008, based on the question: "Please look carefully at the following list of voluntary organisations and activities and say a) which, if any, do you belong to?".

Finally, I have argued that socio-economic factors might play a role for the visibility of European EU citizens. Based on findings by previous research, two factors can be used to determine the size of an EU member state in terms of its socio-economic status, namely the population size and economic power of an EU member state (Boomgaarden et al. 2013; Brüggemann and Kleinen-von Königslöw 2009; Wessler et al. 2008). *Population size* measures the total population of an EU member state on the 1st of January in 2008 in millions (Source: Eurostat[79]) and *GPD* is the logarithm of the gross domestic product at market prices per capita in 2008 measured in Euro (Source for GPD: Eurostat[80]).

As there is no prior research that has aimed to explaining the visibility of citizens in the news coverage, there are no established factors that can explain variance across news stories, media outlets, or countries. Therefore, there are no *control variables* included in the analysis, but all independent variables are based on hypothesis and the aim is to maximise the variance explained.

Table 9.2 provides an overview of the independent variables, their operationalisations and data sources, as well as their means and standard deviations (country scores can be found in Appendix III). In addition, Table 9.3, Table 9.4, and Table 9.5 show the correlations between the independent variables by level of analysis.[81] Higher correlations are found for TV and the share of EU news (-0.671), old EU member states and the share of EU migrants (0.565), old EU member states and GDP (0.603), turnout at European elections and the share of EU migrants (0.673), turnout at European elections and GDP (0.527), the share of EU migrants and GDP (0.829), as well as for associational membership and GDP (0.749). The correlations are still within acceptable limits and they are not

---

[78] EVS (2011). European Values Study 2008: Integrated Dataset (EVS 2008). GESIS Data Archive, Cologne. ZA4800 Data file version 3.0.0, doi:10.4232/1.11004.
[79] Eurostat: Population on 1 January by five year age group, sex and citizenship, Code: migr_pop1ctz, accessed: 02/02/2015.
[80] Eurostat: Main GDP aggregates per capita, Code: nama_10_pc, accessed: 29/09/2015.
[81] For correlations that include at least one categorical variable, Spearman correlation coefficients were calculated, otherwise, Pearson correlations were used.

a priori problematic, as not all independent variables are included in the final model. Relationships are first tested in the bivariate context before the independent variables are included in the final multilevel model.

Table 9.2 Overview independent variables and operationalisations

Level	IV	Operationalisation	Mean	SD	Source
News story	EP election topic	Dummy (EP election=1, otherwise=0)	0.63	0.48	PIREDEU, recode
	Days to election	Number of day to election day	8.96	6.26	PIREDEU, recode
	1st news story	Dummy (1st news story=1, otherwise=0)	0.08	0.26	PIREDEU, recode
	Length	Quartiles	1.81	1.02	PIREDEU
Media outlet	TV	Dummy (TV=1, newspaper=0)	0.41	0.49	PIREDEU, recode
	Quality media	Dummy (Quality = 1, commercial=0)	0.63	0.48	PIREDEU, recode
	EU news	Share of EU news by media outlet	35.32	22.88	PIREDEU, own calculation
Country	Old member state	Dummy (old member state=1, new member state =0)	0.47	0.50	Own calculation
	EU support	Percentage of population that think that their countries membership in the EU is "a good thing"	55.17	13.08	Eurobarometer
	European identity	Percentage of the population that see themselves in the near future as exclusively European or European and national	10.34	5.76	Eurobarometer
	EP turnout	Percentage of the voting population that casted a vote in the 2009 European election	47.57	19.70	Eurostat
	Share EU migrants	Logarithm of the percentage of foreign population of the total population	0.41	1.57	Eurostat
	Intra-EU trade	Percentage of intra-EU trade of total trade	67.76	7.54	Eurostat, own calculation
	Unemployment change	Percentage change in unemployment between 2008 and 2009	-0.11	1.15	Eurostat
	Associational membership	Percentage of the population that is a member in at least one voluntary association	42.80	21.47	European Value Study
	Population size	Total population of an EU member state in millions	19.19	23.68	Eurostat
	GDP	Logarithm of the gross domestic product per capita in Euro	9.95	0.62	Eurostat

9.3. Methodology

Table 9.3 Correlation independent variables at news story level

IV	EP election topic	Days to election	Prominence
Day to election	-0.169**		
Prominence	0.021*	-0.023**	
Length	0.126**	0.010	0.004

Table 9.4 Correlation independent variables at media outlet level

IV	TV	Quality media
Quality	-0.269**	
Share EU news	-0.671**	0.421**

Table 9.5 Correlation independent variables at member state level

IV	Old member state	EU support	European ID	EP turnout	Share EU migrants	EU trade	Unemployment	Ass. Membership	GDP
EU support	0.316								
European ID	0.493**	0.383*							
EP turnout	0.392*	0.064	0.422*						
Share EU migrant	0.565**	0.063	0.447*	0.673**					
EU trade	-0.239	0.165	0.173	0.027	0.053				
Unemployment	0.197	-0.027	-0.050	0.244	0.314	-0.183			
Ass. membership	0.383*	0.383*	0.294	0.286	0.422*	-0.024	0.056		
GDP	0.603**	0.230	0.414*	0.527**	0.829**	-0.037	0.212	0.749**	
Population size	0.498**	-0.028	0.246	-0.140	-0.142	-0.377	-0.054	-0.057	0.045

9.4. Results

9.4.1. Bivariate Analysis

As the number of hypotheses, especially at the country level, is rather high and in order to develop a parsimonious multilevel model, I first test for bivariate relationships between the dependent and independent variables. Therefore, I ran separate multilevel models for the dependent variables and each of the independent variables where the first level is the news story, the second level is the media outlet and the third level the member states. The independent variables that show significant effects in the bivariate contexts in at least one of the cases are then included in the final multivariate model. As it cannot be ruled out that those variables that do not show significant effects in the bivariate regression become significant in a multivariate setting, all independent variables are tested separately in the final multivariate model before they are ultimately excluded from the analysis (for the results see Appendix IV).

Table 9.6 and Table 9.7 show the bivariate regression results for national and European EU citizens. Based on the bivariate regressions, significant effects are found for news that is about the European elections, the distance to the election day, as well as the length of the news story. Furthermore, significant bivariate relationships are found for all three medial-level variables: TV, quality media and the share of EU news that is reported in a media outlet. Regarding the country level variables that concern a member state's relationship to the EU, significant effects are found for European identity, intra-EU trade. For country level variables independent of EU governance, the bivariate models only show a significant relationship for population size. These independent variables are therefore included in the initial multivariate model. Furthermore, when testing the non-significant independent variables again in the multivariate model, a significant effect was found for turnout at European elections, which is consequently also included in the final model.

9.4. Results

Table 9.6 Bivariate analysis national EU citizens

Level	IV	Coefficient	AMV	-2LL	AIC
News story level	EP election topic	1.27*** (0.06)	0.20***	11909.93	11917.93
	Days to election	-0.84*** (0.08)	-0.13***	12388.01	12346.01
	1st news story	0.11 (0.09)	0.02	12450.62	12458.62
	Length	0.99*** (0.09)	0.16***	12337.92	12345.92
Media level	TV	0.35*** (0.09)	0.05***	12438.78	12446.78
	Quality media	-0.12 (0.10)	-0.02	12450.83	12458.83
	Share EU news	-0.63*** (0.17)	-0.10***	12439.24	12447.24
Country level	Old member state	-0.29 (0.19)	-0.05	12450.28	12458.28
	EU support	-0.30 (0.60)	-0.05	12452.19	12460.19
	European identity	-0.48 (0.50)	-0.08	12451.51	12459.51
	EP turnout	-0.53 (0.47)	-0.09	12451.18	12459.18
	EU migrants	-0.06 (0.06)	-0.01	12451.28	12459.28
	Intra-EU trade	1.25 (1.04)	0.20	12450.99	12458.99
	Unemployment change	-0.06 (0.49)	-0.01	12452.41	12460.41
	Ass. membership	0.51 (0.41)	0.08	12450.94	12458.94
	Population size	-0.72* (0.34)	-0.12*	12448.17	12456.17
	GDP	-1.23 (1.73)	-0.20	12451.92	12459.92
N (Level 3)	27				
N (Level 2)	143				
N (Level 1)	12850				

Table 9.6 shows the bivariate regression results for each of the independent variables regressed on the dependent variable "national EU citizens". Note: †p<.1, *p<.05, **p<.01, ***p<.001. Calculations were made using the meqrlogit option in Stata 13. Standard errors in parentheses. Continuous variables were standardised ranging from 0 to 1. Random effects are not reported.

Table 9.7 Bivariate analysis European EU citizens

Level	IV	Coefficient	AMV	-2LL	AIC
News story level	EP election topic	0.19* (0.09)	0.01*	4856.72	4864.72
	Days to election	-0.76*** (0.15)	-0.03***	4833.21	4841.22
	1st news story	-0.23 (0.17)	-0.01	4859.19	4867.19
	Length	0.92*** (0.17)	0.03***	4831.90	4839.90
Media level	TV	-0.23 (0.17)	-0.01	4859.40	4867.40
	Quality media	0.64*** (0.18)	0.02**	4848.21	4856.21
	Share EU news	0.62* (0.30)	0.02†	4856.75	4864.75
Country level	Old member state	0.24 (0.20)	0.01	4859.72	4867.72
	EU support	0.75 (0.62)	0.03	4859.71	4867.71
	European identity	1.59*** (0.39)	0.06***	4848.30	4856.30
	EP turnout	0.56 (0.48)	0.02	4859.85	4867.85
	EU migrants	0.05 (0.06)	0.00	4860.47	4868.47
	Intra-EU trade	1.87† (1.11)	0.07†	4858.37	4866.37
	Unemployment change	-0.24 (0.52)	-0.01	4860.91	4868.91
	Ass. membership	0.45 (0.43)	0.02	4860.08	4868.08
	Population size	-0.13 (0.39)	-0.004	4861.00	4869.00
	GDP	1.54 (1.79)	0.06	4860.40	4868.41
N (Level 3)		27			
N (Level 2)		143			
N (Level 1)		12850			

Table 9.7 shows the bivariate regression results for each of the independent variables is regressed on the dependent variable "European EU citizens". Note: †p<.1, *p<.05, **p<.01, ***p<.001. Calculations were made using the meqrlogit option in Stata 13. Standard errors in parentheses. Continuous variables were standardised ranging from 0 to 1. Random effects are not reported.

9.4. Results

As the significant relationships are discussed in more detail in the next section, I focus in the following on the results that are not significant and therefore excluded from further analyses. At the news story level, I expected that, as EU citizens are seen as less prominent actors (e.g., compared to politicians) by journalists, their visibility is lower in the most important news stories, i.e., the front page news of newspapers and the first news stories of TV news broadcasts (H3). However, whether the news story is the most important news of the day or not does not affect the visibility of national or European EU citizens significantly.

At the country level, I assumed that because the introduction of the EU citizenship was a lengthy process, the media of older EU member states that joined the EU before the introduction of the EU citizenship are more familiar with the idea of the EU citizenship, which should lead to a higher visibility of both national and European EU citizens (H8.1 and H8.2). I furthermore expected that the effect should be stronger for the latter (H8.3), as it reflects the EU growing together to a political community. However, the length of the EU membership does not impact the visibility of EU citizens in the EU news coverage and none of these hypotheses can be supported.

Previous research has shown that in member states where the European integration is contested and seen as negative, news media attention to the EU overall increases. Hence, I anticipated that also the visibility of national EU citizens would be higher in EU member states that are less supportive and hence more sceptical towards the European integration. I assumed that in order to emphasise and exemplify the negative attitudes of the population towards the EU, journalists would include references to national EU citizens more often in their news coverage on EU governance (H9.1). As European EU citizens, on the other hand, represent a supranational and truly European image of the EU citizenship, I expected that they are more visible in EU member states that are more supportive of the EU (H9.2). However, the results cannot provide evidence that EU support plays a role for the visibility of EU citizens in the EU news media coverage.

As the EU introduced a concept of citizenship that goes beyond the nation state, I expected that more interactions among citizens of EU member states would foster a more European understanding of the EU citizenship that is also reflected in the news media coverage. I used the share of EU migrants that live in a member state as one indicator for exchange among EU citizens. However, the share of EU migrants of the total population does not seem to be related to the visibility of European EU citizens. For national EU citizens, as expected (H12.1), no effect was found.

Furthermore, I argued that there might be temporary or rather situational factors that influence a member state's relation to the EU and have an impact on the visibility of EU citizens in the European public sphere. I have identified the recent economic crisis as such an event and expected that the crisis would affect the visibility of national EU citizens in the news coverage (H14.1), but also foster a more European understanding of the EU citizenship that leads to a higher visibility of European EU citizens in countries that are more severely affected by the crisis (H14.2). I used change in unemployment as an indicator for how severely an EU member state is affected by the crisis. However, neither of the hypotheses can be supported based on the empirical results. One reason might be that the economic crisis only started in 2009, when the European elections took place and it might have had stronger effects on the news coverage in the following years.

Regarding country level factors that are independent of EU governance, I assumed that the visibility of national EU citizens would be influenced by the degree to which citizens of a member state generally participate in the political and societal life beyond the electoral process (H15.1). In states where a citizenry is more active, journalists might generally pay more attention to citizens in the political process and hence include citizens to a greater extent into the news coverage. For European EU citizens, on the other hand, an active national citizenry should not influence their visibility, as they measure a more abstract concept of the EU citizenship (H15.2). Using associational membership as a measure for an active national citizenry, as expected, I do not find an effect for European EU citizens. Yet, higher rates in associational membership do not lead to a higher visibility of national EU citizens either.

Finally, I hypothesised that the importance of a member state might influence the visibility of European EU citizens in the news coverage (H16.2). As their own influence is limited, smaller member states have a higher incentive to transfer power to the EU level, as they depend to a greater extent on political and economic cooperation. Therefore, smaller states are more motivated to push the European integration forward. If smaller states are more pro-European, this might also be reflected in a more European vision of the EU citizenship that becomes visible in the news coverage (H16.2), while it should not impact the visibility of national EU citizens (H16.1). I used GDP as one indicator for the economic importance of an EU member state. While GDP, as expected, does not influence the visibility of national EU citizens, it also does not lead to a higher visibility of European EU citizens in the EU news coverage in EU member states with a smaller GDP (compared to EU member states with higher GDP).

9.4.2. Multilevel Analysis

What are the factors that can lead to a higher visibility of EU citizens in the news media coverage on EU governance? This study has proposed that the visibility of EU citizens in the news media coverage might be influenced (1) by features of the respective news story, (2) by certain characteristics of the respective media outlet, as well as (3) by country level factors. Table 9.8 and Table 9.9 show the factors that influence the visibility of national and European EU citizens in the news coverage on EU governance during the 2009 European election campaign. Starting with factors at the news story level, according to the first hypotheses, both national and European EU citizens are more likely to be visible in new stories about the European election compared to non-election stories on EU governance (H1.1 and H1.2). For national EU citizens, the election topic has not only a significantly positive effect on visibility, but the average marginal effects show that it is also the factor that influences their visibility the strongest. For European EU citizens, on the other hand, this cannot be confirmed and the election topic has no significant effect on their visibility. The results for the first hypotheses are therefore mixed.

Related to the election topic, the second set of hypotheses assumed that the closer the election day, the higher the visibility of national and European EU citizens will be (H2.1 and H2.2). The election day, in fact, has an effect on both dependent variables. The negative effect indicates that both national and European EU citizens are significantly less likely to be included in news stories that are reported further away from the election day. Or, in other words, the closer the election day, the more likely it is that citizens are actors in the EU news. This supports the idea that the visibility of citizens in the EU news coverage is not necessarily stable over time, but that there is a dynamic element to the news coverage that influences their visibility.

The last factor located at the news story level that is taken into account in the multivariate model is the length of the news story. In general, space in the news coverage is limited and actors compete for news media attention. As ordinary citizens cannot be considered as elite-actors and lack the news value of prominence, journalist might generally favour to include more prominent actors in the news coverage. However, there might be certain characteristics of a news story that make reporting on EU citizens more likely. As such, I have expected that the length of a news story pays a role, because the longer a news story, the more space there is for additional and less prominent actors to be mentioned (H4.1 and H4.2). The results of the multilevel regression model support this expectation and the length of the news story increases the likelihood of national as well as European EU citizens to become visible in a news story.

Regarding factors that are related to the news outlet, I expected that national EU citizens are more visible on TV and in commercial media outlets than in print and quality media outlets due to a more extensive use of personalisation and episodic framing in the former news outlets (H5.1 and H6.1). Because personalisation and episodic framing do not conform to the notion of the EU citizenship that is measured though the visibility of European EU citizens, no effect of TV was expected (H5.2). As European EU citizens represent a truly supranational vision of the EU citizenship and since quality media can generally be considered as more pro-European, while commercial media sometimes conveys more Eurosceptic views (cf. de Vreese et al., 2006), I expected that European EU citizens are more visible in quality media outlets (H6.2). While TV had a significantly positive effect on the visibility of national EU citizens in the bivariate regression (cf. Table 9.6), this cannot be confirmed in the multivariate model, nor are national EU citizens more visible in commercial media. As expected, the visibility of European EU citizens does not vary depending on whether the respective media outlet is a TV channel or a newspaper. Yet, the quality of the media outlet plays a role and European EU citizens are more likely to be visible in quality than commercial media outlets, which supports H6.2.

European public sphere research generally considers the amount of EU news that is reported as an indicator for how vibrant the European public sphere is (Wessler et al. 2008). A more vibrant European public sphere might include a greater variety of actors, including EU citizens. I therefore expected that the visibility of both national and European EU citizens is higher in news outlets that generally report more on the EU affairs (H7.1 and H7.2), but expected that the effect is stronger for the latter (H7.3). However, contrary to these initial expectations, the share of EU news that is reported by a media outlet seems to have a negative effect on the visibility of national EU citizens, even though the effect is only significant at the 10% level. The bivariate correlations between the independent variables (cf. Table 9.4) have shown that TV reports significantly less EU news than newspapers. Hence, newspapers report more EU news, but the bivariate regressions (cf. Table 9.6) have also shown that newspapers tend to report less on citizens compared to TV channels. This higher share of EU news characteristic for print media might be related to the finding that more reporting on EU news decreases the likelihood of national EU citizens to become visible. For European EU citizens, on the other hand, the bivariate analysis indicated that their visibility is more likely in news outlets that report to a greater extent on EU affairs, supporting the initial expectation (cf. Table 9.7). However, this result can no longer be supported based on the multivariate analysis.

Table 9.8 Explaining the visibility of national EU citizens

	Coefficient	Average marginal effect
Fixed Effects		
Level 1		
EP election story	1.19*** (0.06)	0.18***
Election day	-0.58*** (0.08)	-0.09***
Length	0.88*** (0.10)	0.13***
Level 2		
TV	-0.13 (0.15)	-0.02
Quality media	0.07 (0.10)	0.01
Share EU news	-0.48† (0.29)	-0.07†
Level 3		
European ID	0.56 (0.52)	0.08
EP turnout	-0.92† (0.47)	-0.14†
Intra-EU trade	0.11 (0.99)	0.01
Population size	-1.01** (0.36)	-0.15**
Intercept	-1.76† (0.91)	
Random Effects		
Country	0.13 (0.05)	
Media outlet	0.10 (0.03)	
-2LL	11760.79	
AIC	11786.79	
N (Level 3)	27	
N (Level 2)	143	
N (Level 1)	12850	

Table 9.8 shows the results of the multilevel logistic regression model, where level 1 is the news story, level 2 the news outlet, and level 3 the member state. Note: †p<.1, *p<.05, **p <.01, ***p<.001. Calculations were made using the meqrlogit option in Stata 13. Standard errors in parentheses. Continuous variables were standardised ranging from 0 to 1.

9.4. Results

Table 9.9 Explaining the visibility of European EU citizens

	Coefficient	Average marginal effect
Fixed Effects		
Level 1		
EP election story	0.11 (0.09)	0.004
Election day	-0.73*** (0.15)	-0.029***
Length	1.00*** (0.17)	0.040***
Level 2		
TV	-0.19 (0.26)	-0.008
Quality media	0.66** (0.19)	0.026**
Share EU news	0.08 (0.43)	0.003
Level 3		
European ID	1.97*** (0.47)	0.078***
EP turnout	-0.67 (0.44)	-0.027
Intra-EU trade	0.16 (0.95)	0.007
Population size	-0.54 (0.33)	-0.021
Intercept	-4.37*** (0.93)	
Random Effects		
Country	0.00 (0.00)	
Media outlet	0.30 (0.09)	
-2LL	4769.02	
AIC	4795.02	
N (Level 3)	27	
N (Level 2)	143	
N (Level 1)	12850	

Table 9.9 shows the results of the multilevel logistic regression model, where level 1 is the news story, level 2 the news outlet, and level 3 the member state. Note: †$p < .1$, *$p<.05$, **$p<.01$, ***$p<.001$. Calculations were made using the meqrlogit option in Stata 13. Standard errors in parentheses. Continuous variables were standardised ranging from 0 to 1.

Turning now to the country-level variables that concern a member state's relationship with the EU, I expected that the visibility of national EU citizens is higher in member states where the European integration is more contested and support for the European integration is lower. As negativity is a news value, I assumed that journalists might include citizens to a greater extent in the news coverage to underline negative public attitudes towards to EU. For support for the EU as such, no significant effect was found in the bivariate setting (cf. Table 9.6 and Table 9.7) and the variable was therefore excluded. The extent to which a European identity is developed in a member state is another measure for (diffuse) support for the EU. However, the strength of a European identity does not seem to influence the visibility of national EU citizens either (H10.1).

For European EU citizens, on the other hand, I expected the opposite: A more developed European identity should be reflected in a higher visibility of the supranational image of European EU citizens in the news coverage (H10.2). This can be supported by the empirical results. The more citizens see themselves as European, the higher the likelihood that European EU citizens become visible in the EU news coverage. Moreover, the average marginal effects reveal that European identity is the factor that influences their visibility the strongest.

In the model, turnout is used as an indicator for an active European citizenry and the initial expectation was that the more active and involved citizens of the EU member states are in EU governance, the higher the visibility of national and European EU citizens in the EU news (H11.1 and H11.2). While this cannot be supported for European EU citizens, the effect for national EU citizens goes in the opposite direction as initially hypothesised, although it is only significant at the 10% level. The result means that reporting on national EU citizens as actors is less likely to take place in member states where turnout at European elections is higher. As mentioned earlier, journalists are of the opinion that citizens should have a say in the news coverage (Deuze 2002; Raeymaeckers et al. 2012) and their visibility is especially important during election times. If turnout in a member state is going to be low, there are two possible scenarios that could explain why the effect goes in the opposite direction than initially hypothesised: a) journalists might include citizens to a greater extent in the news coverage to

9.4. Results

encourage them to vote, or b) low turnout is seen as a lack of support for the EU and citizens are included to a greater extent to exemplify citizens' lack of interest in the election.

Furthermore, I have argued that more interactions and exchange among citizens of different EU member states might foster a more European understanding of the EU citizenship that is consequently also reflected in a higher visibility of European EU citizens in the news media. Using intra-EU trade as an indicator for economic interactions, I expected that European EU citizens are more visible in member states where intra-EU trade is higher (H13.2), while it should not influence the visibility of national EU citizens (H13.1). While the initial bivariate analysis supported these hypotheses (see Table 9.7), intra-EU trade has no longer a significantly positive impact on the visibility of European EU citizens in the multivariate model.

Finally, I expected that the visibility of EU citizens is influenced by factors at the country level that are independent of EU governance, such as the importance of a member state in terms of its size. Based on previous research, I have argued that states that are smaller in terms of their population size have higher incentives to transfer decision-making powers to the EU level and they are therefore generally more supportive of a more extensive European integration compared to larger EU member states (see also: Brüggemann and Kleinen-von Königslöw 2013). This more European stance of smaller states should lead to a more European perspective and a more European understanding of the EU citizenship that is reflected in a more European image of the EU citizenship in the news coverage. Hence, European EU citizens are more likely to become visible in EU news of smaller states (H16.2), while it should not affect the visibility of national EU citizens (H16.1). However, the empirical results show the opposite: While the size of a country does not significantly influence the visibility of European EU citizens, it has a negative effect on the visibility of national EU citizens. This might indicate that the media coverage of larger state is generally more elite-centred compared to news of smaller states.

9.5. Conclusion

What are the factors that foster the visibility of national and European EU citizens in the European public sphere? Finding an answer to this question was the main focus of this chapter. This study has developed a number of hypotheses that have identified potential factors at the news story, media outlet, and country level that can explain variance in their visibility in the EU news coverage. To test potential influence factors, I used the PIRDEU media study that includes content analysis data from 27 EU member states that was gathered during the 2009 European elections. To develop a parsimonious model, the hypotheses were first tested using bivariate regressions and significant independent variables were then included in the multivariate model. In line with the three cluster of hypotheses and the structure of the data set, I used a three level logistic regression model where the first level is the news story, the second level is the media outlet and the third the country level.

The results show that reporting on the European Parliament elections and the election campaign fosters the visibility of national EU citizens. The importance of the context of the European election is furthermore supported, as their visibility increases the closer the election day. For European EU citizens, on the other hand, the topical context in which the reporting takes place is less relevant. Their visibility is not higher in election news compared to other topics on EU governance. Yet, also the visibility of European EU citizens increases in the run up to the election day. Furthermore, both national and European EU citizens are more likely to be included as actors in longer rather than shorter news stories. The results moreover show that the quality of reporting is important for the visibility of a supranational, European citizenry in the news coverage, as European EU citizens are significantly more visible in quality than commercial media outlets. The strongest predictor for the visibility of European EU citizens, however, is the extent to which a European identity is developed in a member state. This is furthermore the only variable at the country level that showed a significant effect in the multivariate analysis for the visibility of European EU citizens.

However, this chapter has also revealed several factors that can hinder the visibility of EU citizens in the EU news coverage. I initially expected that visibility of EU citizens would generally be higher in news outlets that report more EU news and might therefore also include a broader range of actors. On the contrary, the results suggest that national EU citizens are less likely to be mentioned as actors in news outlets that report more EU news. The result might be related to the circumstance that it is generally *newspapers* that report more EU news, but they tend at the same time to report less on EU citizens (as the bivariate regressions revealed). Another fining that goes contrary to the hypothesis is that national EU citizens are less likely to be visible in member states where turnout at European elections is higher. Using turnout at the European election as an indicator for an active European citizenry, I expected that turnout affects visibility positively. Here, it might be that journalists in member states with low turnout include citizens to a greater extent in the news coverage to encourage higher turnout rates, or that low turnout is seen as an absence of support for the EU and citizens are included to a greater extent to emphasise citizens' lack of interest in the election campaign. Furthermore, the results show that national EU citizens are less likely to be visible in EU member states that are more important in the European community in terms of their population size, possibly indicating that news media of larger states are generally more focused on elite actors compared to smaller states.

Based on the empirical results, it can first of all be concluded that factors from all three levels are relevant for the visibility of EU citizens in the news media coverage on EU governance. Especially the factors at the news story level have a strong impact on the visibility of national and European EU citizens, but also factors at the media and country level play a role. Furthermore, this study was able to provide evidence that national EU citizen and European EU citizen do not only differ conceptually, as they refer to two different visions of the EU citizenship, but that they can also be differentiated on the basis of the empirical findings.

The visibility of citizens is important, because the news media not only provide citizens with information on public affairs, but by including citizens into their news coverage, governmental actors are also able to learn about what their electorate wants and act according to their preferences. When assuming that the visibility of citizens in the news coverage is important because it facilitates communication between citizens and those who govern, then understanding the factors that can enhance or reduce their visibility is crucial. In the case of the EU, research has identified a democratic as well as communication deficit, as the EU is perceived as a distant institution that is not sufficiently responsible or accountable to the EU citizens (Follesdal and Hix 2006; Meyer 1999; Scharpf 1999). Especially in such a situation, the visibility of EU citizens in the news coverage on EU governance can provide citizens with the opportunity to express their preferences and thereby contribute to responsiveness and accountability of EU governance and improve the EU's overall legitimacy.

This study was able to contribute to a neglected field in European political communication research: The visibility of EU citizens in the European public sphere. Journalists themselves are of the opinion that giving citizens a voice in the news coverage is an important part of their job (Deuze 2002; Raeymaeckers et al. 2012). Especially during election campaigns, the role of the media to facilitate communication between citizens and politicians is heightened. Hence, it is generally a positive finding that the visibility of EU citizens is more likely in the context of the European elections and even increases in the course of the election campaign. This enhances the chances that candidates and political parties who run in the European election are able to learn about the preference of their voters and act accordingly once they have been elected, which improves democratic governance at the EU level.

Yet, the results also indicate that citizens might not be perceived by journalists as the most important actors during election campaigns. Longer news stories that discuss topics more extensively and arguably provide more viewpoints and more space for a greater variety of actors to be included, therefore also have a positive effect on the visibility of EU citizens. With regards to a truly supranational vision of the EU citizenship that becomes visible in the EU news coverage via appearances of European EU citizens, it is important to try to strengthen citizens' identification with the EU as a polity that can improve the mediated representation of a truly European vision of the EU citizenship in the European public sphere.

10. Excursus: Explaining the Visibility of Fellow EU Citizens

This study has primarily been concerned with the visibility of EU citizens in the European public sphere, as well as with the visibility of a truly European citizenry (European EU citizens) and one that remains nationally entrenched (national EU citizens). The main argument is based on the premise that it is via the European public sphere that EU citizens and their preferences become visible to policy makers and can consequently be taken into account when making decisions at the EU level. The aim of this excursus is to move beyond this general conceptual framework that the European public sphere contributes to an exchange between EU citizens and EU governmental actors. Instead, the argument put forward in this excursus is that when thinking about the EU citizenship, the European public sphere fulfils an additional role: To mediate between the citizens of the EU member states.

Theoretically, this chapter builds on previous research on the European public sphere that has introduced the distinction between a vertical and horizontal Europeanisation of the news coverage (Koopmans and Erbe 2004; see also Brüggemann and Kleinen-von Königslöw 2009; Peters et al. 2006; Pfetsch and Koopmans 2006; Wessler et al. 2008). The present study has so far focused on the idea of vertical Europeanisation, which refers to a connection between the national and EU level. Horizontal Europeanisation, on the other hand, refers to a linkage between the member states in form of an increased focus on actors and events taking place in fellow EU member states (Brüggemann and Kleinen-von Königslöw 2009 p.29). It is assumed that reporting on fellow member states is important, because "[i]n an intergovernmental polity, the other member states can no longer be treated as foreign countries whose internal politics are not really relevant for one's own country" (Koopmans and Erbe 2004 p.101). The same argument applies for citizens from fellow EU member states, as news media reporting on citizens from fellow EU member states can contribute to a communicative linkage and exchange between the citizens of the EU member states (Walter forthcoming).

10.1. Theoretical Background

Analysing to what extent citizens from fellow EU member states are visible in the European public sphere is also of interest, as the EU citizenship has introduced a novel form of citizenship that goes beyond the nation state and unites people with different nationalities. Theorising about the EU citizenship, Weiler writes that the premises of democracy is "the existence of a polity with members" (Weiler 1997 p.503) and he argues that such a democratic community cannot "be a bunch of strangers" (ibid.). Since communication today is primarily mediated, it is via the news media that EU citizens can learn about each other. Therefore, the final question of this study is: *What factors foster the visibility of citizens from fellow EU member states in the European public sphere?*

As shown and discussed in Chapter 7, the category of national EU citizens can be further divided into two groups: a) references to a country's own national citizens, and b) references to citizens from fellow EU member states. An example of reporting on a country's own national EU citizens would be a news report by the British newspaper *The Guardian* on the lack of support of the *British* citizens for EU policies. A news report by *The Guardian* on the lack of support of the *Greek* citizens for EU policies, on the other hand, would account for the visibility of EU citizens from fellow member states. Both British and Greek citizens account for national EU citizens, as the EU can be identified as the relevant polity, while it is, at the same time, known from which EU member state the respective citizens are. Figure 10.1 visualises the two different types of reporting on national EU citizens.

Figure 10.1 Reporting about national EU citizens

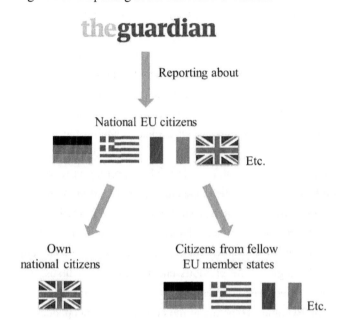

The initial descriptive results presented in Chapter 7 have shown that the levels of visibility of a country's own citizens clearly prevail in the EU news coverage. The only exception is Luxembourg, where the visibility of citizens from the fellow EU member states is higher than the visibility of citizens from Luxembourg. Generally, there is considerable cross-country variance in reporting on citizens from fellow EU member states. The next section presents several hypotheses that aim to explain these different levels of media attention.

10.2. Hypotheses

Research on the European public sphere has to a larger extent focused on the vertical dimension of the European public sphere and aimed to explain variance in media attention to EU news and actors from the EU level (e.g., Vreese and Boomgaarden 2006; Eder 2000; Koopmans and Erbe 2004; Peter and de Vreese

2004). Less is known about the horizontal level of the European public sphere, and especially about how differences in media attention to fellow EU member states can be explained. Research has taken into account two indicators for horizontal Europeanisations: News media reporting on governmental actors and reporting on events taking place in fellow EU member states (Brüggemann and Kleinen-von Königslöw 2009). However, so far, no study has analysed the visibility of fellow EU citizens in the EU news media coverage, an important omission given its importance for contributing to an exchange among the EU citizens.

Regarding potential factors that can explain media reporting on fellow EU citizens, several hypotheses have been developed and are outlined in the following. Since factors that influence the general visibility of citizens in the EU news coverage have already been addressed (see Chapter 9), this excursus is purely interested in factors that can explain news media reporting on *fellow* EU citizens. Following a similar logic as the previous chapter, in this excursus, it is differentiated between (1) media related factors, (2) factors that concern a member states relation to the EU, and (3) factors at the country level independent of EU governance that can potentially influence the visibility of citizens form fellow EU member states. The respective hypotheses are outlined below.

Quality media
Starting with the media related factors, first of all, the visibility of fellow EU citizens might vary depending on the media outlet. As discussed previously, popular media and tabloids in particular sometimes convey more Eurosceptic views (cf. de Vreese et al., 2006) and are considered "agents of national perspectives" (Pfetsch 2008 p.30). This makes popular media outlets less likely to report foreign affairs in general and news on fellow EU member states in particular. When thinking about the visibility of national citizens in EU news, popular media are therefore more likely to report on their own national citizens, rather than on citizens from fellow EU member states. Quality media, on the contrary, have a stronger European focus and report more news from fellow EU member states than popular media (Hepp et al. 2012; Kleinen-von Königslöw 2010).

When it comes to the visibility of actors from fellow EU member states, the contrast is even more striking: A study by Hepp et al. (2012) finds that the share of actors from fellow EU member states that are cited in the media is twice as high in quality media compared to popular media outlets. Because of a more European coverage and a greater focus on actors from fellow EU member states, I expext that:

> H1: *Citizens from fellow EU member states are more visible in the EU news coverage of quality than popular media outlets.*

Europeanisation of news coverage

As I have previously argued, a functioning and vital European public sphere indicates awareness that a shift in governance from the national to the EU level has been taking place (Wessler et al. 2008). If a society is aware of the importance of the European integration process, they might also realise that EU member states have become increasingly interdependent. This insight that fellow EU member state "can no longer be treated as foreign countries" (Koopmans and Erbe 2004 p.101), might affect the visibility of actors from other EU member states, including citizens. Or in other words, a more European coverage might not only be reflected in more news reports on EU governance (vertical Europeanisation), but might also lead to higher levels of visibility of actors from fellow EU member states (horizontal Europeanisation) within EU news. For the visibility of citizens from other EU member states, I expect therefore that:

> H2: *The more EU news a media outlet reports, the higher the visibility of citizens from fellow EU member states compared to media outlets that reports to a lesser extent on EU governance.*

European consolidation

At the member state level, I have identified the length of the EU membership as an indicator for the extent to which member states are involved in this European consolidation process. Over time, the EU member states grow together to a more closely knit political community. The longer the EU membership, the more people realise that national events taking place in fellow EU member states can also affect other member states. One recent example is the Eurozone crisis that has highlighted the interdependency of the EU member states. However, this European consolidation process needs time and is therefore expected to be more advanced for old EU member states. Journalists from long standing EU member states may have become accustomed to paying more attention to the affairs of other member states over time (Kleinen-von Königslöw 2012). The length of the EU membership is therefore likely to be related to news media attention to fellow EU member states and their citizens. Therefore, my expectation is that:

> H3: *Citizens from fellow EU member states are more visible in the EU news coverage of old EU member states than news EU member states.*

European identity
European identity has been discussed as an indicator for (diffuse) support for the European integration (cf. Risse 2003). The strength of a European identity might also be important for reporting on citizens from fellow EU member states. Wessler et al. (2008 p.59) argue that the "more open citizens of a country are to identifying with communities beyond the nation-state, the more the national media will be interested in coverage and discussion of the affairs of other European countries". This argument applies even more so to the visibility of fellow EU citizens in the news coverage, since European identity and the EU citizenship are two interrelated concepts. The more citizens identify with the EU as a political community, the more interested citizens should be in news and opinions of fellow EU citizens. Hence, I expect that:

> H4: *The more developed the European identity in a member state, the higher the visibility of fellow EU citizens_in the EU news coverage.*

10.2. Hypotheses

Dependency on other EU member states

One of the core ideas of the European integration is related to economic cooperation among the European states and the economy is the policy field that has been affected most by the European integration. However, this cooperation also contributed to a greater dependency on other states. Intra-EU trade has already been discussed as an indicator for interaction and exchange among the EU citizens. However, when thinking about news media reporting on fellow EU citizens, it is more about economic dependency and cooperation with other member states. More than 70% of the exports from EU member states go to other states within the EU (Fligstein 2008 p.62). The more a member state depends on trade with fellow EU member states, the more important become events in other member states. When assuming that public opinion should play a role in the decision making process, then also the monitoring of the opinions of citizens in fellow EU member states becomes relevant. Therefore, the hypothesis is:

H5: *Higher levels of trade with fellow EU states are positively related to the visibility of fellow EU citizens_in the EU news coverage.*

Proximity

Independent of EU governance, geographic factors might determine the extent to which news media pay attention to other (member) states and their citizens. In the context of foreign affairs, research has shown that proximity is an important factor that influences the news media coverage (Wu 2003). Some scholars even argue that "the coverage of foreign countries by the news is primarily determined by geographical proximity" (Wilke et al. 2012 p.306). Geographic proximity also increases the number of linkages between countries (Kriesi 2013b p.35). At the same time, proximity is also considered a news value that influences journalists and determines whether or not reporting on other states takes place (Galtung and Ruge 1965). In general, it can be assumed that the higher the number of bordering states, the more adjusted journalists are to report on events and actors from other states. This, as a consequence, is likely to also influence reporting on citizens of other states. In the context of reporting on fellow EU member states, a study by Schuck and de Vreese (2011) found that the total number of neighbouring states has a significantly positive effect on reporting news from fellow EU member states. Therefore, I expect that:

H6: *The higher the number of neighbouring countries of an EU member state, the higher the visibility of fellow EU citizens_in the EU news coverage.*

Importance of a member state

Previous research furthermore suggests that socio-economic factors play a role for reporting of foreign and EU affairs (Boomgaarden et al. 2013; Brüggemann and Kleinen-von Königslöw 2013; Kim and Barnett 1996; Wu 2000). It is assumed that states that are smaller in terms of their economic power and population size ought to be more cosmopolitan in their reporting and for quality newspapers, it has been shown that smaller EU member states include references to other member states and foreign speakers to a greater extent into their coverage than lager states (Brüggemann and Kleinen-von Königslöw 2009). The argument is based on the assumption that smaller states depend to a greater extent on cooperation with other countries compared to larger states: "[W]eaker countries depend more heavily on their neighbours both politically and economically, so that their media outlets will pay more attention to what is going on abroad" (Wessler et al. 2008 p.58). This general pattern of reporting is also likely to be reflected in news media attention to citizens from other EU member states. Therefore, I hypothesise that:

H7: *The lower the socio-economic status of an EU member state, the more visible are citizens from fellow EU member states in the EU news coverage.*

10.3. Methodology

Reporting on fellow EU citizens from other member states is a rare phenomenon as they are visible actors in less than 4% of the EU news included in the sample (see Chapter 7.2). For the analysis of this excursus, I operationalise the dependent variable *Fellow EU citizens* as the percentage of citizens from fellow EU

10.3. Methodology

member states of the category "national EU citizens" (where national EU citizens is a categorical variable that takes the value 1 if national EU citizens are mentioned in a news story and 0 otherwise). Thereby, I account and control for factors that influence the general visibility of national EU citizens, which have already been identified and discussed (see Chapter 9). As there is not sufficient variance at the news story level, I aggregated the data to the media outlet level (mean=19.74, standard deviation=20.68). Thus the media outlet is the unit of analysis in this chapter. Due to missing values, the analysis is based on 138 cases. Even though media outlets might share common characteristics across countries, it is likely that outlets from the same country are not independent of each other, which potentially leads to biased estimates that could distort the results (Arceneaux and Nickerson 2009). Therefore, I use a two level random intercept model that is able account for the clustered structure of the data set.

As independent variables at the news outlet level I use a categorical variable for *Quality media*, while the Europeanisation of the EU news coverage is measured by the *Share of EU news* of the total news coverage by media outlet (further details see Chapter 9.3.2). At the member state level, I use the variable *Old member state* to measure the length of EU membership. It is a categorical variable that takes the value 1 if a member state joined the EU before the eastern enlargement in 2004, and otherwise takes the value 0 (cf. e.g., de Vreese et al. 2006) (see Appendix V for further details on independent variables that are not included in Chapter 9.3.2, and Appendix VI for their correlations). *European identity* measures the extent to which EU citizens see themselves as exclusively or predominantly European, and *Intra-EU trade* measures the percentage of the trade with other EU member states as the percentage of the total trade (see Chapter 9.3.2). As a geographic factor that might influence the visibility of fellow EU member states, *Neighbouring states* takes the total number of sovereign states that share a border with an EU member state into account (cf. Schuck and de Vreese 2011). As socio-economic factors that might influence the visibility of fellow EU citizens, I take the *Population size*, measured as the total population of an EU member state in millions, and *GDP*, measured the logarithm of the gross domestic product, into account (see Chapter 9.3.2).

10.4. Results

Citizenship and nationality have been two closely connected concepts (see, e.g., Janoski and Gran 2002). The EU citizenship, however, challenged this bond by introducing a concept of citizenship that goes beyond the nation state. Today, the EU citizenship unites people from 28 different EU member states. It is via European public sphere that EU citizens can learn about each other. The following analysis is concerned with the question of what factors foster media attention to citizens from fellow EU member states in the EU news coverage. Several hypotheses have been developed taking potential influences at the media and country level into account. As the number of cases is limited, I first test for bivariate relationships between the dependent and independent variables to derive a parsimonious multilevel model. For this purpose, I ran multilevel models for the dependent variable and each of the independent variables separately, where the first level is the media outlet and the second level the member states. The independent variables that show significant effects in the bivariate regression are in a next step included in the final multivariate model. As it cannot be ruled out that those variables that do not show significant effects in the bivariate regression become significant in a multivariate setting, all independent variables are tested separately in the final multivariate model before they are ultimately excluded from the analysis (for the results see Appendix VII).

Table 10.1 shows the bivariate regression results for the visibility of citizens from fellow EU member states in news with main or extensive focus on EU governance. Based on the bivariate regressions, significant effects are found for quality media, European identity, intra-EU trade, as well as the number of neighbouring states. These independent variables are therefore included in the multivariate model. As the significant relationships are discussed in more detail in the context of the multivariate model, I focus in the following on the results that are not significant and therefore excluded from further analysis.

Table 10.1 Bivariate regressions

Level	IV	Coefficient	-2LL	AIC
Media level	Quality media	12.51*** (3.02)	1199.75	1207.75
	Share EU news	6.89 (5.87)	1214.24	1222.24
Country level	Old member state	3.70 (4.87)	1215.04	1223.04
	European identity	50.14*** (8.11)	1192.02	1200.02
	Intra-EU trade	54.46* (23.90)	1210.82	1218.82
	Neighbouring states	23.03* (9.56)	1210.43	1218.43
	Population size	3.16 (8.73)	1215.48	1223.48
	GDP	106.77 (89.28)	1214.21	1222.21
	N (Level 2)	27		
	N (Level 1)	138		

Table 10.1 shows the results of bivariate multilevel regression models, where level 1 is the news outlet, and level 2 the member state. Note: †$p<.1$, *$p<.05$, **$p<.01$, ***$p<.001$. Calculations were made using the meglm option in Stata 13. Standard errors in parentheses. Continuous variables were standardised ranging from 0 to 1. Random effects are not reported.

At the news outlet level, I hypothesised that a higher share of EU news reflects awareness that a shift in governance from the national to the EU level has been taking place (H2). This should be related to the insight that EU member states have become increasingly interdependent. I expected that actors from fellow EU member states, including citizens, are therefore to a larger extent reported in the media outlets that report more EU news, compared to media outlets where the EU is a less prominent topic of the news media coverage. However, based on the empirical analysis, such a relationship cannot be confirmed.

At the member state level, I assumed that growing together as a political community takes time. As the length of the EU membership varies across countries, I predicted that old EU member states would pay more attention to fellow EU citizens compared to member states that joined the EU more recently (H4). Yet, based on the data, there is no evidence that the visibility of fellow EU citizens varies significantly in old and new EU member states. Likewise, the hypothesis that citizens from fellow EU member states are more visible in EU member states with lower the socio-economic status (H7) cannot be confirmed, as neither the size of an EU member state, nor GDP have a significant effect.

Turning now to the multivariate analysis, the results of the multilevel regression (Table 10.2) show that media, as well as country level variables, significantly impact news media reporting on citizens from fellow EU member states.

Table 10.2 Explaining the visibility of citizens from fellow member states

	Coefficient
Fixed Effects	
Level 1	
Quality media	11.92*** (3.00)
Level 2	
European ID	43.20*** (7.99)
Intra-EU trade	36.63* (16.52)
Neighbouring states	7.03 (6.89)
Intercept	-6.48 (4.23)
Random Effects	
Country	0.67 (17.47)
-2LL	1171.21
AIC	1185.21
N (Level 2)	27
N (Level 1)	138

Table 10.2 shows the results of the multilevel regression model, where level 1 is the news outlet, and level 2 the member state. Note: †$p<.1$, *$p<.05$, **$p<.01$, ***$p<.001$. Calculations were made using the meglm option in Stata 13. Standard errors in parentheses. Continuous variables were standardised ranging from 0 to 1.

As expected, quality media has a significantly positive effect on the visibility of fellow EU citizens (H1). More specifically, this result means that when reporting on national EU citizens, quality media refer more often to citizens from other EU member states in comparison to commercial media outlets.

At the country level, I expected that the visibility of fellow EU citizens is higher in EU member states where a European identity is more developed (H4). The rationale is that the more citizens identify with the EU as a political community, the more interested citizens should be in news and opinions of fellow EU citizens. In fact, European identity has the strongest effect in the model. As the variable has been standardised, the result means that an increase in 27 percentage points from the minimum to the maximum leads to a 43% higher share of fellow EU citizens of national EU citizens.

Intra-EU trade has the second strongest effect in the model. Here, H5 argued that trade is an indicator for the extent to which a country depends on cooperation with other EU member states. The more a member state depends on cooperation with fellow EU member states, the more important events taking place in that member state become and public opinion in other member states should be a relevant factor for political decision making. Therefore, higher levels of trade with fellow EU should be positively related to the visibility of fellow EU citizens in the EU news coverage and the hypothesis can be supported.

Finally, independent of EU governance, I expected that geographic factors might influence the extent to which news media pay attention to other (member) states and their citizens. More specially, I expected that the number of neighbouring countries of an EU member state has a positive effect on the visibility of fellow EU citizens. While the bivariate regression showed a positive relationship between the number of neighbouring countries and news media attention to fellow EU citizens, this effect is no longer significant in the multivariate context.

10.5. Conclusion

While the previous chapters have focused on and compared the visibility of national and European EU citizens, this excursus has exclusively concentrated on the former. Within the category of national EU citizens, it has been differentiated between references to a country's own citizens and references to citizens from fellow EU member states. The aim was to identify factors that foster news media attention to citizens from fellow EU member states in the EU news coverage. Using a multilevel regression, the results reveal three relevant factors that influence their visibility. First, the share of fellow EU citizens among references to national EU citizens is higher in quality media outlets, compared to commercial media. This finding is in line with previous research that has shown that quality media generally report more on actors from fellow EU member states (Hepp et al. 2012; Kleinen-von Königslöw 2010). Second, their visibility is higher in EU member states where a European identity is more developed and in member states whose economy depends to a greater extent on trade with other EU member states.

This excursus moved beyond the general theoretical framework of this study, which argues that it is the primary role of the European public sphere to mediate between the EU citizens and EU governmental actors. It highlighted that another role of the European public sphere is to mediate among the EU citizens of the EU member states. Even though news media reporting on citizens from fellow EU member states is a rare phenomenon, it is important for fostering exchange among the EU citizens. The empirical analysis has once again highlighted the importance of exchange among EU member states and a European identity for the visibility of the EU citizenry in the European public sphere.

11. Discussion and Conclusion

This study set out to determine the extent to which EU citizens are visible in the European public sphere. This question has been neglected by previous research, but is highly relevant for accountability, responsiveness and the overall legitimacy of EU governance. When interested in the visibility of EU citizens in the European public sphere, it is important to first understand the relevance of the concept of citizenship for democratic governance. Therefore, this book started out by tracing back the origins of the concept of citizenship (Chapter 2). The theoretical framework has shown that the idea of citizenship is inevitably linked to self-governance of the people, but it also highlighted that the origins of citizenship are not tied to nationality or to the nation state. Based on the literature review, a citizen in this study is understood as an individual who is a member of a democratic political community. Over time, the scope of those political communities has changed. In ancient Greece, it was the city-state, while today it is still the nation state that is seen as the primary political community that citizens belong to. However, the European integration has resulted in a shift in governance from the national to the supranational level and required to extend the scope of citizenship as well. As such, the EU citizenship was legally introduced in 1993.

The scope of the concept of the public sphere has likewise initially been limited to the nation state and has then been extended to the EU level in the course of the European integration (Chapter 3 and Chapter 4). With reference to the work by Gerhards and Neidhardt's (1991), the public sphere in this study is seen as a communication system that mediates between the citizens at the micro-level and the governmental system at the macro-level. The existence of a public sphere at the national and EU level is an essential element of democratic governance, because it ensures that governments are accountable and responsive to the will of the people.

While the notion of a European public sphere has received extensive scholarly attention (e.g., Boomgaarden et al. 2010; Brüggemann and Kleinen-von Königslöw 2009; Hepp et al. 2012; Koopmans 2007; Schuck and de Vreese 2011; Wessler et al. 2008), this stream of research has paid less attention to the fact that at the national level, different normative public sphere theories have been developed. This study has taken the elitist, liberal, discursive, and participatory model of the public sphere into account, as they provide different standpoints as to whether and to what extent citizens ought to be visible in public debates on governance (Ferree et al. 2002a; Downey et al. 2012). Therefore, these differently nuanced normative public sphere theories are highly relevant when interested in analysing the visibility of EU citizens in the European public sphere.

To date, studies on the European public sphere have largely been influenced by the notion of the discursive public sphere (Brüggemann and Schulz-Forberg 2009a; Brüggemann and Kleinen-von Königslöw 2009; Eriksen 2005b; Gripsrud 2007; Hepp et al. 2012; Kleinen-von Königslöw 2012; Koopmans 2007; Peters 2005; Peters et al. 2005; Schlesinger 1999; Splichal 2006; van de Steeg 2002; Trenz 2004; Wessler et al. 2008) and empirical analyses have primarily focused on the question to what extent EU affairs, but also EU-level governmental actors, receive attention in the media of the EU member states (Boomgaarden et al. 2013; Brüggemann and Kleinen-von Königslöw 2009; Peter and de Vreese 2004; Schuck and de Vreese 2011). As the literature review has shown, only very few empirical studies have addressed the visibility of EU citizens in the European public sphere (Garcia-Blanco and Cushion 2010; Hepp et al. 2012; Michailidou and Trenz 2013; Wessler 2007). Based on previous research, it could only be inferred that EU citizens are visible in the European public sphere; however, no broader conclusions or generalisations about their visibility could be drawn, because these studies lack clear definition of what constitutes an EU citizen in the European public sphere.

To address this shortcoming, this study has discussed the visibility of EU citizens in the European public sphere and introduced the distinction between national EU citizens and European EU citizens. National EU citizens account for citizens of the individual EU member states. As the information about the EU member state a citizen comes from is known, the EU citizenry that becomes visible via the European public sphere appears as divided by nationality. European EU citizens, on the other hand, simultaneously represent the citizens of all EU member states. Contrary to national EU citizens, which link back to the national level, European EU citizens represent a truly European and supranational form of citizenship that goes beyond the nation state.

11.1. Main Empirical Findings

To what extent are EU citizens visible in the European public sphere and what are the factors that foster their visibility? To answer these overarching research questions, this study used the PIREDEU data set of the 2009 European Parliament elections that includes content analysis data of news stories form all 27 EU member states that participated in the election. The results show that EU citizens are overall visible in 30% of the news coverage with the main focus being on EU governance. More specifically, 3% of EU news includes vox pops, 8% polls, and 24% EU citizens as actors (Chapter 7). Only the latter category can be used as a simultaneous and comparable measure of the visibility of national and European EU citizens. The findings show that while national EU citizens are visible in 20% of the EU related news coverage, for European EU citizens this is only the case in 5%.

Analysing whether these levels of visibility are high or low is not straight forward, as different normative public sphere theories have different standpoints as to whether and to what extent ordinary citizens ought to participate in debates on governance in the public sphere. Therefore, this study also assessed which normative model of the public sphere corresponds best the empirical levels of visibility of EU citizens. The visibility of EU citizens has been compared to other actor groups and analysed in light of the ideal typical actor structures of the elitist, liberal, discursive as well as participatory public sphere theory (Chapter 8). Furthermore, this study has analysed the overall actor structure of EU news and the visibility of actors from the horizontal/national and vertical/EU level separately. The results for the overall actor structure show that the visibility of EU citizens in the EU news coverage during the 2009 European Parliament election is rather low when compared to governmental actors, and somewhat lower when compared to political parties. However, EU citizens are clearly more visible than civil society actors. These results are overall best described by the actor structure of the discursive public sphere theory, where citizens are not seen as an individual actor group, but are part of informal civil society actors.

However, the results differ strongly when analysing the visibility of national EU citizens in comparison to other actors from the member state level and the visibility of European EU citizens compared to other EU level actors separately. While the horizontal dimension is more inclusive of citizens and civil society actors, the vertical level is clearly elitist and it is nearly exclusively EU governmental actors that are in the centre of attention. As far as the Europeanisation of the news media coverage is concerned, i.e., the extent to which news media include actors from the EU level, the results indicate that this process has thus far mainly been limited to governmental actors. While national and EU level governmental actors are approximately equally visible, EU level intermediary actors and European EU citizens are significantly less visible than their counterparts from the national level. For EU citizens, this means that the mediated image of the EU citizenry that becomes visible in the European public sphere does not reflect a vision of a supranational-European citizenry, but predominantly consists of national EU citizens from the member states. Overall, based on the results of this study, one can differentiate between an *elitist-vertical* and *discursive-horizontal* dimension of the European public sphere.

These observations change when taking the quality of visibility in EU news into account: When it comes to quotations, which are seen as an indicator for the extent to which actors are able to express their opinions directly in the news coverage, citizens are among the least relevant actors. This raises ques-

11.1. Main Empirical Findings

tions regarding whether citizens' opinions on EU governance are in fact reflected in the EU news media coverage on EU governance. If citizens are only mentioned, but not able to express their opinions on EU governance, this limits the extent to which the European public sphere is able to contribute to a meaningful exchange between EU citizens and policy makers at the EU level.

The analyses furthermore revealed that the visibility of EU citizens varies across the EU member states. This has led to the question of how these differences in the visibility of EU citizens can be explained and what factors foster their visibility (Chapter 9). Using a three level logistic regression model, the results showed that the visibility of national and European EU citizens is influenced by factors at the news story, the media outlet, and the member state level. The findings highlight the importance of the context of the European election: If an EU news story reports on the European Parliament elections or the election campaign, national EU citizens are significantly more likely to be included as actors and their visibility increases the closer the election day. For European EU citizens, on the other hand, the thematic context of the European election is not relevant. Yet, also their visibility increases in the run up to the election day. Furthermore, both national and European EU citizens are more likely to be included as actors in longer rather than shorter news stories. The results moreover show that the quality of reporting is important for the visibility of a supranational, European citizenry in the news coverage, as European EU citizens are significantly more visible in quality than commercial media outlets. The strongest predictor for the visibility of European EU citizens, however, is the extent to which a European identity is developed in a member state.

Yet, the analysis revealed that there are also several factors that can hinder the visibility of EU citizens in the EU news coverage. Rather surprisingly, the results suggest that national EU citizens are less visible in news outlets whose coverage is more Europeanised, i.e., in news outlets that report more EU news. Similarly, national EU citizens are less likely to be visible in member states that are larger in terms of their population size and in countries where turnout at European elections is higher.

The final empirical chapter of this study (Chapter 10) moved beyond the general theoretical framework of this study and argued that the European public sphere is also important for an exchange that is taking place among the EU citizens. As the EU is a diverse polity, there should also be a certain degree of mediated communication taking place among the citizens of the EU member states to contribute to an understanding and exchange of opinions among them. Therefore, the excursus addressed the question of how news media attention to citizens from fellow EU member states can be explained. The empirical findings based on a multilevel regression highlight once again the importance of a European identity for visibility. In addition, the results show that the quality of reporting, as well as exchange among EU member states (measured by intra-EU trade) forester the visibility of citizens from fellow EU member states in the news coverage on EU governance.

11.2. Theoretical Implications

Political representation and political communication are at the heart of democracy. Yet, as this study has argued, supranational governance makes the exchange between governmental actors and ordinary citizens more difficult. In general, there are several mechanisms through which citizens can provide their input and ensure that governance is responsive and accountable to them. As such, elections are an important mean for citizens to express their political preferences. Yet, at the EU level, political representation via elections and political parties alone is problematic because European elections are often not about Europe, but rather about national affairs. This study has made the argument and has demonstrated empirically that the visibility of EU citizens in the European public sphere constitutes another mechanism through which EU citizens become visible to governmental actors at the EU level.

This study has provided evidence that EU citizens are visible in 30% of the news coverage on EU governance. Is this good or bad news? The answer to this question is: It depends. *First*, it depends on the democratic theory one has in mind. Supporters of the elitist democratic theory would argue that citizens' participation in the democratic process should be limited to casting a vote and their visibility in public debates is neither needed nor desired. Hence, from this standpoint, the visibility of EU citizens would be considered as too high. The same applies to the liberal public sphere theory, where citizens ought to be represented by civil society actors and not become visible themselves. From the perspective of the participatory theory, on the other hand, the visibility of EU citizens would not be high enough, as they are less visible than EU governmental actors. Only from the perspective of the discursive public sphere theory, their visibility can be considered as sufficiently high. Given these considerable levels of visibility, it is rather surprising that EU citizens have so far been neglected by European public sphere research. Future studies should therefore take EU citizens as actors in the European public sphere into account in their theoretical framework.

By applying different normative public sphere theories to the European level, this study has built on previous research by Ferree and colleauges (2002a), who examined to what extent the news media coverage reflects democratic ideals proposed by normative public sphere theories. This research project contributed to the field of European public sphere research by showing that public sphere theories developed at the national level can be adjusted and used for normative assessment of European political communication. It has furthermore provided ideal types of the actor structures of four different normative public sphere theories that can be used as a basis for further empirical analyses. The findings emphasise that it is important to take the particularities of the European public sphere into account when applying those normative theories to the EU level. Here, this study was able to show that whether the visibility of EU citizens can be considered as high or low also depends on the dimension of the European public sphere. When looking at the horizontal level, which measures, in this study, the visibility of national actors in the EU news coverage, the visibility of national EU citizens is comparatively high and it meets the requirements of the discursive public sphere. However, when analysing the vertical dimension of the European public sphere, which in this study takes only actors from the EU level into account, the visibility of European EU citizens is low. Here, the vertical actor structure clearly reflects the ideal of the elitist public sphere theory.

Previous research has used visibility of governmental actors from the EU level as an indicator for the extent to which the public spheres of the EU member states are "Europeanised" (Boomgaarden et al. 2013; Brüggemann and Kleinen-von Königslöw 2009; Peter and de Vreese 2004; Schuck and de Vreese 2011), assuming that their visibility in the news coverage is needed so that citizens are able to perceive that important decision making powers have been transferred to the EU level. The present study showed that while the visibility of national and EU governmental actors is approximately equally high, the visibility of European EU citizens is far behind the visibility of national EU citizens: The news media first and foremost report on national EU citizens, where it is known from which EU member state the respective citizens are. In the European public sphere, a supranational and truly European image of the EU citizenry is still underdeveloped. This result indicates that a Europeanisation of debates on EU governance has thus far remained mainly limited to EU governmental actors, but not yet spread to other actor groups. The image of the EU citizenry that becomes visible to EU citizens via the European public sphere is one that primarily remains nationally entrenched. As a consequence, the mediated image of the EU citizenship does not, so far, reflect "the creation of one people, but the union of many" (Weiler 1997 p.498). Yet, this study has shown that a European image of the EU citizenry is related to a European identity. Strengthening a European identity can therefore also improve the visibility of a truly European citizenry in the European public sphere. For the EU citizenship to have a positive impact on the legitimacy of EU governance, more than a legal framework is needed. Above all, it depends on support and citizens' identification with the EU as a polity to become a politically meaningful concept.

11.3. Limitations and Suggestions for Future Research

This study has put forward the argument that it is via the European public sphere that opinions and interests of EU citizens can become visible to policy makers and enable public opinion to be taken into account in the decision-making process at the EU level. Empirically, this work has analysed the visibility of EU citizens in the EU news coverage, but not the visibility of their opinions as such. The assumption behind the analysis of their visibility is that it is a measure for their opinions being reported (for a similar argument see Bosch 2014). However, the visibility of ordinary EU citizens in the news coverage on EU governance is only a necessary, yet not sufficient condition for opinions being present in the European public sphere. The different measures of the visibility of EU citizens employed by this study vary to the extent that they are likely to capture the opinions and interests of EU citizens. For example, it can be argued that direct quotations of EU citizens as actors and vox pops are to a greater extent likely to include references to citizens' opinions. More research is needed to measure the presence of the opinions and interests of EU citizens in the European public sphere more directly.

In contrast to previous research, this study has applied a more narrow definition of the European public sphere that is exclusively defined by a reference to EU governance. Hence, empirically, only news stories that explicitly mention the EU, its institutions, politics or policies have been taken into account. Moreover, this study can only provide an image of the visibility of EU citizen in the European public sphere during a short time period of three weeks prior to the 2009 European Parliament elections. The context of the European Parliament elections has a positive impact on the visibility of EU citizens (see Chapter 9). Therefore, a limitation of this study is that it unable to make general statements of the visibility of EU citizens in the European public sphere, but is has rather provided results for the upper-bound of their visibility. This means that this study is carried out under favourable conditions, which lead to a higher visibility of EU citizens in the European public sphere compared to routine periods of the EU news coverage. Hence, this study is unlikely to have underestimated the visibility of EU citizens, rather it has measured the upper-bound of their visibility. Here, more research is needed to analyse the visibility of EU citizens longitudinally, or during routine-periods of EU governance. This would furthermore allow research to examine their visibility across different thematic contexts. For example, this study hypothesised that the economic crisis is related to a higher visibility of EU citizens; yet, no effect was found. As the Eurozone crisis only started out in 2009, when the European election took place, it is possible that it was too early to detect an effect of the economic crisis on the EU news coverage. Hence, future research could also investigate in more detail how such situational factors influence the visibility of EU citizens.

Another limitation concerns the measures for the visibility of EU citizens. As this study has drawn on a pre-defined data set that was not designed to measure the visibility of EU citizens, some approximations had to be made. Ideally, EU citizens would have only been coded if their appearance in the news coverage was unambiguously related to EU politics, policy, or polity. Based on the PIREDEU data set, it is only known that the respective news story discusses EU governance. However, whether the reference to citizens is directly related to EU affairs or appears in another topical context cannot be verified unambiguously. To maximise the likelihood that EU citizens appear in the context of EU governance, I excluded news stories that discuss the EU only briefly, and only included EU news stories that discuss EU affairs extensively or whose main focus is on EU policy, polity or politics in the sample. Yet, this approach is not ideal, since some wrongly classified cases might be included in the data, while other references to EU citizens might be missed.

Furthermore, two measures of the visibility of EU citizens, vox pops and polls, were only coded for news stories about the European election; hence, they only measure the visibility of EU citizens in election news and not in the general EU news coverage. Furthermore, based on the coding scheme, it cannot be unambiguously clarified whether vox pops measure European or national EU citizens, or both, while polls only measure national EU citizens. As this study was interested in a comparative analysis of national and EU citizens, vox pops and polls had to be excluded from further analyses. In this sense, this study has underestimated the visibility of EU citizens.

In Chapter 8, the visibility of EU citizens was analysed in comparison to other actor groups. Also for the operationalisations of governmental actors, political parties, but especially formal and informal society actors, some compromises had to be made that might consequently affect their levels of visibility in EU news. Here, further analyses are needed that employ more nuanced actor schemes that are explicitly designed for the comparison of normative public sphere theories. In addition, the presence of different actors in the public sphere is only one normative criterion of the public sphere theories. Research could build on this work and include additional criteria in the analysis, for example, related to how discussions in the public sphere should take place.

Despite these limitations, the PIREDEU data set provided a unique opportunity for analysing the visibility of EU citizens in the European public sphere in a comparative way across 27 EU member states and 143 different media outlets, thus helping to deliver empirical evidence of a topic of vital importance. In addition, it is currently the only data set available that provides content analysis data from all member states that participated in a European election. Yet, further research is needed that picks up on these issues and carries out content analyses that are explicitly designed for an analysis of the visibility of EU citizens in the news coverage. Such studies might also include further details on how EU citizens are represented in the news coverage. For example, this study has shown that EU citizens are less often than other actor groups able to express their opinions directly in the EU news coverage (see Chapter 8.4.3). This leads to the question to what extent the news media in fact provide space for citizens to express their opinions and standpoints on EU affairs and the European integration more generally.

Overall, this study has been able to contribute to a neglected field in European political communication research: The visibility of EU citizens in the European public sphere. Thus far research had only provided limited evidence that citizens become visible in debates on EU governance, yet, to what extent has remained an open question. In addition to providing empirical evidence to answer this question, this study has contributed to the field by offering a conceptual framework for the analysis of the visibility of EU citizens in the European public sphere by introducing the distinction between national and European EU citizens. Beyond providing evidence as to what extent EU citizens, but also national and European EU citizens become visible in the European public sphere, this study has also been able to shed light on factors that can foster or hinder their visibility. Especially promoting a truly European vision of the EU citizenry in the European public sphere can have a positive impact on the EU's legitimacy and help to close the much debated gap between the EU and its citizens.

References

van Aelst, P. and de Swert, K. 2009. Politics in the News: Do Campaigns Matter? A Comparison of Political News During Election Periods and Routine Periods in Flanders (Belgium). *Communications* 34(2), pp. 149–168.
Alesina, A. and Wacziarg, R. 1999. *Is Europe Going Too Far?* Cambridge.
Althaus, S.L. 2011. What's Good and Bad in Political Communication Research? Normative Standards for Ecaluating Media and Citizen Performance. In: Semetko, H. A. ed. *The SAGE Handbook of Political Communication*. Los Angeles: Sage, pp. 97–112.
Andersen, S.S. and Burns, T. 1996. The European Union and the Erosion of Parliamentary Democracy: A Study of Post-Parliamentary Governance. In: Andersen, S. and Eliassen, K. A. eds. *The European Union: How Democratic Is It?*. London: Sage, pp. 227–252.
Anderson, M., den Boer, M. and Miller, G. 1994. European Citizenship and Cooperation in Justice and Home Affairs. In: Duff, A. Pinder, J. and Pryce, R. eds. *Maastricht and Beyond: Building the European Union*. London, New York: Routledge, pp. 104–122.
Andeweg, R.B. and Thomassen, J.J.A. 2005. Modes of Political Representation: Toward a New Typology. *Legislative Studies Quaterly* XXX(4), pp. 507–528.
Anon 1951. Treaty Establishing the European Coal and Steel Community.
Anon 1957. *Treaty of Rome*.
Anon 2007. Treaty of Lisbon Amending the Treaty on European Union and the Treaty Establishing the European Community. *Official Journal of the European Union* C 306/1.
Anon 2012. Treaty on the Functioning of the European Union. C 326,26.
Arceneaux, K. and Nickerson, D.W. 2009. Modeling Certainty with Clustered Data: A Comparison of Methods. *Political Analysis* 17(2), pp. 177–190.
Aristotle 1990. *Aristotle: In twenty-three volumes. 19. The Nicomachean Ethics*. Rackham, H. ed. Cambridge, Mass: Cambridge University Press.
Aristotle 1995. *Politics. Book III and IV*. Robinson, R. ed. Oxford: Clarendon.
Armingeon, K. and Ceka, B. 2013. The Loss of Trust in the European Union During the Great Recession Since 2007: The Role of Heuristics From the National Political System. *European Union Politics* 15(1), pp. 82–107.
Asp, K. and Esaiasson, P. 1996. The Modernization of Swedish Campaigns: Individualization, Professionalization, and Medialization. In: Swanson, D. L. and Mancini, P. eds. *Politics, Media, and Modern Democracy: An International Study of Innovations in Electoral Campaigns and Their Consequences*. Westport, Conn: Praeger, pp. 73–90.
Bachrach, P. and Botwinick, A. 1992. *Power and Empowerment: A Radical Theory of Participatory Democracy*. Philadelphia: Temple University Press.
Bagchi, A. 2000. Political Citizenship in Britain and Germany. *German Politics* 9(3), pp. 161–180.
Baker, E. 1998. The Media That Citizens Need. *The University of Pennsylvania Law Review* 147(2), pp. 317–408.
Barber, B.R. 1984. *Strong Democracy: Participatory Politics for a New Age*. Berkeley: University of California Press.
de Bardeleben, J. and Viju, C. 2013. Introduction. In: de Bardeleben, J. and Crina, V. eds. *Economic Crisis in Europe: What it Means for the EU and Russia*. Basingstoke: Palgrave MacMillan, pp. 1–18.

Bee, C. and Guerrina, R. 2014a. Framing Civic Engagement, Political Participation and Active Citizenship in Europe. *Journal of Civil Society* 10(1), pp. 1–4.
Bee, C. and Guerrina, R. 2014b. Participation, Dialogue, and Civic Engagement: Understanding the Role of Organized Civil Society in Promoting Active Citizenship in the European Union. *Journal of Civil Society* 10(1), pp. 29–50.
Beetham, D. 1991. *The Legitimation of Power*. Basingstoke: Palgrave.
Beetham, D. 1992. Liberal Democracy and the Limits of Democratization. *Political Studies* 40, pp. 40–53.
Beetham, D. 2011. Legitimacy. In: Badie, B., Berg-Schlosser, D. and Morlino, L. eds. *International Encyclopedia of Political Science*. Los Angeles: Sage, pp. 1414–1425.
Beetham, D. and Lord, C. 1998. Legitimacy and the European Union. In: Weale, A. and Nentwich, M. eds. *Political Theory and the European Union. Legitimacy, Constitutional Choice and Citizenship*. London, New York: Routledge/ECPR Studies in European Political Science, pp. 15–33.
Behr, R.L. and Iyengar, S. 1982. Television News, Real-World Cues, and Changes in the Public Agenda. *Public Opinion Quarterly* 49(1), pp. 38–57.
Beierwaltes, A. 2002. *Demokratie und Medien: Der Begriff der Öffentlichkeit und seine Bedeutung für die Demokratie in Europa*. Baden-Baden: Nomos Verlagsgesellschaft.
Bekkers, R. Völker, B., van der Gaag, M. and Flap, H. 2008. Social Networks and Participants in Voluntary Associations. In: Lin, N. and Erickson, B. eds. *Social Capital: An International Research Program*. Oxford: Oxford University Press, pp. 185–205.
Bellamy, R., Castiglione, D. and Shaw, J. 2006. Introduction: From National to Transnational Citizenship. In: Bellamy, R., Castiglione, D. and Shaw, J. eds. *Making European Ciitzens. Civic Inclusion in a Transational Context*. New York: Palgrave MacMillan, pp. 1–28.
Bellamy, R. 2008. *Citizenship: A Very Short Introduction*. Oxford: Oxford University Press.
Bengtsson, Å.S.A. 2004. Economic Voting: The Effect of Political Context, Volatility and Turnout on Voters' Assignment of Responsibility. *European Journal of Political Research* 43(5), pp. 749–767.
Bennett, W.L. and Entman, R.M. 2001. Mediated Politics: An Introduction. In: Bennett, W. L. and Entman, R. M. eds. *Mediated Politics: Communication in the Future of Democracy*. Cambridge: Cambridge University Press, pp. 1–29.
Bentele, G. and Fähnrich, B. 2010. Personalisierung als Sozialer Mechanismus in Medien und Gesellschaftlichen Organisationen. In: Eisenegger, M. and Wehmeier, S. eds. *Personalisierung der Organisationskommunikation: Theoretische Zugänge, Empirie und Praxis*. Wiesbaden: VS Verlag für Sozialwissenschaften, pp. 51–75.
von dem Berge, B. and Poguntke, T. 2013. Handbuch Parteienforschung. In: Niedermayer, O. ed. *Handbuch Parteienforschung*. Wiesbaden: Springer Fachmedien Wiesbaden, pp. 875–904.
Berkel, B. 2006. *Konflikt als Motor europäischer Öffentlichkeit: Eine Inhaltsanalyse von Tageszeitungen in Deutschland, Frankreich, Großbritannien und Österreich*. Wiesbaden: VS Verlag für Sozialwissenschaften.
Bessette, J. 1980. *Deliberative Democracy: The Majority Principle in Republican Government*. Washington, DC: AEI Press.
Best, H. and Higley, J. 2009. Intoduction: Democratic Elitism Reappraised. *Comparative Sociology* 8(3), pp. 323–344.
Blondel, J., Sinnott, R. and Svensson, P. 1998. *People and Parliament in the European Union: Participation, Democracy, and Legitimacy*. Oxford: Clarendon Press.
Bohman, J. 1998. Survey Article: The Coming of Age of Deliberative Democracy. *Journal of Political Philosophy* 6(4), pp. 400–425.
Bohman, J. 2000. *Public Deliberation: Pluralism, Complexity, and Democracy*. Cambridge, Mass: MIT Press.
Bohman, J. and Rehg, W. 1997. Introduction. In: Bohman, J. and Rehg, W. eds. *Deliberative Democracy: Essays on Reason and Politics*. Cambridge, Mass: MIT Press, pp. IX–XXX.
Boomgaarden, H.G., Vliegenthart, R., de Vreese, C.H. and Schuck, A.R.T. 2010. News on the

Move: Exogenous Events and News Coverage of the European Union. *Journal of European Public Policy* 17(4), pp. 506–526.
Boomgaarden, H.G., Schuck, A.R.T., Elenbaas, M. and de Vreese, C.H. 2011. Mapping EU Attitudes: Conceptual and Empirical Dimensions of Euroscepticism and EU Support. *European Union Politics* 12(2), pp. 241–266.
Boomgaarden, H.G., de Vreese, C.H., Schuck, A.R.T., Azrout, R., Elenbaas, M., van Spanje, J.H.P. and Vliegenthart, R. 2013. Across Time and Space: Explaining Variation in News Coverage of the European Union. *European Journal of Political Research* 52(5), pp. 608–629.
Bosch, B. 2014. Beyond Vox Pop: The Role of News Sourcing and Political Beliefs in Exemplification Effects. *Mass Communication and Society* 17(2), pp. 217–235.
Boykoff, M.T. 2008. The Cultural Politics of Climate Change Discourse in UK Tabloids. *Political Geography* 27(5), pp. 549–569.
Brookes, R., Lewis, J. and Wahl-Jorgensen, K. 2004. The Media Representation of Public Opinion: British Television News Coverage of the 2001 General Election. *Media, Culture & Society* 26(1), pp. 63–80.
Brubaker, R. 1992. *Citizenship and Nationhood in France and Germany*. Cambridge: Harvard University Press.
Brüggemann, M. 2008. *Europäische Öffentlichkeit durch Öffentlichkeitsarbeit? Die Informationspolitik der Europäischen Kommission*. Wiesbaden: VS Verlag für Sozialwissenschaften.
Brüggemann, M. and Kleinen-von Königslöw, K. 2009. 'Let's Talk about Europe': Why Europeanization Shows a Different Face in Different Newspapers. *European Journal of Communication* 24(1), pp. 27–48.
Brüggemann, M. and Kleinen-von Königslöw, K. 2013. Explaining Cosmopolitan Coverage. *European Journal of Communication* 28(4), pp. 361–378.
Brüggemann, M. and Schulz-Forberg, H. 2008. Towards a Pan-European Public Sphere? A Typology of Transnational Media in Europe. In: Wessler, H., Peters, B., Brüggemann, M., Kleinen-von Königslöw, K. and Sifft, S. eds. *Transnationalization of Public Spheres*. Basingstoke, Hampshire: Palgrave MacMillan, pp. 78–94.
Brüggemann, M. and Schulz-Forberg, H. 2009. Becoming Pan-European?: Transnational Media and the European Public Sphere. *International Communication Gazette* 71(8), pp. 693–712.
Bruter, M. 2004. On what citizens mean by feeling 'European': perceptions of news, symbols and borderless-ness. *Journal of Ethnic and Migration Studies* 30(1), pp. 21–39.
Bunting, M. 2009. A New Politics: Beyond Westminster's Bankrupted Practices, a New Idealism is Emerging: Progressive Politics Will Take Root From the Rubble of a Labour Defeat. The Transition Movement Is Giving Us a Glimpse Now. *The Guardian*, p. 23.
Carey, S. 2002. Undivided Loyalties: Is National Identity an Obstacle to European Integration? *European Union Politics* 3(4), pp. 387–413.
Carrell, S. 2009. Labour in Crisis: Kirkcaldy: Even Home Turf Now Tricky Territory for Prime Minister. *The Guardian*, p. 6.
Cerutti, F. 2003. A Political Identity of the Europeans? *Thesis Eleven* 72(1), pp. 26–45.
Closa, C. 1992. The Concept of Citizenship in the Treaty on European Union. *Common Market Law Review* 29, pp. 1137–1169.
Cohen, J. 2003. Deliberation and Democratic Legitimacy. In: Matravers, D. and Pike, J. eds. *Debates in Contemporary Political Philosophy: An Anthology*. London, New York: Routledge, pp. 342–360.
Coicaud, J.-M. 2004. *Legitimacy and Politics: A Contribution to the Study of Political Right and Political Responsibility*. Cambridge: Cambridge University Press.
Commission of the European Communities 1975. *Towards European citizenship. Implementation of point 10 of the final communi- que issued at the European Summit held in Paris on 9 and 10 December 1974, COM (75) 322, A Passport Union*.
Commission of the European Communities 2006a. *White Paper on a European Communication Policy*.

Commission of the European Communities 2006b. White Paper on a European Communication Policy. , pp. 1–13.
Commission of the European Communities 2010. Report from the Commission to the Parliament, the Council and the European Economic and Social Committee under Article 25 TFEU. On Progress towards effective EU Citizenship 2007-2010 [Online] Available at: http://eur-lex.europa.eu/LexUriServ/LexUriServ.do?uri=CELEX:52010DC0602:en:HTML [Accessed: 1 December 2011].
Corrigan, D.M. 1990. Value Coding Consensus in Front Page News Leads. *Journalism & Mass Communication Quarterly* 67(4), pp. 653–662.
Council Decision 2004. *of 26 January 2004 Establishing a Community Action Programme to Promote Active European Citizenship (Civic Participation) 2004/100/EC*.
Council of the European Communities and Commission of the European Communities 1992. Treaty on European Union.
Curran, J. 1991. Rethinking the Media as a Public Sphere. In: Dahlgren, P. and Sparks, C. eds. *Communication and Citizenship: Journalism and the Public Sphere in the New Media Age*. London: Routledge, pp. 27–57.
Curtis, J.E., Baer, D.E. and Grabb, E.G. 2001. Nations of Joiners: Explaining Voluntary Association Membership in Democratic Societies. *American Sociological Review* 66(6), pp. 783–805.
Dahl, R.A. 1994. A Democratic Dilemma: System Effectiveness versus Citizen Participation. *Political Science Quarterly* 109(1), pp. 23–34.
Dahl, R.A. 2000. *On Democracy*. New Haven: Yale University Press.
Dahlgren, P. 2002. In Search of the Talkative Public: Media, Deliberative Democracy and Civic Culture. *Javnost - The Public* 9(3).
Dahrendorf, R. 1967. Aktive und Passive Öffentlichkeit. *Merkur: Deutsche Zeitschrift für Europäisches Denken* 21(12), pp. 1109–1122.
Dalton, R.J. and Duval, R. 1986. The Political Environment and Foreign Policy Opinions: British Attitudes Toward European Integration , 1972-1979. *British Journal of Political Science* 16(1), pp. 113–134.
Daschmann, G. 2000. Vox Pop & Polls: The Impact of Poll Results and Voter Statements in the Media on the Perception of a Climate of Opinion. *International Journal of Public Opinion Research* 12(2), pp. 160–181.
Decker, F. 2002. Governance beyond the nation-state. Reflections on the democratic deficit of the European Union. *Journal of European Public Policy* 9(2), pp. 256–272.
Delanty, G. 2008. European Citizenship: A Critical Assessment. In: Isin, E.F., Neyers, P. and Turner, B.S. eds. *Citizenship Between Past and Future*. New York: Routledge, pp. 61–70.
Déloye, Y. 2000. Exploring the Concept of European Citizenship: A Socio-Historical Approach. *Yearbook of European Studies* 14, pp. 197–219.
Déloye, Y. 2011. Citizenship. In: Badie, B., Berg-Schlosser, D. and Morlino, L. eds. *International Encyclopedia of Political Science*. Los Angeles: Sage, pp. 237–243.
van Deth, J.W. and Kreuter, F. 1998. Membership in Voluntary Associations. In: Van Deth, J. W. ed. *Comparative Politics: The Problem of Equivalence*. London: Routledge, pp. 135–155.
Deuze, M. 2002. National News Cultures: A Comparison of Dutch, German, British, Australian, and U.S. Journalists. *Journalism & Mass Communication Quarterly* 79(1), pp. 134–149.
Dimitrova, D. V. and Strömbäck, J. 2009. Look Who's Talking: Use of Sources in Newspaper Coverage in Sweden and the United States. *Journalism Practice* 3(1), pp. 75–91.
Downey, J., Mihelj, S. and König, T. 2012. Comparing Public Spheres: Normative Models and Empirical Measurements. *European Journal of Communication* 27(4), pp. 337–353.
Easton, D. 1965. *A Systems Analysis of Political Life*. New York: Wiley.
Eder, K. 2000. Zur Transformation Nationalstaatlicher Öffentlichkeit in Europa. Von der Sprachgemeinschaft zur Issuespezifischen Kommunikationsgemeinschaft. *Berliner Journal für Soziologie* 10(2), pp. 167–184.
Eder, K. and Kantner, C. 2000. Transnationale Resonanzstrukturen in Europa. Eine Kritik der Rede vom Öffentlichkeitsdefizit. In: Bach, M. ed. *Die Europäisierung Nationaler Gesellschaften*.

Opladen: Westdeutscher Verlag, pp. 306–331.
EES 2009. European Parliament Election Study 2009, Media Study Data, Advanced Release, 31/03/2010, www.piredeu.eu.
Eichenberg, R.C. and Dalton, R.J. 1993. Europeans and the European Community: The Dynamics of Public Support for European Integration. *International Organization* 47(4), pp. 507–534.
Eichenberg, R.C. and Dalton, R.J. 2007. Post-Maastricht Blues: The Transformation of Citizen Support for European Integration, 1973–2004. *Acta Politica* 42(2-3), pp. 128–152.
Eising, R. 2012. Interessenvermittlung in der Europäischen Union. In: Reutter, W. ed. *Verbände und Interessengruppen in den Ländern der Europäischen Union.* Wiesbaden: VS Verlag für Sozialwissenschaften, pp. 837–860.
Elster, J. 1997. The Market an the Forum: Three Varieties of Political Theory. In: Bohman, J. and Rehg, W. eds. *Deliberative Democracy: Essays on Reason and Politics.* Cambridge, Mass: MIT Press, pp. 3–33.
Engelstad, F. 2009. Democratic Elitism – Conflict and Consensus. *Comparative Sociology* 8(3), pp. 383–401.
Eriksen, E.O. 2004. Conceptualizing European Public Spheres: General, Segmented and Strong Publics. In: *ARENA – Centre for European Studies.*
Eriksen, E.O. 2005. An Emerging European Public Sphere. *European Journal of Social Theory* 8(3), pp. 341–363.
Eriksen, E.O. 2005. An Emerging European Public Sphere. *European Journal of Social Theory* 8(3), pp. 341–363.
Esser, F. 1999. 'Tabloidization' of News: A Comparative Analysis of Anglo-American and German Press Journalism. *European Journal of Communication* 14(3), pp. 291–324.
Etzioni, A. 1995. *The Spirit of Community: Rights, Responsibilities, and the Communitarian Agenda.* London: Fontana.
Eulau, H. and Karps, P.D. 1977. The Puzzle of Representation: Specifying Components of Responsiveness. *Legislative Studies Quaterly* 2(3), pp. 233–254.
European Commission 2007. Eurobarometer 67.1 (February-March 2007). In: *TNS Opinion & Social.* Brussels: GESIS Data Archive, Cologne. ZA4529 Data file Version 3.0.1.
European Commission 2012. Eurobarometer 78, November 2012. *TNS Opinion & Social.*
European Parliament 2014. European Parliament / Results of the 2014 European elections [Online] Available at: http://www.europarl.europa.eu/elections2014-results/en/turnout.html [Accessed: 13 April 2015].
European Parliament and Council 2004. *Directive 2004/38/EC.*
European Youth Forum 2015. About [Online] Available at: http://www.youthforum.org/european-youth-forum/ [Accessed: 14 April 2015].
Evans, J. and Ivaldi, G. 2011. Deriving a Forecast Model for European Election Turnout. *Political Research Quarterly* 65(4), pp. 855–867.
Everson, M. 1995. The Legacy of the Market Citizen. In: Shaw, J. and More, G. eds. *The New Legal Dynamics of the European Union.* Clarendon Press.
Fahrmeier, A. 2007. *Citizenship: Rise and Fall of a Modern Concept.* New Haven, London: Yale University Press.
Featherstone, K. and Radaelli, C.M. 2003. *The Politics of Europeanization.* Oxford, New York: Oxford University Press.
Ferree, M.M., Gamson, W.A., Gerhards, J. and Rucht, D. 2002a. Four Models of the Public Sphere in Modern Democracies. *Theory and Society* 31, pp. 289–325.
Ferree, M.M., Gamson, W.A., Gerhards, J. and Rucht, D. 2002b. *Shaping Abortion Discourse: Democracy and the Public Sphere in Germany and the United States.* Cambridge: Cambridge University Press.
Field, A., Miles, J. and Field, Z. 2012. *Discovering Statistics Using R.* SAGE Publications.
Firmstone, J. 2008. Approaches of the Transnational Press to Reporting Europe. *Journalism* 9(4), pp. 423–442.
Fisher, E. 2004. The European Union in the Age of Accountability. *Oxford Journal of Legal Studies*

24(3), pp. 495–515.
Fishkin, J. 2009. *When the People Speak: Deliberative Democracy and Public Consultation.* Oxford, New York: Oxford University Press.
Fishkin, J.S. 1991. *Democracy and Deliberation: New Directions for Democratic Reform.* New Haven: Yale University Press.
Fligstein, N. 2008. *Euroclash: The EU, European Identity, and the Future of Europe.* Oxford: Oxford University Press.
Follesdal, A. and Hix, S. 2006. Why There is a Democratic Deficit in the EU: A Response to Majone and Moravcsik. *JCMS: Journal of Common Market Studies* 44(3), pp. 533–562.
Franklin, M.N. 2001. How Structural Factors Cause Turnout Variations at European Parliament Elections. *European Union Politics* 2(3), pp. 309–328.
Freudenberger, M. 2013. *Bürgerdialoge in der Europäischen Union - der Weg in eine Europäische Öffentlichkeint? Eine Untersuchung am Beispiel der Europäischen Bürgerkonferenz 2009.* Berlin: LIT Verlag.
Fuchs, D. 1993. *Eine Metatheorie des demokratischen Prozesses. FS III 93-202.* Berlin: Wissenschaftszentrum Berlin für Sozialforschung.
Gabel, M. and Palmer, H.D. 1995. Understanding Variation in Public Support for European Integration. *European Journal of Political Research* 27, pp. 3–19.
Gabel, M. and Whitten, G.D. 1997. Economic Conditions, Economic Perceptions, and Public Support for European Integration. 19(1), pp. 81–96.
Gabel, M.J. 1998. Economic Integration and Mass Politics: Market Liberalization and Public Attitudes in the European Union. *American Journal of Political Science* 42(3), pp. 936–953.
Galtung, J. and Ruge, M.H. 1965. The Structure of Foreign News. *Journal of Peace Research* 2(1), pp. 64–91.
Gans, H.J. 1979. *Deciding What's News: A Study of CBS Evening News, NBC Nightly News, Newsweek, and Time.* Northwestern University Press.
Garcia-Blanco, I. and Cushion, S. 2010. A Partial Europe Without Citizens or EU-Level Political Institutions. *Journalism Studies* 11(3), pp. 393–411.
Gattermann, K. 2013. News about the European Parliament: Patterns and External Drivers of Broadsheet Coverage. *European Union Politics* 14(3), pp. 436–457.
Gerhards, J. 1993a. Europäische Öffentlichkeit durch Massenmedien? In: hrsg. im Auftr. d. Dt. Ges. für Soziologie von Bernhard Schäfers ed. *Lebensverhältnisse und Soziale Konflikte im Neuen Europa.* Opladen: Westdeutscher Verlag, pp. 558–567.
Gerhards, J. 1993b. Westeuropäische Integration und die Schwierigkeit der Entstehung einer Europäischen Öffentlichkeit. *Zeitschrift für Soziologie* 22(2), pp. 96–110.
Gerhards, J. 1997. Diskursive Versus Liberale Öffentlichkeit. Eine Empirische Auseinandersetzung mit Jürgen Habermas. *Kölner Zeitschrift für Soziologie und Sozialpsychologie* 49(1), pp. 1–34.
Gerhards, J. 1998a. Konzeptionen von Öffentlichkeit Unter Heutigen Medienbedingungen. In: Jarren, O. and Krotz, F. eds. *Öffentlichkeit Unter Viel-Kanal-Bedingungen.* Baden-Baden, Hamburg: Nomos-Verlagsgesellschaft, pp. 25–48.
Gerhards, J. 1998b. Öffentlichkeit. In: Jarren, O. ed. *Politische Kommunikation in der Mediengesellschaft: Ein Handbuch mit Lexikon.* Opladen: Westdeutscher Verlag.
Gerhards, J., Neidhardt, F. and Rucht, D. 1998. *Zwischen Palaver und Diskurs: Strukturen Öffentlicher Meinungsbildung am Beispiel der Deutschen Diskussion zur Abtreibung.* Wiesbaden: Westdeutscher Verlag.
Gerhards, J. 2000. Europäisierung von Ökonomie und Politik und die Trägheit der Entstehung einer Europäischen Öffentlichkeit. In: Bach, M. ed. *Sonderheft 40 der Kölner Zeitschrift für Soziologie und Sozialpsychologie. Die Europäisierung Nationaler Gesellschaften.* Opladen: Westdeutscher Verlag, pp. 277–305.
Gerhards, J. 2002. Das Öffentlichkeitsdefizit der EU im Horizont Normativer Öffentlichkeitstheorien. In: *Transnationale Öffentlichkeiten und Identitäten im 20. Jahrhundert.* Frankfurt: Campus Verlag, pp. 135–158.
Gerhards, J. and Neidhardt, F. 1990. *Strukturen und Funktionen moderner Öffentlichkeit.* Berlin.

References

Gerhards, J. and Neidhardt, F. 1991. Strukturen und Funktionen Modernder Öffentlichkeit: Fragestellungen und Ansätze. In: Müller-Doohm, S. and Neumann-Braun, K. eds. *Öffentlichkeit, Kultur, Massenkommunikation*. FS III 90-101. Oldenburg: Universitätsverlag, pp. 31–89.

Gerhards, J. and Neidhardt, F. 1993. Strukturen und Funktionen Moderner Öffentlichkeit. Fragestellungen und Ansätze. In: Langenbucher, W. R. ed. *Politische Kommunikation: Grundlagen, Strukturen, Prozesse*. 2nd ed. Wien: Braumüller, pp. 52–89.

Gerhards, J. and Schäfer, M.S. 2011. Normative Modelle Wissenschaftlicher Öffentlichkeit. Theoretische Systematisierung und Illustration am Fall der Humangenomforschung. In: Ruhrmann, G., Milde, J. and Zillich, A.F. eds. *Molekulare Medizin und Medien*. Wiesbaden: VS Verlag für Sozialwissenschaften, pp. 19–40.

Gibson, J.L. and Duch, R.M. 1991. Elitist Theory and Political Tolerance in Western Europe. *Political Behavior* 13(3), pp. 191–212.

Golub, J. 2000. Globalization, Sovereignty and Policy-Making: Insights from European Integration. In: Holden, B. ed. *Global Democracy. Key Debates*. London, New York: Routledge, pp. 179–201.

Grimm, D. 1995. Does Europe Need a Constitution? *European Law Journal* 1(3), pp. 282–302.

Gripsrud, J. 2007. Television and the European Public Sphere. *European Journal of Communication* 22(4), pp. 479–492.

Gutmann, A. and Thompson, D. 1996. *Why Deliberative Democracy?* Cambridge, Mass: Harvard University Press.

Habermas, J. 1974. The Public Sphere: An Encyclopedia Article (1964). *New German Critique* 3, pp. 49–55.

Habermas, J. 1976. *Legitimation Crisis*. London: Heinemann.

Habermas, J. 1990. *Strukturwandel der Öffentlichkeit. Untersuchung zu einer Kategorie der Bürgerlichen Gesellschaft*. 6th ed. Frankfurt am Main: Suhrkamp.

Habermas, J. 1991. The Public Sphere. In: Mukerji, C. and Schudson, M. eds. *Rethinking Popular Culture: Concemporary Perspectives in Cultural Studies*. Berkeley: University of Californiai Press, pp. 398–404.

Habermas, J. 1992. *Faktizität und Geltung*. Frankfurt am Main: Suhrkamp.

Habermas, J. 1997. Popular Sovereignty as a Precedure. In: Bohman, J. and Rehg, W. eds. *Deliberative Democracy: Essays on Reason and Politics*. Cambridge, Mass: MIT Press, pp. 35–65.

Habermas, J. 2001. Braucht Europa eine Verfassung? In: Habermas, J. ed. *Zeit der Übergänge: Kleine Politische Schriften IX*. Frankfurt am Main: Suhrkamp.

Habermas, J. 2003. Citizenship and National Identity: Some Reflections on the Future of Europe. In: Robertson, R. and White, K. E. eds. *Globalization: Critical Concepts in Sociology, Volume 3*. Taylor & Francis, pp. 155–174.

Habermas, J. 2004. Why Europe Needs a Constitution. In: Eriksen, E. O., Fossum, J.E. and Menéndez, A. eds. *Developing a Constitution for Europe*. London, New York: Routledge, pp. 17–33.

Habermas, J. 2006. Political Communication in Media Society: Does Democracy Still Enjoy an Epistemic Dimension? The Impact of Normative Theory on Empirical Research. *Communication Theory* 16(4), pp. 411–426.

Hague, R. and Harrop, M. 2004. *Comparative Government and Politics. An Introduction*. 6th ed. New York: Palgrave Macmillan.

Haller, M. 2008. *European Integration as an Elite Process: The Failure of a Dream?* New York: Routledge.

Haller, M. 2009. Is the European Union Legitimate? To What Extent? *International Social Science Journal* 60(196), pp. 223–234.

Hardin, R. 1999. *Liberalism, Constitutionalism, and Democracy*. New York: Clarendon Press.

Hardin, R. 2011. Liberalism. In: Badie, B., Berg-Schlosser, D. and Morlino, L. eds. *International Encyclopedia of Political Science*. Los Angeles: Sage, pp. 1428–1433.

Heater, D. 1999. *What is Citizenship?* Cambridge: Polity Press.
Heater, D.B. 2004. *A Brief History of Citizenship*. New York: New York University Press.
Held, D. 1995. *Democracy and the Global Order. From the Modern State to Cosmopolitan Governance*. Stanford: Stanford University Press.
Held, D. 1996. *Models of Democracy*. 2nd ed. Oxford: Polity Press.
Held, D. 2000. The Changing Contours of Political Community. Rethinking Democracy in the Context of Globalization. In: Holden, B. ed. *Global Democracy. Key Debates*. London, New York: Routledge, pp. 17–31.
Henjak, A., Tóka, G. and Sanders, D. 2012. Support for European Integration. In: Sanders, D., Magalhães, P.C. and Tóka, G. eds. *Citizens and the European Polity: Mass Attitudes Towards the European and National Polity*. Oxford: Oxford University Press, pp. 163–211.
Hepp, A., Brüggemann, M., Kleinen-von Königslöw, K., Lingenberg, S. and Möller, J. 2012. *Politische Diskurskulturen in Europa: Die Mehrfachsegmentieung Europäischer Öffentlichkeit*. Wiesbaden: Springer VS.
Herbert, J. 2000. *Journalism in the Digital Age: Theory and Practice for Broadcast, Print and Online Media*. Oxford: Focal Press.
Higley, J. 2011. Elites. In: Badie, B., Berg-Schlosser, D. and Morlino, L. eds. *International Encyclopedia of Political Science*. Los Angeles: Sage, pp. 759–764.
Hirst, P.Q. 1994. *Associative Democracy: New Forms of Economic and Social Governance*. Cambridge: Polity Press.
Hix, S., Noury, A. and Roland, G. 2006. Dimensions of Politics in the European Parliament. *American Journal of Political Science* 50(2), pp. 494–520.
Hix, S. and Høyland, B. 2011. *The Political System of the European Union*. 3rd ed. Basingstoke: Palgrave MacMillan.
Hix, S. and Lord, C. 1997. *Political Parties in the European Union*. Basingstoke: Macmillan Press LTD.
Holden, B. 1988. *Understanding Liberal Democracy*. Oxford: Philip Allan.
Holtz-Bacha, C. and Norris, P. 2010. 'To Entertain, Inform, and Educate': Still the Role of Public Television. *Political Communication* 18(2), pp. 123–140.
Hooghe, L. and Marks, G. 2001. *Multi-Level Governance and European Integration*. Oxford: Rowman & Littlefield.
Hooghe, L. and Marks, G. 2004. Does Identity or Economic Rationality Drive Public Opinion on European Integration? *Political Science and Politics* 37(3), pp. 415–420.
Hooghe, L. and Marks, G. 2005. Calculation, Community and Cues: Public Opinion on European Integration. *European Union Politics* 6(4), pp. 419–443.
Hooghe, M. 2008. Voluntary Associations and Socialization. In: Castiglione, D. ed. *The Handbook of Social Capital*. Oxford: Oxford University Press, pp. 568–593.
Hopmann, D.N. and Shehata, A. 2011. The Contingencies of Ordinary Citizen Appearances in Political Television News. *Journalism Practice* 5(6), pp. 657–671.
Howard, M.M. 2002. The Weakness of Postcommunist Civil Society. *Journal of Democracy* 13(1), pp. 157–169.
Hunold, C. 2011. Deliberative Policy Making. In: Badie, B., Berg-Schlosser, D. and Morlino, L. eds. *International Encyclopedia of Political Science*. Los Angeles, London: Sage, pp. 551–553.
Imig, D. and Tarrow, S. 2003. *Contentious Europeans: Protest and Politics in an Emerging Polity*. Imig, D. and Tarrow, S. eds. Lanham, Md.: Rowman & Littlefield.
Inotai, A. 2013. Macroeconomic Impacts of the 2008-2009 Crisis in Europe. In: DeBardeleben, J. and Viju, C. eds. *Economic Crisi in Europe: What it Means for the EU and Russia*. Basingstoke: Palgrave MacMillan, pp. 21–46.
Isernia, P., Fiket, I., Serriccjio, F. and Westle, B. 2012. But Still It Does Not Move: Functional and Identity-Based Determinants of European Identity. In: Sanders, D., Magalhães, P.C. and Tóka, G. eds. *Citizens anf the European Polity: Mass Attitudes Towards the European and National Polities*. Oxford: Oxford University Press, pp. 110–136.
Isin, E.F. and Turner, B.S. 2002. Citizenship Studies: An Introduction. In: Isin, E. F. and Turner, B.

S. eds. *Handbook of Citizenship Studies*. London: Sage, pp. 1–10.
Isin, E.F. and Turner, B.S. 2007. Investigating Citizenship: An Agenda for Citizenship Studies. *Citizenship Studies* 11(1), pp. 5–17.
Iyengar, S. 1991. *Is Anyone Responsible? How Television Frames Political Issues*. Chicago: University of Chicago Press.
Iyengar, S. and Simon, A. 1993. News Coverage of the Gulf Crisis and Public Opinion: A Study of Agenda-Setting, Priming, and Framing. *Communication Research* 20(3), pp. 365–383.
Jachtenfuchs, M. and Kohler-Koch, B. 2003. Regieren und Institutionenbildung. In: Jachtenfuchs, M. and Kohler-Koch, B. eds. *Europäische Integration*. 2nd ed. Opladen: Leske + Budrich, pp. 11–46.
Janoski, T. 1998. *Citizenship and Civil Society: A Framework of Rights and Obligations in Liberal, Traditional, and Social Democratic Regimes*. Cambridge: Cambridge University Press.
Janoski, T. and Gran, B. 2002. Political Citizenship: Foundations of Rights. In: Isin, E. F. and Turner, B. S. eds. *Handbook of Citizenship Studies*. London: Sage, pp. 13–52.
Just, M.R. 1996. *Crosstalk: Citizens, Candidates, and the Media in a Presidential Campaign*. Chicago: University of Chicago Press.
Kaase, M. 2011. Participation. In: Badie, B., Berg-Schlosser, D. and Morlino, L. eds. *International Encyclopedia of Political Science*. Los Angeles, London: Sage, pp. 1777–1788.
Kern, A., Marien, S. and Hooghe, M. 2015. Economic Crisis and Levels of Political Participation in Europe (2002–2010): The Role of Resources and Grievances. *West European Politics* (January), pp. 1–26.
de Keyser, J. and Raeymaeckers, K. 2012. The Printed Rise of the Common Man: How Web 2.0 Has Changed the Representation of Ordinary People in Newspapers. *Journalism Studies* 13(5-6), pp. 825–835.
Kielmansegg, P.G. 2003. Demokratie und Integration. In: Jachtenfuchs, M. and Kohler-Koch, B. eds. *Europäische Integration*. 2nd ed. Opladen: Leske + Budrich, pp. 49–76.
Kim, K. and Barnett, G.A. 1996. The Determinants of International News Flow: A Network Analysis. *Communication Research* 23(3), pp. 323–352.
Kivisto, P. and Faist, T. 2007. *Citizenship: Discourse, Theory, and Transnational Prospects*. Oxford: Blackwell.
Kleinen-von Königslöw, K. 2010. Europe for the People? The Europeanization of Public Spheres in the Tabloid Press. In: Tréfás, D. and Lucht, J. eds. *Europe on Trial. Shortcomings of the EU with Regard to Democracy, Public Sphere, and Identity*. Insbruck, Wien, Bozen: Studienverlag, pp. 44–60.
Kleinen-von Königslöw, K. 2012. Europe in Crisis? Testing the Stability and Explanatory Factors of the Europeanization of National Public Spheres. *International Communication Gazette* 74(5), pp. 443–463.
Klingemann, H.-D. 1998. Citizens and the State: A Changing Relation? In: Klingemann, H.-D. and Fuchs, D. eds. *Citizens and the State*. Oxford, New York: Oxford University Press, pp. 1–23.
Kocka, J. 2003. Zivilgesellschaft in Historischer Perspektive. *Forschungsjournal Neue Soziale Bewegungen: Konturen der Zivilgesellschaft. Zur Profilierung eines Begriffs* 16(2), pp. 29–37.
Koopmans, R. 2007. Who Inhabits the European Public Sphere? Winners and Losers, Supporters and Opponents in Europeanised Political Debates. *European Journal of Political Research* 46(2), pp. 183–210.
Koopmans, R., Erbe, J. and Meyer, M.F. 2010. The Europeanization of Public Spheres. In: Koopmans, R. and Statham, P. eds. *The Making of a European Public Sphere: Media Discourse and Political Contention*. Cambridge: Cambridge University Press, pp. 63–96.
Koopmans, R. and Erbe, J. 2004. Towards a European Public Sphere? Vertical and Horizontal Dimension of Europeanized Political Communication. *Innovation: The European Journal of Social Science Research* 17(2), pp. 97–118.
Koopmans, R. and Statham, P. 2010a. *The Making of a European Public Sphere: Media Discourse and Political Context*. Cambridge: Cambridge University Press.
Koopmans, R. and Statham, P. 2010b. Theoretical Framework, Research Design, and Method. In:

Koopmans, R. and Statham, P. eds. *The Making of a European Public Sphere: Media Discourse and Political Contention*. Cambridge: Cambridge University Press, pp. 34–59.

Körösényi, A. 2009. Beyond the Happy Consensus about Democratic Elitism. *Comparative Sociology* 8(3), pp. 364–382.

Kostakopoulou, D. 2008. *The Future Governance of Citizenship*. Cambridge: Cambridge University Press.

Kostakopoulou, T. 1998. European Union Citizenship as a Model of Citizenship Beyond the Nation State. Possibilities and Limitations. In: Weale, A. and Nentwich, M. eds. *Political Theory and the European Union. Legitimacy, Constitutional Choice and Citizenship*. London, New York: Routledge/ECPR Studies in European Political Science, pp. 157–169.

Kriesi, H. 2013a. Conclusion: An Assessment of the State of Democracy Given the Challanges of Globalization and Mediatization. In: Kriesi, H., Bochsler, D., Matthes, J., Lavenex, S., Bühlmann, M. and Esser, F. eds. *Democracy in the Age of Globalization and Mediatization*. Basingstoke: Palgrave MacMillan, pp. 202–215.

Kriesi, H. 2013b. Democracy as a Moving Target. In: Kriesi, H., Bochsler, D., Matthes, J., Lavenex, S., Bühlmann, M. and Esser, F. eds. *Democracy in the Age of Globalization and Mediatization*. Basingstoke: Palgrave Macmillan, pp. 19–43.

Kriesi, H. 2013c. Introduction - The New Challenges to Democracy. In: Kriesi, H., Bochsler, D., Matthes, J., Lavenex, S., Bühlmann, M. and Esser, F. eds. *Democracy in the Age of Globalization and Mediatization*. Basigstoke: Palgrave MacMillan, pp. 1–16.

Kuper, R. 1998. The Many Democratic Deficits of the European Union. In: Weale, A. and Nentwich, M. eds. *Political Theory and the European Union. Legitimacy, Constitutional Choice and Citizenship*. London, New York: Routledge/ECPR Studies in European Political Science, pp. 143–157.

Latzer, M. and Saurwein, F. 2006. Europäisierung durch Medien: Ansätze und Erkenntnisse der Öffentlichkeitsforschung. In: Wolfgang R. Langenbucher and Latzer, M. eds. *Europäische Öffentlichkeit und Medialer Wandel: Eine Transdisziplinäre Perspektive*. Wiesbaden: VS Verlag für Sozialwissenschaften, pp. 10–44.

Lefevere, J., de Swert, K. and Walgrave, S. 2011. Effects of Popular Exemplars in Television News. *Communication Research* 39(1), pp. 103–119.

Lewis, J., Wahl-Jorgensen, K. and Inthorn, S. 2004. Images of Citizenship on Television News: Constructing a Passive Public. *Journalism Studies* 5(2), pp. 153–164.

Lewis-Beck, M.S. and Paldam, M. 2000. Economic Voting: An Introduction. *Electoral Studies* 19(2-3), pp. 113–121.

Lightfoot, S. 2006. The Consolidation of Europarties? The 'Party Regulation' and the Development of Political Parties in the European Union. *Representation* 42(4), pp. 303–314.

Lindberg, L.N. and Scheingold, S.A. 1970. *Europe's Would-Be Polity: Patterns of Change in the European Community*. Englewood Cliffs, NJ: Prentice-Hall.

Lingenberg, S. 2006. The Audience's Role in Constituting the European Public Sphere: A Theoretical Approach Based on the Pragmatic Concept of John Dewey. In: Carpentier, N., Pruulmann-Vengerfeldt, P., Nordenstreng, K., Hartmann, M.,Vihalemm, P. and Cammaerts, B. eds. *Researching Media, Democracy and Participation*. Tartu: Tartu University Press, pp. 121–132.

Lingenberg, S. 2010. The Citizen Audience and European Transcultural Public Spheres: Exploring Civic Engagement in European Political Communication. *Communications* 35(1), pp. 45–72.

Linz, J.J. 2009. State Building and Nation Building. *European Review* 1(04), pp. 355–369.

Locke, J. 1821. *Two Treatises of Government*. London: Whitmore and Fenn, and C. Brown.

Lord, C. and Beetham, D. 2001. Legitimizing the EU: Is There a 'Post-parliamentary Basis' for its Legitimation? *Journal of Common Market Studies* 39(3), pp. 443–462.

Lord, C. and Pollack, J. 2012. Representation and Accountability: Communicating Tubes? In: Curtin, D., Mair, P. and Papadopoulos, Y. eds. *Accountability and European Governance*. London, New York: Routledge, pp. 40–60.

Maas, W. 2005. The Evolution of EU Citizenship. *Priceton Workshop on The State of the European*

Union 8.
Maas, W. 2007a. *Creating European Citizens*. Lanham: Rowman & Littfield Publishers.
Maas, W. 2007b. The Evolution of EU Citizenship. In: *Making History: European Integration and Istitutional Change at Fifty*. Oxford: Oxford University Press, pp. 231–245.
Machill, M., Beiler, M. and Fischer, C. 2006. Europe-Topics in Europe's Media. The Debate about the European Public Sphere: A Meta-Analysis of Media Content Analyses. *European Journal of Communication* 21(1), pp. 57–88.
Magnette, P. 2005. *Citizenship: The History of an Idea*. Colchester: ECPR Press.
Maier, J. and Rittberger, B. 2008. Shifting Europe's Boundaries: Mass Media, Public Opinion and the Enlargement of the EU. *European Union Politics* 9(2), pp. 243–267.
Majone, G. 1999. The Regulatory State and its Legitimacy Problems. *West European Politics* 22(1), pp. 1–24.
Maloney, W.A., van Deth, J.W. and Roßteutscher, S. 2008. Civic Orientations: Does Associational Type Matter? *Political Studies* 56(2), pp. 261–287.
Markowski, R. 2011. Responsiveness. In: Badie, B., Berg-Schlosser, D. and Morlino, L. eds. *International Encyclopedia of Political Science*. Los Angeles: Sage, pp. 2301–2306.
Marshall, T.H. 1964. *Class, Citizenship, and Social Development: Essays by T.H. Marshall. With an Introduction by Seymour Martin Lipset*. New York: Doubleday.
Marshall, T.H. 2009. Citizenship and Social Class. In: Manza, J. and Sauder, M. eds. *Inequality and Society*. New York: Norton and Co, pp. 148–154.
Martinsen, R. 2009. Öffentlichkeit in der „Mediendemokratie" aus der Perspektive Konkurrierender Demokratietheorien. In: Marcinkowski, F. and Pfetsch, B. eds. *Politik in der Mediendemokratie*. Wiesbaden: VS Verlag für Sozialwissenschaften, pp. 37–69.
Mattila, M. 2003. Why bother? Determinants of Turnout in the European Elections. *Electoral Studies* 22(3), pp. 449–468.
McLaren, L.M. 2013. Public Support for the European Union: Cost/Benefit Analysis or Perceived Cultural Threat? *The Journal of Politics* 64(2), pp. 551–566.
Medding, P.Y. 1969. 'Elitist' Democracy: An Unsuccessful Critique of a Misunderstood Theory. *The Journal of Politics* 31(3), pp. 641–654.
Meyer, C. 1999. Political Legitimacy and the Invisibility of Politics: Exploring the European Union's Communication Deficit. *Journal of Common Market Studies* 37(4), pp. 617–639.
Meyer, C.O. 2005. The Europeanization of Media Discourse: A Study of Quality Press Coverage of Economic Policy Co-ordination since Amsterdam. *Journal of Common Market Studies* 43(1), pp. 121–148.
Michailidou, A. and Trenz, H.-J. 2010. Mediati(zi)ng EU politics: Online News Coverage of the 2009 European Parliamentary Elections. *Communications* 35, pp. 327–346.
Michailidou, A. and Trenz, H.-J. 2013. Mediatized Representative Politics in the European Union: Towards Audience Democracy? *Journal of European Public Policy* 20(2), pp. 260–277.
Milbrath, L.W. 1972. *Political Participation: How and Why Do People Get Involved in Politics?* Chicago: Rand McNally & Company.
Mill, J.S. 1861. *Considerations on Representative Government*. London: Parker, Son, and Bourn, West Strand.
Mill, J.S. 1989. On Liberty. In: Collin, S. ed. *J. S. Mill: 'On Liberty' and Other Writings*. 1989th ed. Cambridge: Cambridge University Press, pp. 2–126.
Mill, J.S. 1991. *Considerations on Representative Governmet*. Amherst, N.Y.: Prometheus Books.
Milll, J. 1997. Liberty of the Press. In: Bromley, M. and O'Malley, T. eds. *A Journalism Reader*. London, New York: Routledge, pp. 16–21.
Mittag, J. and Wessels, W. 2003. The 'One' and the 'Fifteen'? The Member States Between Procedural Adaptation and Structural Revolution. In: Wessels, W., Maurer, A. and Mittag, J. eds. *Fifteen Into One?: The European Union and Its Member States*. Manchester University Press, pp. 413–454.
Moro, G. 2012. *Citizens in Europe: Civic Activism and the Community. Democratic Experiment*. New York, Heidelberg: Springer.

Mouffe, C. 2000. Deliberative Democracy or Agonistic Pluralism. *Reihe Politikwissenschaft / Political Science Series* 72.

Moy, P. and Rinke, E.M. 2012. Attitudinal and Behavioral Consequences of Published Opinion Polls. In: Holtz-Bacha, C. and Strömbäck, J. eds. *Opinion Polls and the Media: Reflecting and Shaping Public Opinion*. Basingstoke: Palgrave MacMillan, pp. 225–245.

Muir, H. 2009. In the Midst of Non-Stop Misery and Destruction, Who Are the 'Saints' of Trouser-Gate? *The Guardian*, p. 27.

Mulgan, R. 2000. 'Accountability': An Ever-Expanding Concept? *Public Administration* 78(3), pp. 555–573.

Neidhardt, F., Koopmans, R. and Pfetsch, B. 2000. Konstitutionsbedingungen Politischer Öffentlichkeit: Der Fall Europa. In: Klingemann, H.-D. ed. *Zur Zukunft der Demokratie: Herausforderungen im Zeitalter der Globalisierung*. Berlin: Ed. Sigma, pp. 263–293.

Örnebring, H. and Jönsson, A.M. 2004. Tabloid Journalism and the Public Sphere: A Historical Perspective on Tabloid Journalism. *Journalism Studies* 5(3), pp. 283–295.

Ostfeld, M. and Mutz, D. 2014. Revisiting the Effects of Case Reports in the News. *Political Communication* 31(1), pp. 53–72.

Parekh, B. 1992. The Cultural Particularity of Liberal Democracy. *Political Studies* XL(Special Issue), pp. 160–175.

Pateman, C. 1970. *Participation and Democratic Theory*. Cambridge: Cambridge University Press.

Pedersen, M.N. 1996. The Euro-Parties and European Parties: New Arenas, New Challanges and New Strategies. In: Andersen, S. S. and Eliassen, K. A. eds. *The European Union: How Democratic Is It?*. London: Sage.

Persson, T. 2009. Civil Society Participation and Accountability. In: Gustavsson, S., Karlsson, C. and Persson, T. eds. *The Illusion of Accountability in the European Union*. London: Routledge, pp. 141–154.

Peter, J., Lauf, E. and Semetko, H.A.. 2004. Television Coverage of the 1999 European Parliamentary Elections. *Political Communication* 21(4), pp. 415–433.

Peter, J. and de Vreese, C.H. 2004. In Search of Europe: A Cross-National Comparative Study of the European Union in National Television News. *The Harvard International Journal of Press/Politics* 9(4), pp. 3–24.

Peters 1994. Der Sinn von Öffentlichkeit. In: Neidhardt, F. ed. *Öffentlichkeit, Öffentliche Meinung, Soziale Bewegungen*. Opladen: Westdeutscher Verlag, pp. 42–76.

Peters, B., Sifft, S., Wimmel, A., Brüggemann, M. and Kleinen-von Königslöw, K. 2005. 7 National and Transnational Public Spheres: The Case of the EU. *European Review* 13(1), pp. 139–160.

Peters, B. 2005. Public Discourse, Identity and the Problem of Democratic Legitimacy. In: Eriksen, E. O. ed. *Making the European Polity: Reflexive Integration in the EU*. London: Routledge, pp. 84–124.

Peters, B. , Weßler, H., Sifft, S., Wimmel, A., Brüggemann, M. and Kleinen-von Königslöw, K. 2006. Die Transnationalisierung von Öffentlichkeit am Beispiel der Europäischen Union. In: Leibfried, S. and Zürn, M. eds. *Transformationen des Staates?*. Frankfurt am Main: Suhrkamp Verlag, pp. 230–261.

Peters, B. 2007. *Der Sinn von Öffentlichkeit*. Weßler, H. ed. Frankfurt am Main: Suhrkamp.

Peters, B. 2008. On Public Deliberation and Public Culture, 1993-2005. In: Wessler, H. ed. *Public Deliberation and Public Culture: The Writings of Bernhard Peters*. Basingstoke: Palgrave Macmillan, pp. 68–118.

Pfetsch, B. 2008. Agents of Transnational Debate Across Europe: The Press in Emerging European Public Sphere. *Javnost - The Public* 15(4), pp. 21–40.

Pfetsch, B. and Koopmans, R. 2006. Unter Falschem Verdacht - Massenmedien und die Europäisierung der Politischen Öffentlichkeit in Deutschland. In: Langenbucher, W. R. and Latzer, M. eds. *Europäische Öffentlichkeit und Medialer Wandel: Eine Transdisziplinäre Perspektive*. Wiesbaden: VS Verlag für Sozialwissenschaften, pp. 179–191.

Pitkin, H.F. 1967. *The Concept of Political Representation*. Berkeley and Los Angeles: University of California Press.

Pollack, M.A. 1997. Representing Diffuse Interests in EC Policy-Making. *Journal of European Public Policy* 4(4), pp. 572–590.
Pollack, M.A. and Ruhlman, M.A. 2009. The Heroic Age of European Integration is Over: Institutional and Policy Developments, 1957–2007. In: Phinnemore, D. and Warleigh-Lack, A. eds. *Reflections on European Integration. 50 Years of the Treaty of Rome*. New York: Palgrave MacMillan, pp. 43–73.
Powell, G.B. 2004. The Chain of Responsiveness. *Journal of Democracy* 15(4), pp. 91–105.
Preuß, U.K. 1996. Two Challenges to European Citizenship. *Political Studies* XLIV, pp. 534–552.
Price, V. and Roberts, D.F. 1987. Public Opinion Processes. In: *Handbook of Communication Science*. Newbury Park: Sage, pp. 781–816.
Radaelli, C.M. 2003. The Europeanization of Public Policy. In: Featherstone, K. and Radaelli, C. M. eds. *The Politics of Europeanization*. Oxford: Oxford University Press, pp. 27–56.
Raeymaeckers, K., Paulussen, S. and de Keyser, J. 2012. A Survey of Professional Journalists in Flanders (Belgium). In: Weaver, D. H. and Willnat, L. eds. *The Global Journalist in the 21st Century*. New York: Taylor & Francis, pp. 141–154.
Raunio, T. 1999. Always One Step Behind? National Legislatures and the European Union. *Government and Opposition* 34(2), pp. 180–202.
Rawls, J. 1997. The Idea of Public Reason. In: Bohman, J. and Rehg, W. eds. *Deliberative Democracy: Essays on Reason and Politics*. Cambridge, Mass: MIT Press, pp. 94–141.
Reif, K. and Schmitt, H. 1980. Nine Second-Order National Elections - A Conceptual Framework for the Analysos of European Election Results. *European Journal of Political Research* 8(1), pp. 3–44.
Reisner, B.A.E. 1992. The News Conference: How Daily Newspaper Editors Construct the Front Page. *Journalism Quaterly* 69(4), pp. 971–986.
Risse, T. 2003. The Euro Between National and European Identity. *Journal of European Public Policy* 10(4), pp. 487–505.
Rousseau, J.-J. 1994. *The Social Contract*. Oxford, New York: Oxford University Press.
Rucht, D. 1993. Parteien, Verbände und Bewegungen als Systeme Politischer Interessenvermittlung. In: Niedermayer, O. and Stöss, R. eds. *Stand und Perspektiven der Parteienforschung in Deutschland*. Opladen: Westdeutscher Verlag, pp. 251–275.
Rucht, D. 2001. Lobbying or Protest? Strategies to Influence EU Environmental Policies. In: Imig, D. R. and Tarrow, S. G. eds. *Contentious Europeans: Protest and Politics in an Emerging Polity*. Oxford: Rowman & Littlefield, pp. 125–142.
Rucht, D. 2005. Europäische Zivilgesellschaft: Akteure, Konzepte, Strategien. In: Knodt, M. and Finke, B. eds. *Europäische Zivilgesellschaft: Akteure, Konzepte, Strategien*. Wiesbaden: VS Verlag für Sozialwissenschaften, pp. 31–54.
Rucht, D. 2009. Von Zivilgesellschaft zu Zivilität: Konzeptuelle Überlegungen und Möglichkeiten der Empirischen Analyse. In: Frantz, C. and Holger Kolb eds. *Transnationale Zivilgesellschaft in Europa: Traditionen, Muster, Hindernisse, Chancen*. Münster: Waxmann, pp. 75–102.
Rumford, C. 2003. European Civil Society or Transnational Social Space?: Conceptions of Society in Discourses of EU Citizenship, Governance and the Democratic Deficit: an Emerging Agenda. *European Journal of Social Theory* 6(1), pp. 25–43.
Ruzza, C. 2004. *Europe and Civil Society: Movement Coalitions and European Governance*. Manchester: Manchester University Press.
Safran, W. 1997. Citizenship and Nationality in Democratic Systems: Approaches to Defining and Acquiring Membership in the Political Community. *International Political Science Review* 18(3), pp. 313–335.
Sanders, D., Magalhães, P.C. and Tóka, G. 2012. *Citizens and the European Polity*. Oxford: Oxford University Press.
Saward, M. 2013. The Dynamics of European Citizenship: Enactment, Extension and Assertion. *Comparative European Politics* 11(1), pp. 49–69.
Scharpf, F.W. 1999. *Regieren in Europa: Effektiv und demokratisch?* Frankfurt: Campus Verlag.
Schlesinger, P. 1999. Changing Spaces of Political Communication: The Case of the European

Union. *Political Communication* 16(3), pp. 263–279.
Schlesinger, P. and Kevin, D. 2000. Can the European Union Become a Sphere of Publics? In: Eriksen, E. O. and Fossum, J. E. eds. *Democracy in the European Union: Integration Through Deliberation?*. London, New York: Routledge, pp. 206–229.
Schmidt, V.A. 2006. *Democracy in Europe: The EU and National Polities*. Oxford, New York: Oxford University Press.
Schmitt-Beck, R. and Farrell, D.M. 2002. Studying Political Campaigns and Their Effects. In: Farrell, D. M. and Schmitt-Beck, R. eds. *Do Political Campaigns Matter? Campaign Effects in Elections and Referendums*. London, New York: Routledge, pp. 1–21.
Schuck, A.R.. and de Vreese, C.H. 2011. Finding Europe: Mapping and Explaining Antecedents of 'Europeanness' in News about the 2009 European Parliamentary Elections. *Studies in Communication / Media (SCM)* 1(2), pp. 267–294.
Schuck, A.R.T., Xezonakis, G., Banducci, S.A. and de Vreese, C.H. 2010. *European Parliament Election Study 2009, Media Study*. Cologne.
Schuck, A.R.T., Azrout, R., Boomgaarden, H.G., Elenbaas, M., van Spanje, J., Vliegenthart, R. and de Vreese, C.H. 2011. Media Visibility and Framing of the European Parliament Election 2009: A Media Content Analysisin 27 Countries. In: Maier, M., Strömbäck, J. and Kaid, L.L. eds. *Political Communication in European Parliamentary Elections*. Farnham: Ashgate, pp. 175–196.
Schuck, A.R.T., Xezonakis, G., Elenbaas, M. and Banducci, S.A. 2011. Party Contestation and Europe on the News Agenda: The 2009 European Parliamentary Elections. *Electoral Studies* 30(1), pp. 41–52.
Schuck, A.R.T., Vliegenthart, R., Boomgaarden, H.G., Elenbaas, M., Azrout, R., van Spanje, J. and de Vreese, C.H.. 2013. Explaining Campaign News Coverage: How Medium, Time, and Context Explain Variation in the Media Framing of the 2009 European Parliamentary Elections. *Journal of Political Marketing* 12(1), pp. 8–28.
Schuck, P.H. 2000. Citizenship in Federal Systems. *The American Journal of Comparative Law* 48(2), pp. 195–226.
Schumpeter, J.A. 1943. *Capitalism, Socialism and Democracy*. 5th ed. London, New York: Routledge.
Semetko, H.A. and Valkenburg, P.M. 2000. Framing European Politics: A Content Analysis of Press and Television News. *Journal of Communication* 50(2), pp. 93–109.
Sifft, S., Brüggemann, M., Kleinen-von Königslöw, K., Peters, B. and Wimmel, A. 2007. Segmented Europeanization: Exploring the Legitimacy of the European Union from a Public Discourse Perspective. *Journal of Common Market Studies* 45(1), pp. 127–155.
Sigalas, E. 2010. Cross-Border Mobility and European Identity: The Eeffectiveness of Intergroup Contact During the ERASMUS Year Abroad. *European Union Politics* 11(2), pp. 241–265.
Smith, R.M. 2002. Modern Citizenship. In: Isin, E. F. and Turner, B. S. eds. *Handbook of Citizenship Studies*. London: Sage, pp. 105–116.
Sniderman, P.M., Fletcher, J.F., Russell, P.H., Tetlock, P.E. and Gaines, B.J. 1991. The Fallacy of Democratic Elitism: Elite Competition and Commitment to Civil Liberties. *British Journal of Political Science* 21(3), pp. 349–370.
Sparks, C. 2000. Introduction: The Panic over Tabloid News. In: Sparks, C. and Tulloch, J. eds. *Tabloid Tales: Global Debates Over Media Standards*. Oxford: Rowman & Littfield Publishers, pp. 1–40.
Splichal, S. 2006. In Search of a Strong European Public Sphere: Some Critical Observations on Conceptualizations of Publicness and the (European) Public Sphere. *Media, Culture & Society* 28(5), pp. 695–714.
Statham, P. 2007. Political Communication, European Integration and the Transformation of National Public Spheres: A Comparison of Britain and France. In: Fossum, J. E. and Schlesinger, P. eds. *The European Union and the Public Sphere: A Communicative Space in the Making?*. London: Routledge, pp. 110–134.
Statham, P. 2008. Making Europe News: How Journalists View Their Role and Media Performance.

Journalism 9(4), pp. 398–422.
Statham, P. 2010. What kind of Europeanized Public Politics? In: Koopmans, R. and Statham, P. eds. *The Making of a European Public Sphere: Media Discourse and Political Contention*. Cambridge: Campus Verlag, pp. 277–306.
van de Steeg, M. 2002. Rethinking the Conditions for a Public Sphere in the European Union. *European Journal of Social Theory* 5(4), pp. 499–519.
Steinberger, J. 1978. *Locke, Rousseau, and the Idea of Consent: An Inquiry into the Liberal Democratic Theory of Political Obligation*. Westport: Greenwood Press.
Steinbrecher, M. and Rattinger, H. 2012. Electoral Turnout at National and European Levels. In: *Citizens anf the European Polity: Mass Attitudes Towards the European and National Polities*. Oxford: Oxford University Press, pp. 88–109.
Strohmeier, G. 2007. Die EU zwischen Legitimität und Effektivität. *Aus Politik und Zeitgeschichte* 10, pp. 24–30.
Taylor, D. 1989. Citizenship and Social Power. *Critical Social Policy* 9(26), pp. 19–31.
Taylor, M. 2009. Party of Mavericks Believe They Can Push Labour into Fourth Place. *The Guardian*, p. 7.
Tenscher, J. and Maier, M. 2009. European Parliamentary Elections 2004: Studies on Political Campaigning and Media Framing of a Second-Order Event. *Journal of Political Marketing* 8(1), pp. 1–6.
Teorell, J. 2006. Political Participation andThree Theories of Democracy: A Research Inventory and Agenda. *European Journal of Political Research* 45(5), pp. 787–810.
Thomassen, J. and Schmitt, H. 1999. Introduction: Political Representation and Legitimacy in the European Union. In: Schmitt, H. and Thomassen, J. eds. *Political Representation and Legitimacy in the European Union*. Oxford: Oxford University Press, pp. 3–22.
Thompson, J.B. 1995. *The Media and Modernity: A Social Theory of the Media*. Cambridge: Polity Press.
Thorhallsson, B. 2006. The Size of States in the European Union: Theoretical and Conceptual Perspectives. *Journal of European Integration* 28(1), pp. 7–31.
Tindemans, L. 1976. *European Union, Report to the Council. Tindemans' Report. Bulletin EC 1/76*.
Traynor, I. 2009. Anti-Immigrant and Europhobic - Far Right Parties Ride Populist Wave: From Portugal to Poland, Disillusionment with Brussels and a Record Low Turnout Could Give Extremists a Breakthrough. *The Guardian*, p. 14.
Trenz, H.-J. 2004. Media Coverage on European Governance: Exploring the European Public Sphere in National Quality Newspapers. *European Journal of Communication* 19(3), pp. 291–319.
Trenz, H.-J. and Eder, K. 2004. The Democratizing Dynamics of a European Public Sphere: Towards a Theory of Democratic Functionalism. *European Journal of Social Theory* 7(1), pp. 5–25.
Turner, B.S. 1990. Outline of a Theory of Citizenship. *Sociology* 24(2), pp. 189–217.
Turner, B.S. 1993. Contemporary Problems in the Theory of Citizenship. In: Turner, B. S. ed. *Citizenship and Social Theory*. London: Sage, pp. 1–18.
Vetters, R., Jentges, E. and Trenz, H.-J. 2009. Whose Project is it? Media Debates on the Ratification of the EU Constitutional Treaty. *Journal of European Public Policy* 16(3), pp. 412–430.
de Vreese, C.H. 2001. 'Europe' in the News: A Cross-National Comparative Study of the News Coverage of Key EU Events. *European Union Politics* 2(3), pp. 283–307.
de Vreese, C.H. 2003. *Framing Europe: Television News and European Integration*. Amsterdam: Het Spinhuis.
de Vreese, C.H. 2004. Primed by the Euro: The Impact of a Referendum Campaign on Public Opinion and Evaluations of Government and Political Leaders. *Scandinavian Political Studies* 27(1), pp. 45–64.
de Vreese, C.H., Banducci, S.A., Semetko, H.A. and Boomgaarden, H.G. 2006. The News Coverage of the 2004 European Parliamentary Election Campaign in 25 Countries. *European Union*

Politics 7(4), pp. 477–504.
de Vreese, C.H. 2007. The EU as a Public Sphere. *Living Reviews in European Governance* 2(3 [Online Article]).
de Vreese, C.H. and Boomgaarden, H.G. 2006. Media Effects on Public Opinion about the Enlargement of the European Union. *Journal of Common Market Studies* 44(2), pp. 419–436.
de Vreese, C.H. and Semetko, H.A. 2002. Public Perception on Polls and Support for Restrictions on the Publication of Polls: Denmark's 2000 Euro Referendum. *International Journal of Public Opinion Research* 14(4), pp. 367–390.
de Vreese, C.H. and Semetko, H.A. 2004. News Matters : Influences on the Vote in the Danish 2000 Euro Referendum Campaign. *European Journal of Political Research* 43(5), pp. 699–722.
Walker, J.L. 1966. A Critique of the Elitist Theory of Democracy. *The American Political Science Review* 60(2), pp. 285–295.
Wallace, H. 2009. Some Reflections on 50 Years of Experience since the Signature of the Treaties of Rome. In: Phinnemore, D. and Warleigh-Lack, A. eds. *Reflections on European Integration. 50 Years of the Treaty of Rome.* New York: Palgrave MacMillan, pp. 11–21.
Walter, S. Forthcoming. A Network Perspective on European Union News: Explaining Relationships of Horizontal Reporting across EU Member States. *Mass Communication and Society*.
Walzer, M. 1989. Citizenship. In: Ball, T. ed. *Political Innovation and Conceptual Change.* Cambridge: Cambridge University Press, pp. 211–219.
Walzer, M. 1990. The Communitarian Critique of Liberalism. *Political Theory* 18(1), pp. 6–23.
Walzer, M. 1994. *Thick and Thin: Moral Argument at Home and Abroad.* Notre Dame: University of Notre Dame Press.
Ward, D. 2004. *The European Union Democratic Deficit and the Public Sphere: An Evaluation of EU Media Policy.* Amsterdam: IOS Press.
Warren, M. 1992. Democratic Theory and Self-Transformation. *The American Political Science Review* 86(1), pp. 8–23.
Warren, M.E. 2002. What Can Democratic Participation Mean Today? *Political Theory* 30(5), pp. 677–701.
Warren, M.E. 2004. What Can Democratic Participation Mean Today? In: Laycock, D. ed. *Representation and Democratic Theory.* Vancouver: UBC Press, pp. 197–219.
Weber, M. 1968. *Economy and Society: An Outline of Interpretive Sociology.* 2. Roth, G. ed. New York: Bedminster Press.
Weber, M. 2011. Objectivity in Social Science and Social Policy. In: Shils, E. A. and Finch, H. A. eds. *Methodology of Social Sciences.* News Brunswick: Transaction Publishers, pp. 49–112.
Weiler, J.H.H. 1997. To Be a European Citizen - Eros and Civilization. *Journal of European Public Policy* 4(4), pp. 495–519.
Welzel, C., Inglehart, R. and Deutsch, F. 2005. Social Capital, Voluntary Associations and Collective Action: Which Aspects of Social Capital Have the Greatest 'Civic' Payoff? *Journal of Civil Society* 1(2), pp. 121–146.
Wessler, H. 2007. Politische Öffentlichkeit Jenseits des Nationalstaats? In: Jarren, O., Lachenmeier, D. and Steiner, A. eds. *Entgrenzte Demokratie? Herausforderungen für die Politische Interessenvermittlung.* Baden-Baden: Nomos, pp. 49–71.
Wessler, H., Peters, B., Brüggemann, M., Kleinen-von Königslöw, K. and Sifft, S. 2008. *Transnationalization of Public Spheres.* Houndmills, Baskingstoke, Hampshire: Palgrave MacMillan.
Wessler, H. 2008. *Transnationalization of Public Spheres.* Basingstoke, Hampshire: Palgrave MacMillan.
Wessler, H. and Rinke, E.M. 2013. Öffentlichkeit. In: Mau, S. and Schöneck, N. M. eds. *Handwörterbuch zur Gesellschaft Deutschlands.* 3rd ed. Wiesbaden: Springer VS, pp. 637–650.
Wessler, H. and Rinke, E.M. 2014. Deliberative Performance of Television News in Three Types of Democracy: Insights From the U.S., Germany, and Russia. *Journal of Communication* 64(5), pp. 827–851.

Wiener, A. 1998. *'European' Citizenship Practice: Building Institutions of a Non-State*. Boulder, Colo: Westview Press.
Wilke, J., Heimprecht, C. and Cohen, A. 2012. The geography of foreign news on television: A comparative study of 17 countries. *International Communication Gazette* 74(4), pp. 301–322.
Wilke, J. and Reinemann, C. 2007. Invisible Second-Order Campaigns? A Longitudinal Study of the Coverage of the European Parliamentary Elections 1979–2004 in Four German Quality Newspapers. *Communications* 32(3), pp. 299–322.
Wimmel, A. 2005. Transnationale Diskurse in der europäischen Medienöffentlichkeit: Die Debatte zum EU-Beitritt der Türkei. *Politische Vierteljahresschrift* 46(3), pp. 459–483.
Wonka, A., Baumgartner, F.R., Mahoney, C. and Berkhout, J. 2010. Measuring the Size and Scope of the EU Interest Group Population. *European Union Politics* 11(3), pp. 463–476.
Wu, D.H. 2003. Homogeneity Around the World? Comparing the Systemic Determinants of International News Flow between Developed and Developing Countries. *Gazette: The International Journal for Communication Studies* 65(1), pp. 9–24.
Wu, H.D. 1998. Investigating the Determinants pf International News Flow: A Meta-Analysis. *International Communication Gazette* 60(6), pp. 493–512.
Wu, H.D. 2000. Systemic Determinants of International News Coverage: A Comparison of 38 Countries. *Journal of Communication* 50(2), pp. 110–130.
Yuval-Davis, N. 1999. The 'Multi-Layered Citizen'. *International Feminist Journal of Politics* 1(1), pp. 119–136.
Zaller, J. 2003. A New Standard of News Quality: Burglar Alarms for the Monitorial Citizen. *Political Communication* 20(2), pp. 109–130.

Appendix I Classification of Media Outlets

Media outlet	Classification
Austria: Der Standard	Quality media
Austria: Die Presse	Quality media
Austria: Neue Kronen Zeitung	Commercial media
Austria: ZiB 19.30 (ORF1)	Quality media
Austria: Aktuell 19.20 (ATV)	Commercial media
Belgium: De Morgen	Quality media
Belgium: De Standard	Quality media
Belgium: Het Laatste Nieuws	Commercial media
Belgium: La Derniere Heure	Commercial media
Belgium: La Libre Belgique	Quality media
Belgium: Le Soir	Quality media
Belgium: Het Journaal 19.00 (VRT)	Quality media
Belgium: VTM-Nieuws 19.00 (VTM)	Commercial media
Belgium: JT Meteo 19.30 (La Une)	Quality media
Belgium: Le Journal 19.00 (RTL-TV)	Commercial media
Bulgaria: 24 Chasa	Commercial media
Bulgaria: Dnevnik	Quality media
Bulgaria: Trud	Quality media
Bulgaria: bTV 19:00 (bTV)	Commercial media
Bulgaria: 20:00 (BNT kanal 1)	Quality media
Cyprus: Fileleytheros	Quality media
Cyprus: Haravgi	Quality media
Cyprus: Simerini	Quality media
Cyprus: 20.00 (RIK1)	Quality media
Cyprus: Ant1 20.15 (Antenna)	Commercial media
Czech. Rep.: Blesk	Commercial media
Czech. Rep.: Mlada Fronta	Quality media
Czech. Rep.: Pravo	Quality media
Czech Republic: Udalosti 19.00 (Ceska televize)	Quality media
Czech Republic: Televizni noviny 19.30 (TV Nova)	Commercial media
Denmark: Ekstra Bladet	Commercial media
Denmark: Morgenavisen Jyllandsp.	Quality media
Denmark: Politiken	Quality media
Denmark: Nyhederne 19.00 (TV2)	Commercial media
Denmark: TV-avisen 21.00 (DR 1)	Quality media
Estonia: Eesti Ekspress Wochenblatt	Quality media
Estonia: Postimees	Quality media
Estonia: SL Öhtuleht	Commercial media
Estonia: Aktuaalne kaamera 21.00 (ETV)	Quality media
Estonia: Reporter 19.00 (Kanal2)	Commercial media
Finland: Aamulehti	Quality media
Finland: Helsingin Sanomat	Quality media
Finland: Iltasanomat	Commercial media
Finland: Tv-uutiset ja sää 20.30 (YLE TV1)	Quality media
Finland: Kymmenen uutiset 22:00 (MTV3)	Commercial media
France: Le Figaro	Quality media
France: Le Monde	Quality media
France: Libération	Quality media
France : Le Journal 20.00 (TF1)	Quality media

France : Le Journal 20.00 (F2) — Commercial media
Germany: Bild — Commercial media
Germany: FAZ — Quality media
Germany: SZ — Quality media
Germany: Tagesschau 20.00 (ARD) — Quality media
Germany: Heute 19.00 (ZDF) — Quality media
Germany: RTL aktuell 18.45 (RTL) — Commercial media
Germany: 18.30 (SAT1) — Commercial media
Greece: Eleftherotypia — Quality media
Greece: Kathimerini — Quality media
Greece: Ta Nea — Quality media
Greece: 20.00 (Mega) — Commercial media
Greece: (21.00) — Quality media
Hungary: Blikk — Commercial media
Hungary: Magyar Nemzet — Quality media
Hungary: Nepszabadsag — Quality media
Hungary: Hírádó 20:30 (M2) — Quality media
Hungary: Esti Híradó 18:30 (RTL Klub) — Commercial media
Ireland: Irish Independent — Quality media
Ireland: The Irish Times — Quality media
Ireland: The (Daily) Star — Commercial media
Ireland: Nine News 21.00 (RTEI1) — Quality media
Ireland: TV3 News 17:30 (TV3) — Commercial media
Italy: Il Corriere della Sera — Quality media
Italy: Il Giornale — Quality media
Italy: La Repubblica — Quality media
Italy: TG1 20.00 (RaiUno) — Quality media
Italy: TG5 20.00 (Canale5) — Commercial media
Latvia: Diena — Quality media
Latvia: Latvijas Avize — Commercial media
Latvia: Vesti segodnya — Quality media
Latvia: Panor?mas 20:30 (LTV) — Quality media
Latvia: T Zi?as 20:00 (LNT) — Commercial media
Lithuania: Lietuvos rytas — Quality media
Lithuania: Respublika — Quality media
Lithuania: Vakaro zinios — Commercial media
Lithuania: Panorama 20.30 (LTV) — Quality media
Lithuania: TV3 inios 18.45 (TV3) — Commercial media
Luxembourg: Tageblatt — Quality media
Luxembourg: Voix du Luxembourg — Quality media
Luxembourg: Wort (D) — Quality media
Luxembourg: De Journal 19.30 (RTL) — Commercial media
Malta: Nazzjon — Quality media
Malta: Orizzont — Quality media
Malta: The Times (engl.) — Quality media
Malta: L-A?barijiet TVM 20.00 (TVM) — Quality media
Malta: One News 19.30 (One TV) — Commercial media
NET — Commercial media
Netherlands: De Telegraaf — Commercial media
Netherlands: De Volkskrant — Quality media
Netherlands: NRC Handelsblad — Quality media
Netherlands: RTL Nieuws 19.30 (RTL) — Commercial media
Netherlands: NOS Journaal 20.00 — Quality media

Poland: Fakt	Commercial media
Poland: Gazeta Wyborcza	Quality media
Poland: Rzeczpospolita	Quality media
Poland: Wiadomo?ci 19:30 (TVP1)	Quality media
Poland: FAKTY 19:00 (TVN)	Commercial media
Portugal: Correio da Manha	Commercial media
Portugal: Jornal de Notícias	Quality media
Portugal: Publico	Quality media
Portugal: Telejornal 20:00 (RTP1)	Quality media
Portugal: Jornal Nacional (20:00) (TVI)	Commercial media
Romania: Evenimentul Zilei	Quality media
Romania: Jurnalul National	Quality media
Romania: Libertatea	Commercial media
Romania: Telejurnal 20:00 (TVR1)	Quality media
Romania: Stirile 19.00 (Pro TV)	Commercial media
Slovakia: Daily Pravda	Quality media
Slovakia: Nový cas	Commercial media
Slovakia: Sme/Práca	Quality media
Slovakia: Spravy 19:30 (STV 1)	Quality media
Slovakia: Televizne Noviny 19:00 (TV Markiza)	Commercial media
Slovenia: Dnevnik	Quality media
Slovenia: Slovenske Novice	Commercial media
Slovenia: The Delo	Quality media
Slovenia: Dnevnik 19.00 (TV S1)	Quality media
Slovenia: 24UR 19.00 (POP TV)	Commercial media
Spain: ABC	Quality media
Spain: El Mundo	Commercial media
Spain: El Pais	Quality media
Spain: Telediario-2 21.00 (TVE1)	Quality media
Spain: Telecinco 20.30 (Tele5)	Commercial media
Spain: Noticias2 21.00 (Antena3)	Commercial media
Sweden: Aftonbladet	Commercial media
Sweden: Dagens Nyheter	Quality media
Sweden: Svenska Dagbladet	Quality media
Sweden: Rapport 19.30 (TV2)	Quality media
Sweden: Nyheterna 18.25 (TV4)	Commercial media
UK: Daily Telegraph	Quality media
UK: Guardian	Quality media
UK: Sun	Commercial media
UK: BBC1 News at 10	Quality media
UK: ITV News at 10	Commercial media

Appendix II Tables for Results in Chapter 8

Table 8.4 Horizontal and vertical actor structure (news story level)

Actor Group	Percentage	Difference to grand mean	T	Sig.
Horizontal				
Governmental actors	57.41	-27.96	n.a.	n.a.
Political parties	32.61	-1.35	n.a.	n.a.
Formal civil society	7.11	-1.56	n.a.	n.a.
Informal civil society	4.4	-0.78	n.a.	n.a.
Citizens	19.81	-4.07	n.a.	n.a.
Vertical				
Governmental actors	52.45	-32.92	n.a.	n.a.
Political parties	2.38	-31.58	n.a.	n.a.
Formal civil society	1.81	-6.86	n.a.	n.a.
Informal civil society	0.8	-4.38	n.a.	n.a.
Citizens	4.82	-19.06	n.a.	n.a.

Table 8.5 Horizontal and vertical actor structure (actor level)

Actor Group	Percentage	Difference to grand mean	Chi^2	Sig.
Horizontal				
Governmental actors	52.71	-11.05	779.50	0.000
Political parties	27.52	7.61	504.07	0.000
Formal civil society	4.92	0.82	24.40	0.000
Informal civil society	2.67	0.52	18.25	0.000
Citizens	12.18	2.10	69.61	0.000
Vertical				
Governmental actors	87.68	23.92	2461.80	0.000
Political parties	3.43	-16.48	1846.14	0.000
Formal civil society	2.33	-1.77	81.00	0.000
Informal civil society	1.02	-1.13	63.34	0.000
Citizens	5.54	-4.54	229.71	0.000

Table 8.6 Overall actor structure by EU member state (news story level)

Country	Actor group	Percentage	Difference to grand mean	T	Sig.
Austria	Governmental actors	83.36	-2.01	-1.36	0.176
	Political parties	35.18	1.22	0.64	0.521
	Formal civil society	10.46	1.79	1.47	0.143
	Informal civil society	6.18	1.00	1.04	0.297
	Citizens	17.43	-6.45	-4.27	0.000
Belgium	Governmental actors	77.26	-8.11	-4.11	0.000
	Political parties	22.74	-11.22	-5.69	0.000
	Formal civil society	16.56	7.89	4.51	0.000
	Informal civil society	3.09	-2.09	-2.57	0.011
	Citizens	28.92	5.04	2.36	0.019
Bulgaria	Governmental actors	85.21	-0.16	-0.12	0.908
	Political parties	30.89	-3.07	-1.73	0.083
	Formal civil society	12.30	3.63	2.89	0.004
	Informal civil society	4.98	-0.20	-0.24	0.808
	Citizens	19.18	-4.70	-3.12	0.002
Cyprus	Governmental actors	85.48	0.11	0.11	0.911
	Political parties	42.74	8.78	6.23	0.000
	Formal civil society	7.46	-1.21	-1.61	0.107
	Informal civil society	1.62	-3.56	-9.89	0.000
	Citizens	32.52	8.64	6.48	0.000
Czech Rep	Governmental actors	81.02	-4.35	-1.29	0.198
	Political parties	33.58	-0.38	-0.1	0.925
	Formal civil society	2.19	-6.48	-5.16	0.000
	Informal civil society	2.92	-2.26	-1.57	0.120
	Citizens	32.12	8.24	2.06	0.042
Denmark	Governmental actors	93.63	8.26	5.98	0.000
	Political parties	32.80	-1.16	-0.44	0.663
	Formal civil society	6.05	-2.62	-1.94	0.053
	Informal civil society	7.96	2.78	1.82	0.070
	Citizens	34.08	10.20	3.81	0.000
Estonia	Governmental actors	80.87	-4.50	-1.22	0.224
	Political parties	30.43	-3.53	-0.82	0.415
	Formal civil society	9.57	0.90	0.33	0.746
	Informal civil society	13.04	7.86	2.49	0.014
	Citizens	37.39	13.51	2.98	0.004
Finland	Governmental actors	85.48	0.11	0.06	0.955
	Political parties	22.90	-11.06	-4.63	0.000
	Formal civil society	7.74	-0.93	-0.61	0.542
	Informal civil society	6.45	1.27	0.91	0.364

	Citizens	43.55	19.67	6.97	0.000
France	Governmental actors	80.27	-5.10	-3.30	0.001
	Political parties	45.63	11.67	6.03	0.000
	Formal civil society	8.28	-0.39	-0.36	0.718
	Informal civil society	7.68	2.50	2.42	0.016
	Citizens	23.19	-0.69	-0.42	0.675
Germany	Governmental actors	84.8	-0.57	-0.29	0.775
	Political parties	17.33	-16.63	-7.96	0.000
	Formal civil society	12.46	3.79	2.08	0.038
	Informal civil society	7.60	2.42	1.65	0.099
	Citizens	12.16	-11.72	-6.5	0.000
Greece	Governmental actors	83.67	-1.70	-1.76	0.079
	Political parties	46.05	12.09	9.26	0.000
	Formal civil society	5.63	-3.04	-5.04	0.000
	Informal civil society	2.88	-2.30	-5.24	0.000
	Citizens	23.47	-0.41	-0.37	0.714
Hungary	Governmental actors	82.89	-2.48	-1.27	0.204
	Political parties	37.97	4.01	1.6	0.112
	Formal civil society	9.09	0.42	0.28	0.778
	Informal civil society	4.81	-0.37	-0.33	0.741
	Citizens	20.32	-3.56	-1.71	0.088
Ireland	Governmental actors	88.17	2.80	1.59	0.113
	Political parties	35.5	1.54	0.59	0.554
	Formal civil society	7.10	-1.57	-1.12	0.263
	Informal civil society	5.92	0.74	0.57	0.567
	Citizens	20.71	-3.17	-1.44	0.152
Italy	Governmental actors	81.51	-3.86	-1.08	0.283
	Political parties	33.61	-0.35	-0.08	0.937
	Formal civil society	3.36	-5.31	-3.20	0.002
	Informal civil society	2.52	-2.66	-1.84	0.068
	Citizens	10.08	-13.80	-4.98	0.000
Latvia	Governmental actors	93.89	8.52	6.26	0.000
	Political parties	23.15	-10.81	-4.51	0.000
	Formal civil society	13.83	5.16	2.63	0.009
	Informal civil society	10.93	5.75	3.25	0.001
	Citizens	40.19	16.31	5.86	0.000
Lithuania	Governmental actors	88.79	3.42	1.16	0.247
	Political parties	3.45	-30.51	-17.93	0.000
	Formal civil society	6.90	-1.77	-0.75	0.454
	Informal civil society	2.59	-2.59	-1.75	0.082
	Citizens	12.07	-11.81	-3.89	0.000
Luxembourg	Governmental actors	92.76	7.39	5.99	0.000

	Political parties	24.66	-9.3	-4.53	0.000
	Formal civil society	11.09	2.42	1.62	0.107
	Informal civil society	4.75	-0.43	-0.42	0.672
	Citizens	20.14	-3.74	-1.96	0.051
Malta	Governmental actors	78.36	-7.01	-4.83	0.000
	Political parties	27.49	-6.47	-4.11	0.000
	Formal civil society	5.97	-2.70	-3.23	0.001
	Informal civil society	1.49	-3.69	-8.62	0.000
	Citizens	15.55	-8.33	-6.52	0.000
Netherlands	Governmental actors	91.48	6.11	4.37	0.000
	Political parties	26.32	-7.64	-3.46	0.001
	Formal civil society	10.53	1.86	1.21	0.228
	Informal civil society	7.52	2.34	1.77	0.078
	Citizens	27.57	3.69	1.65	0.100
Poland	Governmental actors	82.27	-3.10	-1.95	0.051
	Political parties	29.95	-4.01	-2.11	0.035
	Formal civil society	9.12	0.45	0.38	0.705
	Informal civil society	13.77	8.59	6.00	0.000
	Citizens	13.77	-10.11	-7.07	0.000
Portugal	Governmental actors	90.74	5.37	4.51	0.000
	Political parties	36.36	2.40	1.22	0.224
	Formal civil society	9.09	0.42	0.36	0.722
	Informal civil society	3.37	-1.81	-2.45	0.015
	Citizens	22.39	-1.49	-0.87	0.385
Romania	Governmental actors	90.43	5.06	2.35	0.020
	Political parties	15.96	-18.00	-6.72	0.000
	Formal civil society	4.26	-4.41	-2.99	0.003
	Informal civil society	1.60	-3.58	-3.91	0.000
	Citizens	40.43	16.55	4.61	0.000
Slovakia	Governmental actors	89.57	4.20	1.99	0.048
	Political parties	25.12	-8.84	-2.95	0.003
	Formal civil society	4.74	-3.93	-2.68	0.008
	Informal civil society	7.11	1.93	1.09	0.278
	Citizens	30.33	6.45	2.03	0.043
Slovenia	Governmental actors	89.73	4.36	3.46	0.001
	Political parties	20.03	-13.93	-8.40	0.000
	Formal civil society	9.93	1.26	1.02	0.309
	Informal civil society	7.88	2.70	2.42	0.016
	Citizens	19.52	-4.36	-2.66	0.008
Spain	Governmental actors	90.39	5.02	4.66	0.000
	Political parties	48.06	14.10	7.72	0.000
	Formal civil society	7.88	-0.79	-0.81	0.421

Appendix II

	Informal civil society	3.47	-1.71	-2.55	0.011
	Citizens	22.30	-1.58	-1.04	0.298
Sweden	Governmental actors	81.5	-3.87	-2.27	0.024
	Political parties	31.21	-2.75	-1.35	0.178
	Formal civil society	8.09	-0.58	-0.48	0.630
	Informal civil society	6.55	1.37	1.26	0.208
	Citizens	24.47	0.59	0.31	0.755
UK	Governmental actors	81.54	-3.83	-1.38	0.171
	Political parties	46.15	12.19	3.41	0.001
	Formal civil society	13.33	4.66	1.91	0.058
	Informal civil society	5.64	0.46	0.28	0.781
	Citizens	24.62	0.74	0.24	0.812

Table 8.7 Overall actor structure by EU member state (actor level)

Country	Actor group	Percentage	Difference to grand mean	Chi^2	Sig.
Austria	Governmental actors	63.30	-0.46	0.15	0.698
	Political parties	21.44	1.53	2.00	0.117
	Formal civil society	5.10	1.00	4.00	0.038
	Informal civil society	2.55	0.40	2.00	0.156
	Citizens	7.60	-2.48	12.00	0.000
Belgium	Governmental actors	60.77	-2.99	4.00	0.035
	Political parties	15.34	-4.57	15.00	0.000
	Formal civil society	8.97	4.87	67.00	0.000
	Informal civil society	1.68	-0.47	0.85	0.357
	Citizens	13.24	3.16	12.63	0.000
Bulgaria	Governmental actors	62.67	-1.09	1.00	0.318
	Political parties	20.38	0.47	0.27	0.605
	Formal civil society	5.78	1.68	14.00	0.000
	Informal civil society	2.06	-0.09	0.00	1.000
	Citizens	9.11	-0.97	2.00	0.155
Cyprus	Governmental actors	59.76	-4.00	24.00	0.000
	Political parties	24.19	4.28	39.00	0.000
	Formal civil society	3.33	-0.77	5.00	0.022
	Informal civil society	0.52	-1.63	43.00	0.000
	Citizens	12.2	2.12	17.00	0.000
Czech Rep	Governmental actors	58.56	-5.2	4.00	0.041
	Political parties	23.76	3.85	3.00	0.069
	Formal civil society	1.10	-3.00	8.00	0.004
	Informal civil society	1.38	-0.77	0.82	0.365
	Citizens	15.19	5.11	10.00	0.001
Denmark	Governmental actors	68.61	4.85	11.00	0.000

	Political parties	14.80	-5.11	18.00	0.000
	Formal civil society	1.79	-2.31	15.00	0.000
	Informal civil society	2.60	0.45	2.00	0.211
	Citizens	12.20	2.12	5.00	0.021
Estonia	Governmental actors	56.99	-6.77	7.00	0.007
	Political parties	16.44	-3.47	3.00	0.098
	Formal civil society	4.38	0.28	0.08	0.785
	Informal civil society	4.66	2.51	12.00	0.000
	Citizens	17.53	7.45	22.00	0.000
Finland	Governmental actors	61.68	-2.08	2.00	0.180
	Political parties	14.76	-5.15	16.00	0.000
	Formal civil society	3.64	-0.46	0.52	0.472
	Informal civil society	2.22	0.07	0.13	0.718
	Citizens	17.69	7.61	61.00	0.000
France	Governmental actors	57.12	-6.64	39.00	0.000
	Political parties	25.74	5.83	43.00	0.000
	Formal civil society	4.00	-0.10	0.050	0.818
	Informal civil society	2.76	0.61	5.00	0.027
	Citizens	10.39	0.31	0.21	0.650
Germany	Governmental actors	67.58	3.82	5.00	0.023
	Political parties	14.90	-5.01	13.00	0.000
	Formal civil society	7.99	3.89	31.00	0.000
	Informal civil society	3.81	1.66	12.00	0.000
	Citizens	5.72	-4.36	17.00	0.000
Greece	Governmental actors	58.05	-5.71	55.00	0.000
	Political parties	29.13	9.22	201.00	0.000
	Formal civil society	2.34	-1.76	32.00	0.000
	Informal civil society	1.17	-0.98	16.00	0.000
	Citizens	9.32	-0.76	3.00	0.111
Hungary	Governmental actors	62.05	-1.71	1.00	0.255
	Political parties	22.32	2.41	4.00	0.053
	Formal civil society	4.43	0.33	0.28	0.596
	Informal civil society	2.07	-0.08	0.00	1.000
	Citizens	9.13	-0.95	1.00	0.310
Ireland	Governmental actors	66.76	3.00	4.00	0.046
	Political parties	17.96	-1.95	2.00	0.117
	Formal civil society	4.01	-0.09	0.02	0.889
	Informal civil society	2.20	0.05	0.10	0.758
	Citizens	9.07	-1.01	1.00	0.283
Italy	Governmental actors	74.14	10.38	15.00	0.000
	Political parties	19.63	-0.28	0.02	0.898
	Formal civil society	1.25	-2.85	7.00	0.010

	Informal civil society	0.93	-1.22	2.00	0.157
	Citizens	4.05	-6.03	13.00	0.000
Latvia	Governmental actors	67.46	3.70	6.00	0.012
	Political parties	8.52	-11.39	87.00	0.000
	Formal civil society	5.77	1.67	7.00	0.006
	Informal civil society	3.67	1.52	13.00	0.000
	Citizens	14.57	4.49	23.00	0.000
Lithuania	Governmental actors	82.52	18.76	31.00	0.000
	Political parties	2.91	-17.00	37.00	0.000
	Formal civil society	4.85	0.75	0.30	0.585
	Informal civil society	1.46	-0.69	0.37	0.543
	Citizens	8.25	-1.83	0.76	0.384
Luxembourg	Governmental actors	69.21	5.45	17.00	0.000
	Political parties	14.63	-5.28	23.00	0.000
	Formal civil society	6.26	2.16	15.00	0.000
	Informal civil society	1.67	-0.48	0.99	0.321
	Citizens	8.22	-1.86	5.00	0.024
Malta	Governmental actors	68.13	4.37	12.00	0.000
	Political parties	18.85	-1.06	1.00	0.317
	Formal civil society	3.50	-0.60	1.00	0.253
	Informal civil society	0.89	-1.26	10.00	0.002
	Citizens	8.64	-1.44	3.00	0.071
Netherlands	Governmental actors	67.21	3.45	6.00	0.013
	Political parties	14.03	-5.88	26.00	0.000
	Formal civil society	4.49	0.39	0.45	0.501
	Informal civil society	3.10	0.95	6.00	0.012
	Citizens	11.17	1.09	2.00	0.213
Poland	Governmental actors	64.52	0.76	0.41	0.521
	Political parties	19.67	-0.24	0.06	0.807
	Formal civil society	4.10	0.00	0.00	1.000
	Informal civil society	6.32	4.17	136.00	0.000
	Citizens	5.39	-4.69	41.00	0.000
Portugal	Governmental actors	67.78	4.02	12.00	0.000
	Political parties	18.94	-0.97	1.00	0.315
	Formal civil society	3.56	-0.54	1.00	0.264
	Informal civil society	1.87	-0.28	0.32	0.573
	Citizens	7.86	-2.22	9.00	0.002
Romania	Governmental actors	68.06	4.30	5.00	0.033
	Political parties	9.72	-10.19	5.00	0.033
	Formal civil society	1.56	-2.54	9.00	0.002
	Informal civil society	0.52	-1.63	7.00	0.009
	Citizens	20.14	10.06	62.00	0.000

Country	Actor group	Percentage	Difference to grand mean	T	Sig.
Slovakia	Governmental actors	67.90	4.14	5.00	0.029
	Political parties	13.43	-6.48	17.00	0.000
	Formal civil society	2.16	-1.94	6.00	0.013
	Informal civil society	2.78	0.63	2.00	0.203
	Citizens	13.73	3.65	9.00	0.002
Slovenia	Governmental actors	72.18	8.42	54.00	0.000
	Political parties	10.90	-9.01	91.00	0.000
	Formal civil society	5.37	1.27	7.00	0.008
	Informal civil society	3.63	1.48	21.00	0.000
	Citizens	7.92	-2.16	9.00	0.002
Spain	Governmental actors	64.33	0.57	0.34	0.562
	Political parties	23.98	4.07	24.00	0.000
	Formal civil society	3.03	-1.07	7.00	0.009
	Informal civil society	1.05	-1.10	12.00	0.000
	Citizens	7.60	-2.48	16.00	0.000
Sweden	Governmental actors	64.18	0.42	0.12	0.735
	Political parties	17.07	-2.84	8.00	0.006
	Formal civil society	3.70	-0.40	0.60	0.437
	Informal civil society	2.60	0.45	2.00	0.148
	Citizens	12.46	2.38	9.00	0.003
UK	Governmental actors	59.07	-4.69	6.00	0.016
	Political parties	23.43	3.52	5.00	0.029
	Formal civil society	6.10	2.00	6.00	0.013
	Informal civil society	2.09	-0.06	0.00	0.962
	Citizens	9.31	-0.77	0.41	0.524

Table 8.8 Horizontal actor structure by EU member state (news story level)

Country	Actor group	Percentage	Difference to grand mean	T	Sig.
Austria	Governmental actors	61.81	4.40	2.27	0.023
	Political parties	34.07	1.46	0.78	0.439
	Formal civil society	8.56	1.45	1.30	0.194
	Informal civil society	5.23	0.83	0.94	0.350
	Citizens	14.58	-5.23	-3.72	0.000
Belgium	Governmental actors	37.31	-20.10	-8.84	0.000
	Political parties	20.31	-12.30	-6.50	0.000
	Formal civil society	12.8	5.69	3.62	0.000
	Informal civil society	2.65	-1.75	-2.32	0.021
	Citizens	21.63	1.82	0.94	0.347
Bulgaria	Governmental actors	54.61	-2.80	-1.47	0.143
	Political parties	29.28	-3.33	-1.91	0.057

	Formal civil society	11.13	4.02	3.34	0.001
	Informal civil society	3.37	-1.03	-1.50	0.135
	Citizens	16.84	-2.97	-2.08	0.038
Cyprus	Governmental actors	54.99	-2.42	-1.71	0.088
	Political parties	41.44	8.83	6.29	0.000
	Formal civil society	6.00	-1.11	-1.64	0.102
	Informal civil society	1.38	-3.02	-9.09	0.000
	Citizens	27.01	7.20	5.69	0.000
Czech Rep	Governmental actors	56.93	-0.48	-0.11	0.911
	Political parties	32.85	0.24	0.06	0.953
	Formal civil society	1.46	-5.65	-5.49	0.000
	Informal civil society	2.92	-1.48	-1.03	0.307
	Citizens	27.74	7.93	2.07	0.041
Denmark	Governmental actors	57.32	-0.09	-0.03	0.976
	Political parties	31.21	-1.40	-0.53	0.593
	Formal civil society	5.73	-1.38	-1.05	0.295
	Informal civil society	7.96	3.56	2.33	0.021
	Citizens	29.62	9.81	3.80	0.000
Estonia	Governmental actors	50.43	-6.98	-1.49	0.139
	Political parties	27.83	-4.78	-1.14	0.257
	Formal civil society	7.83	0.72	0.29	0.776
	Informal civil society	11.3	6.90	2.33	0.022
	Citizens	35.65	15.84	3.53	0.001
Finland	Governmental actors	43.55	-13.86	-4.91	0.000
	Political parties	21.61	-11.00	-4.7	0.000
	Formal civil society	5.81	-1.30	-0.98	0.328
	Informal civil society	5.48	1.08	0.84	0.403
	Citizens	38.71	18.90	6.82	0.000
France	Governmental actors	56.48	-0.93	-0.49	0.628
	Political parties	43.07	10.46	5.44	0.000
	Formal civil society	6.63	-0.48	-0.50	0.617
	Informal civil society	6.78	2.38	2.44	0.015
	Citizens	18.07	-1.74	-1.16	0.245
Germany	Governmental actors	48.63	-8.78	-3.18	0.002
	Political parties	14.89	-17.72	-9.01	0.000
	Formal civil society	10.33	3.22	1.92	0.056
	Informal civil society	4.86	0.46	0.39	0.697
	Citizens	8.21	-11.60	-7.66	0.000
Greece	Governmental actors	60.88	3.47	2.71	0.007
	Political parties	45.23	12.62	9.68	0.000
	Formal civil society	4.05	-3.06	-5.93	0.000
	Informal civil society	2.26	-2.14	-5.48	0.000

	Citizens	17.50	-2.31	-2.32	0.021
Hungary	Governmental actors	61.76	4.35	1.73	0.084
	Political parties	36.63	4.02	1.61	0.108
	Formal civil society	6.68	-0.43	-0.33	0.742
	Informal civil society	4.01	-0.39	-0.38	0.702
	Citizens	16.31	-3.50	-1.83	0.068
Ireland	Governmental actors	67.75	10.34	4.06	0.000
	Political parties	34.62	2.01	0.77	0.440
	Formal civil society	6.80	-0.31	-0.22	0.824
	Informal civil society	4.73	0.33	0.29	0.773
	Citizens	19.23	-0.58	-0.27	0.787
Italy	Governmental actors	58.82	1.41	0.31	0.756
	Political parties	30.25	-2.36	-0.56	0.578
	Formal civil society	3.36	-3.75	-2.26	0.026
	Informal civil society	1.68	-2.72	-2.3	0.023
	Citizens	7.56	-12.25	-5.03	0.000
Latvia	Governmental actors	65.27	7.86	2.91	0.004
	Political parties	22.51	-10.10	-4.26	0.000
	Formal civil society	12.54	5.43	2.89	0.004
	Informal civil society	9.00	4.60	2.83	0.005
	Citizens	36.98	17.17	6.26	0.000
Lithuania	Governmental actors	30.17	-27.24	-6.36	0.000
	Political parties	3.45	-29.16	-17.14	0.000
	Formal civil society	6.03	-1.08	-0.48	0.629
	Informal civil society	0.86	-3.54	-4.10	0.000
	Citizens	11.21	-8.60	-2.93	0.004
Luxembourg	Governmental actors	33.71	-23.70	-10.53	0.000
	Political parties	21.72	-10.89	-5.55	0.000
	Formal civil society	7.01	-0.10	-0.08	0.937
	Informal civil society	4.07	-0.33	-0.35	0.728
	Citizens	11.99	-7.82	-5.06	0.000
Malta	Governmental actors	60.95	3.54	2.05	0.040
	Political parties	25.75	-6.86	-4.45	0.000
	Formal civil society	4.73	-2.38	-3.18	0.002
	Informal civil society	0.75	-3.65	-12.03	0.000
	Citizens	13.56	-6.25	-5.18	0.000
Netherlands	Governmental actors	53.38	-4.03	-1.61	0.108
	Political parties	25.81	-6.80	-3.10	0.002
	Formal civil society	6.77	-0.34	-0.27	0.785
	Informal civil society	6.77	2.37	1.88	0.061
	Citizens	22.31	2.50	1.20	0.232
Poland	Governmental actors	57.14	-0.27	-0.13	0.897

	Political parties	29.09	-3.52	-1.87	0.062
	Formal civil society	8.61	1.50	1.29	0.199
	Informal civil society	12.74	8.34	6.02	0.000
	Citizens	12.22	-7.59	-5.58	0.000
Portugal	Governmental actors	67.17	9.76	5.06	0.000
	Political parties	35.02	2.41	1.23	0.220
	Formal civil society	8.59	1.48	1.28	0.200
	Informal civil society	2.86	-1.54	-2.25	0.025
	Citizens	18.01	-1.80	-1.14	0.255
Romania	Governmental actors	59.04	1.63	0.45	0.650
	Political parties	13.30	-19.31	-7.78	0.000
	Formal civil society	3.19	-3.92	-3.05	0.003
	Informal civil society	1.60	-2.80	-3.06	0.003
	Citizens	34.04	14.23	4.11	0.000
Slovakia	Governmental actors	56.4	-1.01	-0.30	0.768
	Political parties	24.17	-8.44	-2.86	0.005
	Formal civil society	4.27	-2.84	-2.04	0.043
	Informal civil society	6.64	2.24	1.30	0.195
	Citizens	29.38	9.57	3.05	0.003
Slovenia	Governmental actors	62.84	5.43	2.71	0.007
	Political parties	19.35	-13.26	-8.11	0.000
	Formal civil society	8.39	1.28	1.12	0.265
	Informal civil society	7.53	3.13	2.87	0.004
	Citizens	16.61	-3.20	-2.08	0.038
Spain	Governmental actors	71.03	13.62	8.21	0.000
	Political parties	46.86	14.25	7.81	0.000
	Formal civil society	6.28	-0.83	-0.94	0.347
	Informal civil society	2.67	-1.73	-2.94	0.003
	Citizens	18.42	-1.39	-0.98	0.329
Sweden	Governmental actors	55.49	-1.92	-0.88	0.380
	Political parties	30.83	-1.78	-0.88	0.380
	Formal civil society	6.94	-0.17	-0.16	0.876
	Informal civil society	6.36	1.96	1.83	0.068
	Citizens	22.54	2.73	1.49	0.137
UK	Governmental actors	64.62	7.21	2.10	0.037
	Political parties	46.15	13.54	3.78	0.000
	Formal civil society	13.33	6.22	2.55	0.012
	Informal civil society	5.13	0.73	0.46	0.646
	Citizens	22.56	2.75	0.92	0.360

Table 8.9 Horizontal actor structure by EU member state (actor level)

Country	Actor group	Percentage	Difference to grand mean	Chi^2	Sig.
Austria	Governmental actors	53.65	0.94	0.42	0.515
	Political parties	28.71	1.19	0.86	0.354
	Formal civil society	5.73	0.81	1.69	0.194
	Informal civil society	2.98	0.31	0.45	0.503
	Citizens	8.94	-3.24	12.05	0.000
Belgium	Governmental actors	41.58	-11.13	31.96	0.000
	Political parties	25.04	-2.48	1.99	0.159
	Formal civil society	12.75	7.83	81.26	0.000
	Informal civil society	2.28	-0.39	0.39	0.535
	Citizens	18.36	6.18	22.71	0.000
Bulgaria	Governmental actors	49.78	-2.93	4.49	0.034
	Political parties	28.32	0.80	0.42	0.517
	Formal civil society	7.81	2.89	22.67	0.000
	Informal civil society	2.26	-0.41	0.84	0.360
	Citizens	11.82	-0.36	0.15	0.695
Cyprus	Governmental actors	46.43	-6.28	35.63	0.000
	Political parties	33.82	6.30	44.29	0.000
	Formal civil society	4.01	-0.91	3.98	0.046
	Informal civil society	0.69	-1.98	36.27	0.000
	Citizens	15.04	2.86	16.98	0.000
Czech Rep	Governmental actors	49.28	-3.43	1.30	0.254
	Political parties	30.58	3.06	1.29	0.257
	Formal civil society	1.08	-3.84	8.73	0.003
	Informal civil society	1.80	-0.87	0.81	0.369
	Citizens	17.27	5.09	6.63	0.010
Denmark	Governmental actors	51.14	-1.57	0.64	0.425
	Political parties	23.59	-3.93	4.97	0.026
	Formal civil society	2.89	-2.03	5.67	0.017
	Informal civil society	4.41	1.74	7.39	0.007
	Citizens	17.96	5.78	19.82	0.000
Estonia	Governmental actors	42.08	-10.63	10.78	0.001
	Political parties	21.67	-5.85	4.09	0.043
	Formal civil society	5.42	0.50	0.13	0.722
	Informal civil society	6.25	3.58	11.59	0.000
	Citizens	24.58	12.4	33.93	0.000
Finland	Governmental actors	39.5	-13.21	38.50	0.000
	Political parties	24.56	-2.96	2.43	0.119
	Formal civil society	4.80	-0.12	0.02	0.903
	Informal civil society	3.38	0.71	1.06	0.302

Appendix II

	Citizens	27.76	15.58	121.97	0.000
France	Governmental actors	48.71	-4.00	9.85	0.002
	Political parties	32.68	5.16	20.31	0.000
	Formal civil society	4.18	-0.74	1.81	0.179
	Informal civil society	3.26	0.59	2.00	0.158
	Citizens	11.18	-1.00	1.44	0.230
Germany	Governmental actors	55.05	2.34	1.08	0.298
	Political parties	21.98	-5.54	7.64	0.006
	Formal civil society	11.88	6.96	50.12	0.000
	Informal civil society	4.16	1.49	4.18	0.041
	Citizens	6.93	-5.25	12.85	0.000
Greece	Governmental actors	50.69	-2.02	4.93	0.026
	Political parties	36.75	9.23	125.37	0.000
	Formal civil society	2.27	-2.65	48.05	0.000
	Informal civil society	1.18	-1.49	27.52	0.000
	Citizens	9.12	-3.06	26.99	0.000
Hungary	Governmental actors	56.24	3.53	3.84	0.050
	Political parties	26.99	-0.53	0.11	0.741
	Formal civil society	4.67	-0.25	0.10	0.747
	Informal civil society	2.40	-0.27	0.22	0.637
	Citizens	9.71	-2.47	4.41	0.036
Ireland	Governmental actors	60.07	7.36	17.06	0.000
	Political parties	22.37	-5.15	10.45	0.001
	Formal civil society	4.57	-0.35	0.20	0.656
	Informal civil society	2.10	-0.57	0.98	0.322
	Citizens	10.88	-1.30	1.25	0.264
Italy	Governmental actors	68.4	15.69	22.60	0.000
	Political parties	24.68	-2.84	0.93	0.335
	Formal civil society	1.73	-3.19	5.00	0.025
	Informal civil society	0.87	-1.80	2.89	0.089
	Citizens	4.33	-7.85	13.26	0.000
Latvia	Governmental actors	55.04	2.33	1.51	0.219
	Political parties	11.76	-15.76	87.31	0.000
	Formal civil society	8.12	3.20	15.04	0.000
	Informal civil society	4.62	1.95	10.00	0.002
	Citizens	20.45	8.27	43.73	0.000
Lithuania	Governmental actors	61.45	8.74	2.53	0.112
	Political parties	7.23	-20.29	17.10	0.000
	Formal civil society	10.84	5.92	6.19	0.013
	Informal civil society	1.20	-1.47	0.69	0.408
	Citizens	19.28	7.10	3.89	0.049
Luxembourg	Governmental actors	42.21	-10.5	22.83	0.000

	Political parties	32.70	5.18	6.92	0.009
	Formal civil society	9.89	4.97	26.73	0.000
	Informal civil society	3.61	0.94	1.75	0.186
	Citizens	11.6	-0.58	0.16	0.685
Malta	Governmental actors	62.96	10.25	45.07	0.000
	Political parties	22.96	-4.56	11.19	0.000
	Formal civil society	3.68	-1.24	3.55	0.060
	Informal civil society	0.54	-2.13	19.32	0.000
	Citizens	9.87	-2.31	5.39	0.020
Netherlands	Governmental actors	51.55	-1.16	0.37	0.542
	Political parties	23.31	-4.21	6.15	0.013
	Formal civil society	5.08	0.16	0.04	0.838
	Informal civil society	4.80	2.13	11.82	0.000
	Citizens	15.25	3.07	6.05	0.014
Poland	Governmental actors	54.08	1.37	0.88	0.348
	Political parties	26.14	-1.38	1.11	0.292
	Formal civil society	5.39	0.47	0.56	0.453
	Informal civil society	7.92	5.25	114.39	0.000
	Citizens	6.45	-5.73	36.50	0.000
Portugal	Governmental actors	62.47	9.76	50.23	0.000
	Political parties	23.07	-4.45	13.12	0.000
	Formal civil society	4.19	-0.73	1.48	0.224
	Informal civil society	2.10	-0.57	1.68	0.195
	Citizens	8.17	-4.01	20.02	0.000
Romania	Governmental actors	58.14	5.43	4.01	0.045
	Political parties	13.37	-14.15	34.21	0.000
	Formal civil society	2.03	-2.89	6.08	0.014
	Informal civil society	0.87	-1.80	4.26	0.039
	Citizens	25.58	13.4	56.31	0.000
Slovakia	Governmental actors	52.45	-0.26	0.01	0.916
	Political parties	20.10	-7.42	11.12	0.000
	Formal civil society	3.19	-1.73	2.59	0.108
	Informal civil society	4.17	1.50	3.43	0.064
	Citizens	20.1	7.92	23.34	0.000
Slovenia	Governmental actors	58.58	5.87	14.98	0.000
	Political parties	17.35	-10.17	56.74	0.000
	Formal civil society	7.52	2.60	15.40	0.000
	Informal civil society	5.75	3.08	37.82	0.000
	Citizens	10.80	-1.38	1.95	0.163
Spain	Governmental actors	58.26	5.55	22.29	0.000
	Political parties	29.75	2.23	4.49	0.034
	Formal civil society	3.00	-1.92	14.60	0.000

	Informal civil society	1.03	-1.64	19.38	0.000
	Citizens	7.95	-4.23	30.72	0.000
Sweden	Governmental actors	49.04	-3.67	5.41	0.020
	Political parties	24.95	-2.57	3.31	0.069
	Formal civil society	4.82	-0.10	0.02	0.884
	Informal civil society	3.66	0.99	3.72	0.054
	Citizens	17.53	5.35	26.36	0.000
UK	Governmental actors	51.76	-0.95	0.18	0.668
	Political parties	28.32	0.80	0.16	0.688
	Formal civil society	7.23	2.31	5.68	0.017
	Informal civil society	2.15	-0.52	0.53	0.468
	Citizens	10.55	-1.63	1.26	0.263

Table 8.10 Vertical actor structure by EU member state (news story level)

Country	Actor group	Percentage	Difference to grand mean	T	Sig.
Austria	Governmental actors	46.75	-5.70	-2.87	0.004
	Political parties	1.27	-1.11	-2.50	0.013
	Formal civil society	2.06	0.25	0.44	0.659
	Informal civil society	0.95	0.15	0.31	0.755
	Citizens	2.85	-1.97	-2.97	0.003
Belgium	Governmental actors	60.93	8.48	3.69	0.000
	Political parties	3.09	0.71	0.87	0.383
	Formal civil society	3.75	1.94	2.17	0.030
	Informal civil society	0.66	-0.14	-0.44	0.660
	Citizens	7.73	2.91	2.31	0.021
Bulgaria	Governmental actors	54.32	1.87	0.98	0.327
	Political parties	2.78	0.40	0.64	0.524
	Formal civil society	1.46	-0.35	-0.75	0.452
	Informal civil society	1.61	0.81	1.62	0.106
	Citizens	3.22	-1.60	-2.37	0.018
Cyprus	Governmental actors	57.34	4.89	3.47	0.001
	Political parties	6.08	3.70	5.44	0.000
	Formal civil society	2.11	0.30	0.73	0.466
	Informal civil society	0.24	-0.56	-4.18	0.000
	Citizens	7.06	2.24	3.07	0.002
Czech Rep	Governmental actors	41.61	-10.84	-2.57	0.011
	Political parties	0.73	-1.65	-2.26	0.025
	Formal civil society	0.73	-1.08	-1.48	0.141
	Informal civil society	0.00	-0.80		0.000
	Citizens	5.11	0.29	0.15	0.878

Denmark	Governmental actors	78.98	26.53	11.52	0.000
	Political parties	2.55	0.17	0.19	0.851
	Formal civil society	0.32	-1.49	-4.68	0.000
	Informal civil society	0.00	-0.80		0.000
	Citizens	5.41	0.59	0.46	0.643
Estonia	Governmental actors	61.74	9.29	2.04	0.044
	Political parties	3.48	1.10	0.64	0.523
	Formal civil society	2.61	0.80	0.54	0.594
	Informal civil society	1.74	0.94	0.74	0.459
	Citizens	3.48	-1.34	-0.78	0.436
Finland	Governmental actors	75.81	23.36	9.59	0.000
	Political parties	1.29	-1.09	-1.70	0.091
	Formal civil society	1.94	0.13	0.16	0.873
	Informal civil society	0.97	0.17	0.25	0.805
	Citizens	5.48	0.66	0.51	0.609
France	Governmental actors	42.62	-9.83	-5.12	0.000
	Political parties	3.61	1.23	1.70	0.089
	Formal civil society	1.81	0.00	-0.01	0.996
	Informal civil society	0.90	0.10	0.20	0.841
	Citizens	6.02	1.20	1.30	0.193
Germany	Governmental actors	59.88	7.43	2.75	0.006
	Political parties	3.04	0.66	0.70	0.487
	Formal civil society	2.13	0.32	0.40	0.690
	Informal civil society	2.74	1.94	2.12	0.035
	Citizens	3.95	-0.87	-0.81	0.420
Greece	Governmental actors	37.06	-15.39	-12.16	0.000
	Political parties	1.10	-1.28	-4.69	0.000
	Formal civil society	1.65	-0.16	-0.49	0.626
	Informal civil society	0.62	-0.18	-1.03	0.301
	Citizens	6.52	1.70	2.63	0.009
Hungary	Governmental actors	40.64	-11.81	-4.64	0.000
	Political parties	3.48	1.10	1.16	0.249
	Formal civil society	2.67	0.86	1.03	0.302
	Informal civil society	0.80	0.00	-0.06	0.952
	Citizens	5.08	0.26	0.23	0.819
Ireland	Governmental actors	41.72	-10.73	-4.00	0.000
	Political parties	1.18	-1.20	-2.03	0.043
	Formal civil society	0.89	-0.92	-1.81	0.072
	Informal civil society	1.48	0.68	0.99	0.324
	Citizens	2.07	-2.75	-3.54	0.000
Italy	Governmental actors	43.7	-8.75	-1.92	0.058
	Political parties	4.2	1.82	0.99	0.326

Appendix II

	Formal civil society	0.00	-1.81		0.000
	Informal civil society	0.84	0.04	0.01	0.990
	Citizens	2.52	-2.30	-1.59	0.114
Latvia	Governmental actors	74.6	22.15	8.96	0.000
	Political parties	2.57	0.19	0.21	0.831
	Formal civil society	1.61	-0.20	-0.28	0.777
	Informal civil society	1.93	1.13	1.41	0.160
	Citizens	3.86	-0.96	-0.88	0.380
Lithuania	Governmental actors	82.76	30.31	8.60	0.000
	Political parties	0.00	-2.38		0.000
	Formal civil society	0.86	-0.95	-1.10	0.274
	Informal civil society	1.72	0.92	0.74	0.463
	Citizens	0.86	-3.96	-4.59	0.000
Luxembourg	Governmental actors	87.56	35.11	22.34	0.000
	Political parties	4.52	2.14	2.17	0.031
	Formal civil society	5.43	3.62	3.36	0.001
	Informal civil society	0.90	0.10	0.17	0.868
	Citizens	9.28	4.46	3.23	0.001
Malta	Governmental actors	30.35	-22.10	-13.62	0.000
	Political parties	1.87	-0.51	-1.08	0.282
	Formal civil society	1.24	-0.57	-1.45	0.148
	Informal civil society	0.75	-0.05	-0.28	0.783
	Citizens	1.99	-2.83	-5.74	0.000
Netherlands	Governmental actors	74.19	21.74	9.91	0.000
	Political parties	1.25	-1.13	-2.02	0.044
	Formal civil society	4.26	2.45	2.42	0.016
	Informal civil society	0.75	-0.05	-0.18	0.857
	Citizens	6.27	1.45	1.19	0.235
Poland	Governmental actors	49.91	-2.54	-1.22	0.222
	Political parties	2.24	-0.14	-0.23	0.817
	Formal civil society	0.52	-1.29	-4.35	0.000
	Informal civil society	1.55	0.75	1.40	0.161
	Citizens	2.07	-2.75	-4.66	0.000
Portugal	Governmental actors	39.73	-12.72	-6.33	0.000
	Political parties	2.02	-0.36	-0.62	0.534
	Formal civil society	0.67	-1.14	-3.38	0.001
	Informal civil society	0.67	-0.13	-0.47	0.641
	Citizens	4.38	-0.44	-0.53	0.598
Romania	Governmental actors	64.36	11.91	3.40	0.001
	Political parties	3.19	0.81	0.63	0.529
	Formal civil society	1.06	-0.75	-1.00	0.321
	Informal civil society	0.00	-0.80		0.000

	Citizens	13.83	9.01	3.57	0.000
Slovakia	Governmental actors	64.93	12.48	3.79	0.000
	Political parties	0.95	-1.43	-2.14	0.033
	Formal civil society	0.47	-1.34	-2.82	0.005
	Informal civil society	0.47	-0.33	-0.75	0.453
	Citizens	3.32	-1.50	-1.22	0.225
Slovenia	Governmental actors	67.47	15.02	7.74	0.000
	Political parties	0.68	-1.70	-4.96	0.000
	Formal civil society	2.05	0.24	0.42	0.677
	Informal civil society	0.34	-0.46	-2.02	0.044
	Citizens	4.11	-0.71	-0.86	0.388
Spain	Governmental actors	39.79	-12.66	-7.08	0.000
	Political parties	1.60	-0.78	-1.69	0.091
	Formal civil society	1.87	0.06	0.12	0.905
	Informal civil society	0.80	0.00	-0.09	0.929
	Citizens	4.27	-0.55	-0.74	0.459
Sweden	Governmental actors	60.12	7.67	3.56	0.000
	Political parties	0.58	-1.80	-5.41	0.000
	Formal civil society	1.16	-0.65	-1.39	0.164
	Informal civil society	0.39	-0.41	-1.63	0.103
	Citizens	1.93	-2.89	-4.79	0.000
UK	Governmental actors	36.92	-15.53	-4.48	0.000
	Political parties	0.51	-1.87	-3.64	0.000
	Formal civil society	0.51	-1.30	-2.53	0.012
	Informal civil society	0.51	-0.29	-0.62	0.537
	Citizens	2.05	-2.77	-2.72	0.007

Table 8.11 Vertical actor structure by EU member state (actor level)

Country	Actor group	Percentage	Difference to grand mean	Chi^2	Sig.
Austria	Governmental actors	88.52	0.84	0.31	0.578
	Political parties	2.46	-0.97	1.36	0.244
	Formal civil society	3.48	1.15	2.72	0.099
	Informal civil society	1.43	0.41	0.80	0.371
	Citizens	4.10	-1.44	1.89	0.169
Belgium	Governmental actors	84.46	-3.22	4.87	0.027
	Political parties	3.37	-0.06	0.01	0.937
	Formal civil society	4.31	1.98	8.54	0.003
	Informal civil society	0.94	-0.08	0.03	0.856
	Citizens	6.93	1.39	2.69	0.101
Bulgaria	Governmental actors	88.97	1.29	0.99	0.321
	Political parties	4.17	0.74	1.03	0.309

Appendix II

	Formal civil society	1.64	-0.69	1.34	0.247
	Informal civil society	1.64	0.62	2.37	0.124
	Citizens	3.58	-1.96	4.78	0.029
Cyprus	Governmental actors	84.18	-3.50	13.43	0.000
	Political parties	6.54	3.11	32.32	0.000
	Formal civil society	2.08	-0.25	0.32	0.569
	Informal civil society	0.22	-0.80	8.22	0.004
	Citizens	6.98	1.44	4.68	0.030
Czech Rep	Governmental actors	89.29	1.61	0.20	0.655
	Political parties	1.19	-2.24	0.26	0.259
	Formal civil society	1.19	-1.14	0.48	0.491
	Informal civil society	0.00	-1.02	0.86	0.353
	Citizens	8.33	2.79	1.24	0.266
Denmark	Governmental actors	93.67	5.99	14.87	0.000
	Political parties	2.18	-1.25	2.11	0.146
	Formal civil society	0.22	-2.11	8.91	0.003
	Informal civil society	0.00	-1.02	4.70	0.030
	Citizens	3.93	-1.61	2.21	0.137
Estonia	Governmental actors	85.60	-2.08	0.50	0.482
	Political parties	6.40	2.97	3.25	0.071
	Formal civil society	2.40	0.07	0.00	0.956
	Informal civil society	1.60	0.58	0.42	0.519
	Citizens	4.00	-1.54	0.56	0.453
Finland	Governmental actors	90.87	3.19	3.91	0.048
	Political parties	1.87	-1.56	3.08	0.080
	Formal civil society	2.11	-0.22	0.09	0.769
	Informal civil society	0.70	-0.32	0.41	0.522
	Citizens	4.45	-1.09	0.95	0.330
France	Governmental actors	82.12	-5.56	14.77	0.000
	Political parties	5.11	1.68	4.35	0.037
	Formal civil society	3.47	1.14	2.95	0.086
	Informal civil society	1.28	0.26	0.35	0.555
	Citizens	8.03	2.49	6.08	0.014
Germany	Governmental actors	86.53	-1.15	0.40	0.527
	Political parties	4.19	0.76	0.56	0.455
	Formal civil society	2.10	-0.23	0.08	0.783
	Informal civil society	3.29	2.27	15.78	0.000
	Citizens	3.89	-1.65	1.70	0.192
Greece	Governmental actors	83.88	-3.80	11.72	0.000
	Political parties	2.38	-1.05	3.09	0.079
	Formal civil society	2.58	0.25	0.26	0.611
	Informal civil society	1.14	0.12	0.13	0.723

	Citizens	10.02	4.48	32.46	0.000
Hungary	Governmental actors	79.18	-8.50	17.37	0.000
	Political parties	8.55	5.12	20.13	0.000
	Formal civil society	3.72	1.39	2.22	0.137
	Informal civil society	1.12	0.10	0.03	0.874
	Citizens	7.43	1.89	1.79	0.181
Ireland	Governmental actors	89.5	1.82	0.71	0.398
	Political parties	2.94	-0.49	0.17	0.679
	Formal civil society	2.10	-0.23	0.05	0.820
	Informal civil society	2.52	1.50	5.10	0.024
	Citizens	2.94	-2.6	3.04	0.081
Italy	Governmental actors	88.89	1.21	0.12	0.728
	Political parties	6.67	3.24	2.80	0.095
	Formal civil society	0.00	-2.33	2.14	0.143
	Informal civil society	1.11	0.09	0.01	0.929
	Citizens	3.33	-2.21	0.84	0.361
Latvia	Governmental actors	90.98	3.30	3.71	0.054
	Political parties	2.39	-1.04	1.22	0.270
	Formal civil society	1.33	-1.00	1.63	0.202
	Informal civil society	1.86	0.84	2.50	0.114
	Citizens	3.45	-2.09	3.10	0.078
Lithuania	Governmental actors	96.75	9.07	9.33	0.002
	Political parties	0.00	-3.43	4.37	0.037
	Formal civil society	0.81	-1.52	1.23	0.267
	Informal civil society	1.63	0.61	0.45	0.504
	Citizens	0.81	-4.73	5.25	0.022
Luxembourg	Governmental actors	85.97	-1.71	2.14	0.144
	Political parties	3.42	-0.01	0.00	1.000
	Formal civil society	4.01	1.68	9.45	0.002
	Informal civil society	0.47	-0.55	2.42	0.119
	Citizens	6.13	0.59	0.52	0.470
Malta	Governmental actors	84.88	-2.80	2.41	0.121
	Political parties	5.52	2.09	4.33	0.037
	Formal civil society	2.91	0.58	0.49	0.482
	Informal civil society	2.03	1.01	3.35	0.067
	Citizens	4.65	-0.89	0.51	0.475
Netherlands	Governmental actors	88.61	0.93	0.40	0.528
	Political parties	1.35	-2.08	6.66	0.010
	Formal civil society	3.67	1.34	3.85	0.050
	Informal civil society	0.77	-0.25	0.30	0.585
	Citizens	5.60	0.06	0.00	0.957
Poland	Governmental actors	90.91	3.23	4.53	0.033

	Political parties	3.31	-0.12	0.02	0.879
	Formal civil society	0.83	-1.50	4.72	0.030
	Informal civil society	2.27	1.25	6.96	0.008
	Citizens	2.69	-2.85	7.39	0.007
Portugal	Governmental actors	86.79	-0.89	0.28	0.600
	Political parties	4.15	0.72	0.57	0.452
	Formal civil society	1.30	-1.03	1.77	0.183
	Informal civil society	1.04	0.02	0.00	1.000
	Citizens	6.74	1.20	1.01	0.315
Romania	Governmental actors	82.76	-4.92	5.07	0.024
	Political parties	4.31	0.88	0.52	0.469
	Formal civil society	0.86	-1.47	2.17	0.141
	Informal civil society	0.00	-1.02	2.38	0.123
	Citizens	12.07	6.53	18.13	0.000
Slovakia	Governmental actors	94.17	6.49	9.25	0.002
	Political parties	2.08	-1.35	1.30	0.253
	Formal civil society	0.42	-1.91	3.84	0.050
	Informal civil society	0.42	-0.60	2.38	0.123
	Citizens	2.92	-2.62	3.13	0.077
Slovenia	Governmental actors	93.7	6.02	23.14	0.000
	Political parties	0.70	-2.73	15.87	0.000
	Formal civil society	1.96	-0.37	0.40	0.528
	Informal civil society	0.28	-0.74	3.79	0.052
	Citizens	3.36	-2.18	6.26	0.012
Spain	Governmental actors	86.22	-1.46	1.01	0.315
	Political parties	3.17	-0.26	0.11	0.738
	Formal civil society	3.17	0.84	0.40	0.528
	Informal civil society	1.12	0.10	0.05	0.821
	Citizens	6.33	0.79	0.61	0.436
Sweden	Governmental actors	95.43	7.75	27.42	0.000
	Political parties	0.80	-2.63	10.45	0.001
	Formal civil society	1.39	-0.94	1.88	0.170
	Informal civil society	0.40	-0.62	1.89	0.170
	Citizens	1.99	-3.55	11.94	0.000
UK	Governmental actors	92.79	5.11	2.67	0.102
	Political parties	0.90	-2.53	2.14	0.143
	Formal civil society	0.90	-1.43	0.99	0.320
	Informal civil society	1.80	0.78	0.67	0.414
	Citizens	3.60	-1.94	0.79	0.373

Table 8.12 Actor structure based on quotations, absolute (news story level)

Level	Actor Group	Percentage	Difference to grand mean	T	Sig.
Overall	Governmental actors	73.12	-12.25	n.a.	n.a.
	Political parties	5.02	-28.94	n.a.	n.a.
	Formal civil society	7.60	-1.07	n.a.	n.a.
	Informal civil society	7.41	2.23	n.a.	n.a.
	Citizens	6.84	-17.04	n.a.	n.a.
Horizontal	Governmental actors	70.89	13.48	n.a.	n.a.
	Political parties	5.28	-27.33	n.a.	n.a.
	Formal civil society	8.15	1.04	n.a.	n.a.
	Informal civil society	7.88	3.48	n.a.	n.a.
	Citizens	7.79	-12.02	n.a.	n.a.
Vertical	Governmental actors	87.76	35.31	n.a.	n.a.
	Political parties	2.7	0.32	n.a.	n.a.
	Formal civil society	3.88	2.07	n.a.	n.a.
	Informal civil society	4.14	3.34	n.a.	n.a.
	Citizens	1.51	-3.31	n.a.	n.a.

Table 8.13 Actor structure based on quotations, absolute (actor level)

Level	Actor Group	Percentage	Difference to grand mean	Chi^2	Sig.
Overall	Governmental actors	75.56	11.80	479.28	0.000
	Political parties	4.2	-15.71	1365.43	0.000
	Formal civil society	6.68	2.58	116.86	0.000
	Informal civil society	6.17	4.02	471.08	0.000
	Citizens	7.39	-2.69	64.90	0.000
Horizontal	Governmental actors	72.63	19.92	976.30	0.000
	Political parties	4.62	-22.9	1827.43	0.000
	Formal civil society	7.29	2.37	65.42	0.000
	Informal civil society	6.7	4.03	281.41	0.000
	Citizens	8.77	-3.41	69.55	0.000
Vertical	Governmental actors	88.12	0.44	0.29	0.591
	Political parties	2.41	-1.02	5.23	0.022
	Formal civil society	4.11	1.78	20.12	0.000
	Informal civil society	3.89	2.87	94.83	0.000
	Citizens	1.48	-4.06	55.10	0.000

Table 8.14 Actor structure based on quotations, relative (news story level)

Level	Actor Group	Percentage	Difference to grand mean	T	Sig.
Overall	Governmental actors	44.61	-40.76	n.a.	n.a.
	Political parties	7.07	-26.89	n.a.	n.a.
	Formal civil society	45.69	37.02	n.a.	n.a.
	Informal civil society	74.59	69.41	n.a.	n.a.
	Citizens	14.93	-8.95	n.a.	n.a.
Horizontal	Governmental actors	53.65	-3.76	n.a.	n.a.
	Political parties	7.04	-25.57	n.a.	n.a.
	Formal civil society	49.78	42.67	n.a.	n.a.
	Informal civil society	77.74	73.34	n.a.	n.a.
	Citizens	17.09	-2.72	n.a.	n.a.
Vertical	Governmental actors	19.79	-32.66	n.a.	n.a.
	Political parties	13.4	11.02	n.a.	n.a.
	Formal civil society	25.32	23.51	n.a.	n.a.
	Informal civil society	58.88	58.08	n.a.	n.a.
	Citizens	3.71	-1.11	n.a.	n.a.

Table 8.15 Actor structure based on quotations, relative (actor level)

Level	Actor Group	Percentage	Difference to grand mean	Chi^2	Sig.
Overall	Governmental actors	30.15	-33.61	n.a.	n.a.
	Political parties	5.37	-14.54	n.a.	n.a.
	Formal civil society	41.49	37.39	n.a.	n.a.
	Informal civil society	73.04	70.89	n.a.	n.a.
	Citizens	18.64	8.56	n.a.	n.a.
Horizontal	Governmental actors	41.54	-11.17	n.a.	n.a.
	Political parties	5.06	-22.46	n.a.	n.a.
	Formal civil society	44.68	39.76	n.a.	n.a.
	Informal civil society	75.65	72.98	n.a.	n.a.
	Citizens	21.70	9.52	n.a.	n.a.
Vertical	Governmental actors	15.31	-72.37	n.a.	n.a.
	Political parties	10.68	7.25	n.a.	n.a.
	Formal civil society	26.88	24.55	n.a.	n.a.
	Informal civil society	58.20	57.18	n.a.	n.a.
	Citizens	4.60	-0.94	n.a.	n.a.

Appendix III Country Level Scores for Independent Variables Chapter 9

State	Old member state	EU support	European ID	EP Turnout	EU migrants
Austria	0	38.2	8.16	45.97	3.44
Belgium	1	65.53	19.30	90.39	6.18
Bulgaria	0	51.46	14.36	38.99	0.10
Cyprus	0	43.7	14.20	59.4	10.30
Czech Rep.	0	46.16	7.27	28.2	1.27
Denmark	1	63.82	10.24	59.54	1.70
Estonia	0	61.24	4.10	43.9	0.62
Finland	0	46.81	4.15	40.3	0.89
France	1	49.7	16.5	40.63	2.02
Germany	1	62.49	16.13	43.3	3.06
Greece	1	44.99	5.02	52.61	1.41
Hungary	0	31.78	6.00	36.31	1.00
Ireland	1	71.31	6.45	58.64	9.04
Italy	1	43.22	9.99	65.05	1.57
Latvia	0	27.33	5.84	53.7	0.23
Lithuania	0	57.89	4.46	20.98	0.11
Luxembourg	1	73.63	29.61	90.75	36.59
Malta	0	48.44	2.81	78.79	2.00
Netherlands	1	81.65	15.28	36.75	1.60
Poland	0	65.04	5.34	24.53	0.07
Portugal	1	53.96	7.27	36.78	1.09
Romania	0	69.72	12.41	27.67	0.03
Slovakia	0	59.72	10.51	19.64	0.48
Slovenia	0	59.29	7.69	28.33	0.20
Spain	1	68.01	11.51	44.90	4.67
Sweden	0	58.99	6.21	45.53	2.62
UK	1	34.69	12.16	34.70	2.64

State	Intra EU trade	Unemployment. change	Association.. Membership	GDP	Population size
Austria	75.15	-0.60	40.40	35100	8307989
Belgium	73.4	-0.50	66.14	33200	10666866
Bulgaria	57.93	-1.30	18.67	4800	7518002
Cyprus	68.1	-0.20	24.30	23900	776333
Czech Rep.	80.98	-0.90	44.22	15400	10343422
Denmark	70.66	-0.40	92.93	43900	5475791
Estonia	75.53	0.90	39.91	12300	1338440
Finland	58.9	-0.50	73.19	36500	5300484
France	66.19	-0.60	44.66	31000	64007193
Germany	63.47	-1.10	42.47	31100	82217837
Greece	56.79	-0.60	25.33	21600	11182224
Hungary	73.18	0.40	20.70	10700	10045401
Ireland	65.65	1.70	64.59	41600	4457765
Italy	56.72	0.60	37.99	27600	58652875
Latvia	72.82	1.60	28.19	11200	2191810
Lithuania	58.74	1.50	26.40	10200	3212605
Luxembourg	80.78	0.70	63.93	76700	483799
Malta	62.1	-0.50	21.47	15000	407832
Netherlands	64.24	-0.50	87.59	38700	16405399
Poland	74.53	-2.50	16.50	9500	38115641
Portugal	74.64	-0.50	18.13	16900	10553339
Romania	70.01	-0.80	23.64	6900	20635460
Slovakia	79.1	-1.60	27.80	12100	5376064
Slovenia	69.74	-0.50	52.65	18800	2010269
Spain	63.4	3.10	24.70	24300	45668939
Sweden	64.41	0.10	62.51	38200	9182927
UK	53.09	0.30	55.6	30800	61571647

Appendix IV Excluded Independent Variables Chapter 9

1st news story

	National EU citizens	European EU citizens
Fixed Effects		
Level 1		
EP election story	1.18*** (0.06)	0.11 (0.09)
Election day	-0.58*** (0.08)	-0.74***(0.15)
Length	0.88*** (0.10)	0.98*** (0.17)
1st news story	0.04 (0.08)	-0.26 (.17)
Level 2		
TV	-0.15 (0.15)	-0.26 (0.259)
Quality media	0.07 (0.10)	0.66** (0.20)
Share EU news	-0.53†(0.29)	-0.08 (0.43)
Level 3		
European ID	0.05 (0.48)	1.56*** (0.40)
Intra-EU trade	0.51 (1.04)	0.42 (1.01)
Population size	-0.76* (0.36)	-0.33 (0.32)
Intercept	-2.42** (0.91)	-4.71*** (0.96)
Random Effects		
Country	0.15 (0.06)	0.01 (0.05)
Media outlet	0.10 (0.03)	0.29 (0.10)
-2LL	11764.22	4768.95
AIC	11790.22	4794.95
N (Level 3)	27	27
N (Level 2)	143	143
N (Level 1)	12850	12850

Note: † p < .1, * p < .05, ** p < .01, *** p<.001. Calculations were made using the meqrlogit option in Stata 13. Standard errors in parentheses. Continuous variables were standardised ranging from 0 to 1.

Old EU member state

	National EU citizens	European EU citizens
Fixed Effects		
Level 1		
EP election story	1.19*** (0.06)	0.11 (0.09)
Election day	-0.58*** (0.08)	-0.73*** (0.15)
Length	0.88*** (0.10)	0.98*** (0.17)
Level 2		
TV	-0.15 (0.15)	-0.25 (0.26)
Quality media	0.07 (0.10)	0.66** (0.20)
Share EU news	0.53† (0.29)	-0.06 (0.43)
Level 3		
European ID	0.28 (0.53)	1.57** (0.45)
Intra-EU trade	0.30 (1.04)	0.43 (1.01)
Population size	0.65† (0.38)	-0.35 (0.34)
Old EU member state	-0.21 (0.22)	0.02 (0.19)
Intercept	-2.25* (0.91)	-4.75*** (0.96)
Random Effects		
Country	0.15 (0.06)	0.01 (0.05)
Media outlet	0.10 (0.03)	0.29 (0.10)
-2LL	11763.50	4771.288
AIC	11789.50	4797.29
N (Level 3)	27	27
N (Level 2)	143	143
N (Level 1)	12850	12850

Note: † $p < .1$, * $p < .05$, ** $p < .01$, *** $p<.001$. Calculations were made using the meqrlogit option in Stata 13. Standard errors in parentheses. Continuous variables were standardised ranging from 0 to 1.

EU support

	National EU citizens	European EU citizens
Fixed Effects		
Level 1		
EP election story	1.18*** (0.06)	0.11 (0.09)
Election day	-0.58*** (0.08)	-0.73*** (0.15)
Length	0.88*** (0.10)	0.98*** (0.17)
Level 2		
TV	-0.16 (0.15)	-0.25 (0.26)
Quality media	0.07 (0.10)	0.66** (0.20)
Share EU news	-0.54† (0.29)	-0.07 (0.43)
Level 3		
European ID	0.12 (0.51)	1.62*** (0.44)
Intra-EU trade	0.53 (1.03)	0.42 (1.00)
Population size	-0.77* (0.36)	-0.34 (0.32)
EU support	-0.21 (0.58)	-0.011 (0.54)
Intercept	-2.30* (0.95)	-4.67*** (1.01)
Random Effects		
Country	0.15 (0.06)	0.01 (0.05)
Media outlet	0.10 (0.03)	0.29 (0.10)
-2LL	11764.26	4771.25
AIC	11790.26	4797.25
N (Level 3)	27	27
N (Level 2)	143	143
N (Level 1)	12850	12850

Note: † $p < .1$, * $p < .05$, ** $p < .01$, *** $p < .001$. Calculations were made using the meqrlogit option in Stata 13. Standard errors in parentheses. Continuous variables were standardised ranging from 0 to 1.

EP turnout

	National EU citizens	European EU citizens
Fixed Effects		
Level 1		
EP election story	1.19*** (0.06)	0.11 (0.09)
Election day	-0.58*** (0.08)	-0.73*** (0.15)
Length	0.88*** (0.10)	1.00*** (0.17)
Level 2		
TV	-0.13 (0.15)	-0.19 (0.26)
Quality media	0.07 (0.10)	0.66**(0.19)
Share EU news	-0.48† (0.29)	0.08 (0.43)
Level 3		
European ID	0.56 (0.52)	1.98*** (0.47)
Intra-EU trade	0.11 (0.99)	0.17 (0.95)
Population size	-1.01** (0.36)	-0.54 (0.33)
EP turnout	-0.92 † (0.47)	-0.67 (0.44)
Intercept	-1.76† (0.91)	-4.37***
Random Effects		
Country	0.13 (0.05)	0.00 (0.00)
Media outlet	0.10 (0.03)	0.30 (0.09)
-2LL	11760.79	4769.02
AIC	11786.79	4795.02
N (Level 3)	27	27
N (Level 2)	143	143
N (Level 1)	12850	12850

Note: † $p < .1$, * $p < .05$, ** $p < .01$, *** $p<.001$. Calculations were made using the meqrlogit option in Stata 13. Standard errors in parentheses. Continuous variables were standardised ranging from 0 to 1.

EU migrants

	National EU citizens	European EU citizens
Fixed Effects		
Level 1		
EP election story	1.19*** (0.06)	0.12 (0.09)
Election day	-0.58*** (0.08)	-0.73*** (0.15)
Length	0.88*** (0.10)	0.98*** (0.17)
Level 2		
TV	-0.14 (0.15)	-0.20 (0.26)
Quality media	0.07 (0.10)	0.66** (0.19)
Share EU news	-0.50† (0.29)	0.09 (0.43)
Level 3		
European ID	0.37 (0.50)	1.88*** (0.44)
Intra-EU trade	0.42 (0.99)	0.39 (0.98)
Population size	-0.79* (0.35)	-0.37 (0.31)
EU migrants	-3.13 (2.10)	-2.87 (1.96)
Intercept	-2.45** (0.87)	-4.89 (0.94)
Random Effects		
Country	0.14 (0.05)	0.01 (0.05)
Media outlet	0.10 (0.03)	0.28 (0.10)
-2LL	11762.26	4769.16
AIC	11788.26	4795.16
N (Level 3)	27	27
N (Level 2)	143	143
N (Level 1)	12850	12850

Note: † $p < .1$, * $p < .05$, ** $p < .01$, *** $p<.001$. Calculations were made using the meqrlogit option in Stata 13. Standard errors in parentheses. Continuous variables were standardised ranging from 0 to 1.

Unemployment change

	National EU citizens	European EU citizens
Fixed Effects		
Level 1		
EP election story	1.18*** (0.06)	0.11 (0.09)
Election day	-0.58*** (0.08)	-0.73*** (0.15)
Length	0.88*** (0.10)	0.98*** (0.17)
Level 2		
TV	-0.15 (0.15)	-0.25 (0.26)
Quality media	0.07 (0.10)	0.65** (0.20)
Share EU news	-0.54 (0.29)	-0.06 (0.43)
Level 3		
European ID	0.05 (0.48)	1.60*** (0.40)
Intra-EU trade	0.50 (1.06)	0.38 (1.01)
Population size	-0.76† (0.37)	-0.34 (0.32)
Unemployment change	-0.03 (0.43)	-0.15 (0.39)
Intercept	-2.39 (0.98)	-4.64*** (0.98)
Random Effects		
Country	0.15 (0.06)	0.01 (0.05)
Media outlet	0.10 (0.03)	0.29 (0.10)
-2LL	11764.39	4771.14
AIC	11790.39	4797.14
N (Level 3)	27	27
N (Level 2)	143	143
N (Level 1)	12850	12850

Note: † $p < .1$, * $p < .05$, ** $p < .01$, *** $p<.001$. Calculations were made using the meqrlogit option in Stata 13. Standard errors in parentheses. Continuous variables were standardised ranging from 0 to 1.

Associational membership

	National EU citizens	European EU citizens
Fixed Effects		
Level 1		
EP election story	1.18*** (0.06)	0.11
Election day	-0.58*** (0.08)	-0.73***
Length	0.88*** (0.10)	0.98***
Level 2		
TV	-0.13 (0.15)	-0.26
Quality media	0.07 (0.10)	0.66**
Share EU news	-0.50† (0.29)	-0.08
Level 3		
European ID	-0.20 (0.49)	1.62***
Intra-EU trade	0.74 (1.01)	0.39
Population size	-0.66† (0.36)	-0.35
Ass. membership	0.55 (0.38)	-0.08
Intercept	-2.81** (0.93)	-4.67***
Random Effects		
Country	0.14 (0.05)	0.01 (0.05)
Media outlet	0.10 (0.03)	0.29 (0.10)
-2LL	11762.34	4771.238
AIC	11788.34	4797.24
N (Level 3)	27	27
N (Level 2)	143	143
N (Level 1)	12850	12850

Note: † p < .1, * p < .05, ** p < .01, *** p<.001. Calculations were made using the meqrlogit option in Stata 13. Standard errors in parentheses. Continuous variables were standardised ranging from 0 to 1.

GDP

	National EU citizens	European EU citizens
Fixed Effects		
Level 1		
EP election story	1.19*** (0.06)	0.11 (0.09)
Election day	-0.58*** (0.08)	-0.73*** (0.15)
Length	0.88*** (0.10)	0.98*** (0.17)
Level 2		
TV	-0.15 (0.15)	-0.24 (0.26)
Quality media	0.07 (0.10)	0.66** (0.20)
Share EU news	-0.53† (0.29)	-0.02 (0.43)
Level 3		
European ID	0.17 (0.51)	1.74*** (0.44)
Intra-EU trade	0.45 (1.03)	0.42 (0.99)
Population size	-0.76* (0.36)	-0.33 (0.32)
GDP	-0.98 (1.66)	-1.40 (1.50)
Intercept	-1.54 (1.72)	-3.59* (1.53)
Random Effects		
Country	0.15 (0-06)	0.01 (0.05)
Media outlet	0.10 (0.03)	0.29 (0.10)
-2LL	11764.04	4770.42
AIC	11790.04	4796.42
N (Level 3)	27	27
N (Level 2)	143	143
N (Level 1)	12850	12850

Note: † $p < .1$, * $p < .05$, ** $p < .01$, *** $p<.001$. Calculations were made using the meqrlogit option in Stata 13. Standard errors in parentheses. Continuous variables were standardised ranging from 0 to 1.

Appendix V Country Level Scores for Independent Variables Chapter 10

State	Old member state	Neighbouring states
Austria	1	6
Belgium	1	4
Bulgaria	0	2
Cyprus	0	0
Czech Rep.	0	4
Denmark	1	2
Estonia	0	1
Finland	1	1
France	1	5
Germany	1	8
Greece	1	1
Hungary	0	4
Ireland	1	1
Italy	1	3
Latvia	0	2
Lithuania	0	2
Luxembourg	1	3
Malta	0	0
Netherlands	1	2
Poland	0	4
Portugal	1	1
Romania	0	2
Slovakia	0	4
Slovenia	0	3
Spain	1	2
Sweden	1	2
UK	1	1

Appendix VI Correlations of Independent Variables Chapter 10

IV	Old member state	European ID	EU trade	Neighbour. states	GDP
European ID	0.340				
EU trade	-0.258	0.173			
Neighbour. states	0.034	0.310	0.319		
GDP	0.833**	0.414*	-0.037	0.095	
Population size	0.440*	0.246	-0.377	0.482*	0.152

For correlations that include at least one categorical variable, Spearman correlation coefficients were calculated, otherwise, Pearson correlations were used.

Appendix VII Excluded Independent Variables Chapter 10

Share EU news

	Coefficient
Fixed Effects	
Level 1	
Quality media	11.90*** (3.30)
Share EU news	0.09*** (5.74)
Level 2	
European ID	43.20* (7.99)
Intra-EU trade	36.63* (16.52)
Neighbouring states	7.05 (6.93)
Intercept	-35.97** (13.72)
Random Effects	
Country	0.61 (18.02)
-2LL	1171.20
AIC	1187.21
N (Level 2)	27
N (Level 1)	138

Note: † $p < .1$, * $p < .05$, ** $p < .01$, *** $p < .001$. Calculations were made using the meglm option in Stata 13. Standard errors in parentheses. Continuous variables were standardised ranging from 0 to 1.

Old member state

	Coefficient
Fixed Effects	
Level 1	
Quality media	11.91*** (3.00)
Level 2	
European ID	43.99*** (8.61)
Intra-EU trade	34.92† (17.91)
Neighbouring states	7.30 (6.97)
Old EU member state	-0.84 (3.39)
Intercept	-34.39* (14.99)
Random Effects	
Country	0.71 (17.41)
-2LL	1171.14
AIC	1187.14
N (Level 2)	27
N (Level 1)	138

Note: † $p < .1$, * $p < .05$, ** $p < .01$, *** $p < .001$. Calculations were made using the meglm option in Stata 13. Standard errors in parentheses. Continuous variables were standardised ranging from 0 to 1.

Population size

	Coefficient
Fixed Effects	
Level 1	
Quality media	11.87*** (2.99)
Level 2	
European ID	44.50*** (8.09)
Intra-EU trade	25.01 (21.79)
Neighbouring states	11.97 (9.16)
Population size	-6.37 (7.87)
Intercept	-26.81 (17.59)
Random Effects	
Country	0.00 (0.00)
-2LL	1170.55
AIC	1184.55
N (Level 2)	27
N (Level 1)	138

Note: † $p < .1$, * $p < .05$, ** $p < .01$, *** $p < .001$. Calculations were made using the meglm option in Stata 13. Standard errors in parentheses. Continuous variables were standardised ranging from 0 to 1.

GDP

	Coefficient
Fixed Effects	
Level 1	
Quality media	11.94*** (3.00)
Level 2	
European ID	44.53*** (8.58)
Intra-EU trade	35.80* (16.60)
Neighbouring states	7.07 (6.87)
GDP	-24.62 (59.39)
Intercept	-12.38 (58.45)
Random Effects	
Country	0.37 (17.36)
-2LL	1171.03
AIC	1187.03
N (Level 2)	27
N (Level 1)	138

Note: † $p < .1$, * $p < .05$, ** $p < .01$, *** $p < .001$. Calculations were made using the meglm option in Stata 13. Standard errors in parentheses. Continuous variables were standardised ranging from 0 to 1.

Printed by Books on Demand, Germany